The Distance Education Evolution: Issues and Case Studies

Dominique Monolescu
Temple University, USA

Catherine Schifter
Temple University, USA

Linda Greenwood
Temple University, USA

D1451211

Information Science Publishing

Hershey • London • Melbourne • Singapore

Acquisition Editor:	Mehdi Khosrow-Pour
Senior Managing Editor:	Jan Travers
Managing Editor:	Amanda Appicello
Development Editor:	Michele Rossi
Copy Editor:	Jane Conley
Typesetter:	Jennifer Wetzel
Cover Design:	Michelle Waters
Printed at:	Integrated Book Technology

Published in the United States of America by
Information Science Publishing (an imprint of Idea Group Inc.)
701 E. Chocolate Avenue, Suite 200
Hershey PA 17033
Tel: 717-533-8845
Fax: 717-533-8661
E-mail: cust@idea-group.com
Web site: http://www.idea-group.com

and in the United Kingdom by
Information Science Publishing (an imprint of Idea Group Inc.)
3 Henrietta Street
Covent Garden
London WC2E 8LU
Tel: 44 20 7240 0856
Fax: 44 20 7379 3313
Web site: http://www.eurospan.co.uk

Library of Congress Cataloging-in-Publication Data

The distance education evolution : issues and case studies / [edited by] Dominique Monolescu, Catherine Schifter, and Linda Greenwood.
    p. cm.
Includes bibliographical references.
   ISBN 1-59140-120-8 (hardcover) -- ISBN 1-59140-121-6 (ebook)
  1. Distance education--Computer-assisted instruction. 2. Education, Higher--Computer-assisted instruction. 3. Educational technology. I. Monolescu, Dominique. II. Schifter, Catherine. III. Greenwood, Linda, 1951-
   LC5803.C65D545 2004
   371.3'58--dc21

                                                       2003008767

Paperback ISBN 1-59140-224-7

British Cataloguing in Publication Data
A Cataloguing in Publication record for this book is available from the British Library.

All work contributed to this book is new, previously-unpublished material. The views expressed in this book are those of the authors, but not necessarily of the publisher.

NEW Titles
from Information Science Publishing

- **Instructional Design in the Real World: A View from the Trenches**
  Anne-Marie Armstrong
  ISBN: 1-59140-150-X: eISBN 1-59140-151-8, © 2004
- **Personal Web Usage in the Workplace: A Guide to Effective Human Resources Management**
  Murugan Anandarajan & Claire Simmers
  ISBN: 1-59140-148-8; eISBN 1-59140-149-6, © 2004
- **Social, Ethical and Policy Implications of Information Technology**
  Linda L. Brennan & Victoria Johnson
  ISBN: 1-59140-168-2; eISBN 1-59140-169-0, © 2004
- **Readings in Virtual Research Ethics: Issues and Controversies**
  Elizabeth A. Buchanan
  ISBN: 1-59140-152-6; eISBN 1-59140-153-4, © 2004
- **E-ffective Writing for e-Learning Environments**
  Katy Campbell
  ISBN: 1-59140-124-0; eISBN 1-59140-125-9, © 2004
- **Development and Management of Virtual Schools: Issues and Trends**
  Catherine Cavanaugh
  ISBN: 1-59140-154-2; eISBN 1-59140-155-0, © 2004
- **The Distance Education Evolution: Issues and Case Studies**
  Dominique Monolescu, Catherine Schifter & Linda Greenwood
  ISBN: 1-59140-120-8; eISBN 1-59140-121-6, © 2004
- **Distance Learning and University Effectiveness: Changing Educational Paradigms for Online Learning**
  Caroline Howard, Karen Schenk & Richard Discenza
  ISBN: 1-59140-178-X; eISBN 1-59140-179-8, © 2004
- **Managing Psychological Factors in Information Systems Work: An Orientation to Emotional Intelligence**
  Eugene Kaluzniacky
  ISBN: 1-59140-198-4; eISBN 1-59140-199-2, © 2004
- **Developing an Online Curriculum: Techniques and Technologies**
  Lynnette R. Porter
  ISBN: 1-59140-136-4; eISBN 1-59140-137-2, © 2004
- **Online Collaborative Learning: Theory and Practice**
  Tim S. Roberts
  ISBN: 1-59140-174-7; eISBN 1-59140-175-5, © 2004

Excellent additions to your institution's library! Recommend these titles to your librarian!

To receive a copy of the Idea Group Inc. catalog, please contact 1/717-533-8845, fax 1/717-533-8661,or visit the IGI Online Bookstore at: http://www.idea-group.com!

Note: All IGI books are also available as ebooks on netlibrary.com as well as other ebook sources. Contact Ms. Carrie Skovrinskie at <cskovrinskie@idea-group.com> to receive a complete list of sources where you can obtain ebook information or IGI titles.

The Distance Education Evolution: Issues and Case Studies

Table of Contents

Section II: Case Studies in Distance Education

Foreword

Education is the foundation upon which a free and just society is built. If continuous and concerted efforts are not made to provide quality education that is accessible to successive generations of citizens, that foundation will crumble. Although these precepts have been stated many times, they bear repeating. The editors and authors of this book believe that by sharing our insights into and experiences with distance education we can add our efforts to those who are committed to exploring and evaluating innovations in education. The predominant orientation of this book is practical, not theoretical; however, it is not meant to be a definitive "how-to" book on distance education but a heuristic guide for those involved or interested in effective distance education. Although theory is not the focus of this book, practice informed by theory is the guiding principle for a number of chapters in this volume.

Technology has been instrumental in the evolution of distance education and has resulted in modes of delivery that now enable a "virtual" multimedia learning environment. Many distance education instructors now include audio and video clips of their lectures on class websites, and students can upload their own multimedia presentations and interact synchronously with instructors and other students. Although technology plays an important role in distance education, blind adherence to its dictates is a formula for disaster. The emphasis on educational goals is a mantra oft repeated in this volume and one that must predominate in this age of rapid technological innovation. Without a pedagogical framework to guide its use, technology is nothing more than so many "bells and whistles."

This book is an effort to provide educators, administrators, and students with a way to gain some perspective on distance education and to evaluate both its strengths and weaknesses. Distance education initiatives need to be comprehensively evaluated and fully supported by their institutions if they are to succeed. The goal of providing quality education that is accessible to all is a goal that must be emphasized and vigorously pursued, especially given an academic culture that increasingly stresses the bottom line.

Linda Greenwood
Temple University, USA

Preface

Distance education (DE) has a long, rich history of over 100 years. The beginning of DE was correspondence study. In 1892, Penn State University was one of three universities to initiate a new way of reaching out to students capitalizing on the newly developed system of Rural Free Delivery (RFD). While RFD has been credited with many outcomes, the role of RFD in establishing DE is not well known.

RFD provided a vehicle for mail to reach out to the people who were the American pioneers, the folks who moved away from the big cities in the Eastern United States to live in the heartland of America and beyond — the farmers who often lived far from schools of higher education but wanted an education just the same. Before RFD was established by the U.S. Postal System, people were required to go to an institution of higher education; after RFD was established, some institutions like Penn State recognized an opportunity to take higher education to the public.

Since the advent of RFD and paper-oriented correspondence study, newer technologies came into play to offer unique opportunities for DE: the radio (1920s), instructional television (1950s), satellite downlinks (late 1970s and early 1980s), cable TV (1970s), and videoconferencing (VDC) through interactive compressed video (1980s). Each of these delivery methods was considered to be revolutionary in reaching out to the population of people who could not afford to come to higher education institutions. The one characteristic that all of these forms of DE had in common, with the exception of VDC, was that instruction was one-way out to the student, or asynchronous. Interaction between the student and the instructor was difficult and time consuming using the U.S. Mail. VDC was the only medium for DE where the instructor and students were connected in real-time or synchronously, using T-1 telephone lines to send compressed video and audio between sites, and it was the first DE delivery mode to begin to mimic the traditional classroom interaction that was clearly missing from previous distance education delivery methods.

Today the Internet and World Wide Web have revolutionized DE once more. The biggest difference between DE online and the preceding methods is the opportunity to exploit the multimedia and interaction capabilities of the Web. While many online DE courses are asynchronous, interaction with instructors is faster with electronic mail, which can be almost instantaneous.

Most institutions of higher education in the United States have some form of an online DE program or initiative. Many of these programs were started because administrators and faculty thought they "should" include online DE options for their students or be behind the curve in higher education. Others approached online DE methodically, looking at long-standing models and taking steps to insure support for both faculty and students. This book is our attempt to provide a large case study of one institution of higher education that has moved slowly and deliberately into online DE. The audience for this book is administrators and faculty in institutions of higher education looking for guidance in developing and expanding online DE initiatives, faculty who are looking for case studies of how online DE might be useful in their disciplines, and students studying the phenomenon of distance education.

Section 1: Distance Education Issues in Higher Education

The first section of this book will take the reader through a series of discussions that describe, analyze, explain, and hypothesize about online DE programs in higher education. Each chapter will provide insight and advice for various stages of planning and development of an online DE program.

In *Creating an Online Program*, Sandy Kyrish notes that good planning is key to the development of a successful online DE. Initial planning should primarily center on two issues: identifying the educational goal of the program, and identifying the practical issues of implementation. Planners must recognize that while online learning is a technology-based activity, it must be organized around clear educational goals — and these goals must be strongly aligned with one or more key areas for the institution. She suggests common tools and strategies that can be used to help identify key goals.

In Chapter 2, *Faculty Participation in Distance Education Programs: Practices and Plans*, I present research into two questions for administrators of online DE initiatives. Faculty must be involved for a DE program to be successful. What motivates or inhibits faculty participation in online DE on any one campus? Campus culture is one factor to be considered. One practice nationally has been to compensate faculty in some way other than regular pay, except on those campuses where participation in DE is a condition of faculty appointment. But what models of compensation are used and in what settings? Research on both of these questions is presented with suggestions on how to apply the results.

In Chapter 3, John Sorrentino asks *Can a Viable DE Program Stay Behind the Technology Wave?* He questions whether distance education programs should strive to be on the cutting edge of information technology. Using economics as a heuristic, the general perspective taken is that of the Value Net to discuss and explain the education process. Dr. Sorrentino then discusses and compares the mechanics of an online course he taught to MBA students to the same course he taught in a face-to-face format. He concludes by suggesting a cost-benefit analysis to determine whether DE programs should be behind, with or ahead of the technology wave.

An important issue in online DE is accessibility to information. Rosangela Boyd and Bonnie Moulton discuss accessibility issues related to online education in Chapter 4, *Universal Design for Online Education: Access for All.* They present an overview of the challenges faced by students with disabilities in accessing and interacting with online course materials and activities. In order to address the potential barriers to full participation, national and international guidelines are examined, with particular emphasis on their implications for specific course components. The authors provide advice for validating website accessibility and a list of resources for those interested in obtaining further information about the impact of the Americans with Disabilities Act (ADA) and IDEA.

Stella Shields, Gisela Gil-Egui, and Concetta Stewart present a compelling case for team work in online DE in their chapter entitled *Certain about Uncertainty: Strategies and Practices for Virtual Teamwork in Online Classrooms.* They make the clear distinction that virtual teamwork, not virtual group work, is the goal since the team has a common purpose while the group is more amorphous. They discuss the importance of trust and community of practice within the online DE experiences and provide several provocative suggestions for those considering including virtual teams in their online DE courses.

In Chapter 6, Donald Hantula and Darleen Pawlowicz propose that *Education Mirrors Industry: On the Not-So Surprising Rise of Internet Distance Education*. Online DE is analyzed as a natural consequence of end of the century industrial transformations. From this perspective, previous distance and technologically based educational innovations are discussed, not as having failed, but as not matching prevailing economic and social conditions. Implications for adapting educational practices to new economic realities away from the industrial model of the twentieth century are presented, especially in terms of matching instructional technology to educational outcomes, virtual collaboration, and how "natural" the media effects are to the consumer.

In the chapter *Evaluating a Distance Education Program*, Dominique Monolescu and I discuss the importance of ongoing evaluation of DE programs. With a brief description of why program evaluation is important for any education program, key questions for online DE programs are identified. A case study of the Temple University Online Learning Program's ongoing evaluation process is presented as one example of how evaluation can lead to important programmatic and institutional change.

Lastly, through some closing remarks for the issues section of this book, Gisela Gil-Egui makes the case for developing clear copyright policies within institutions wishing to embark in online education endeavors. She illustrates her point by providing a brief narrative of the challenges faced by different actors at Temple University in their attempt to generate a consensual intellectual property policy — one that considers new aspects emerging in light of new technologies for content creation and distribution.

Section 2: Case Studies in Distance Education

In Section 2 of this book, a series of case studies are presented from a number of different disciplines. Each chapter presents insights, issues to be considered, and suggestions for future course developments.

In Chapter 8, *Creating and Using Multiple Media in an Online Course*, Maurice Wright discusses the adaptation of a traditional, fundamentals course of the science of musical sound and the methods used to code and transform musical sound using digital computers for online delivery. Practical choices for technology, which reflect the conflicting benefits of choosing simple versus more sophisticated technology, are outlined. He presents an anecdotal comparison between an online and a face-to-face course section, along with ideas for future development.

Karen Turner, in the chapter *Teaching a Studies-in-Race Course Online: The Challenges and the Rewards*, presents a case study of whether a course dealing with the potentially volatile issue of race can be effectively taught in an online environment. This course was developed to effectively incorporate online instruction with race studies aimed at teaching racial sensitivity to journalism students. Dr. Turner presents student evidence from her course of the success of teaching a sensitive issue online. She projects the potential impact of her approach to a course on race-related issues in the news on students' understanding and dialogue about race.

Transformation of a traditional face-to-face course to an online DE course is the subject of Elizabeth Leebron's chapter entitled *Media Entrepreneurship as an Online Course: A Case Study*. She discusses the importance of reconsidering pedagogical issues like requirements, assessments, participation, and more. This case study, unlike the others in this book, presents a hybrid model of DE. While the majority of the course discussed in this chapter is online, the final requirement is an oral presentation. Dr. Leebron discusses the importance of retaining this requirement for this course, and how face-to-face encounters enhance the DE experience overall.

One of the most commonly used forms of interactivity in online DE courses, as well as face-to-face courses, is the academic listserv, and yet the impact of these listserv discussions is assumed to be positive without much proof. Julie-Ann McFann presents a case study of academic listservs in Chapter 11, *The Uses and Impact of Academic Listservs on University Teaching: An Exploratory Study*. While her research was not limited to online DE courses, the outcomes of her work and the overall case study are directly related to understanding the importance and purpose of online discussions through listservs by all who participate.

Based on the process of Personalized Systems of Instructions (PSI), Erica Davis Blann and Donald Hantula present a case study of a social psychology course in *Design and Evaluation of an Internet-Based Personalized Instructional System for Social Psychology,* Chapter 12. They discuss how the course was designed to capitalize on the unique advantages of the PSI system while using the Internet to overcome some of its noted administrative drawbacks, including how the asynchronous nature of the Internet and the automated features built into Blackboard made it possible for students to attend lectures, take assessments, and communicate with the instructor and other class members from any where, at any time. Their case study demonstrates that the combination of PSI and the Internet produce an effective instructional.

In the *Conclusion*, Dominique Monolescu discusses the lessons learned through initiating and developing the Temple University Online Learning Program and how the book chapters illuminate that process and issues involved.

References

A Century of Commitment. (October 25, 2000). Available online at: http://www.worldcampus.psu.edu/pub/home/de/de_century.shtml. Accessed October 18, 2002.

Downey, G.J. (undated website). *Mail-Order Distribution and Rural Free Delivery.* Available online at: http://www.journalism.wisc.edu/~downey/classes/geographies-of-info/pdf/mail-order-and-RFD.pdf. Accessed October 18, 2002.

Thorbahn, M. (undated website). *100 years of Americana: Rural Free Delivery Celebrates a Milestone.* Available online at: http://www.si.edu/opa/researchreports/9789/89rfd.htm. Accessed October 18, 2002.

Catherine Schifter
Temple University, USA

Acknowledgments

This book is the product of the collaborative efforts of many dedicated individuals. My co-editors and I are especially appreciative of the authors for their adherence to our many deadlines and for their gracious acceptance of our reviews and comments. We would also like to express our gratitude to Nicole Brewer and SungBok Park who contributed their efforts and expertise to this project. In various ways, this project also enjoyed the support of Temple University administrators and staff.

The creation of this book has been a stimulating and enlightening experience and we hope that it will be a useful addition to the literature on distance education.

Dominique Monolescu, Catherine Schifter and Linda Greenwood
Temple University, USA

Section I

Distance Education
Issues in
Higher Education

Chapter I

Creating an Online Program

Sandy Kyrish

Temple University, USA

Abstract

Good planning is key to the development of a successful online learning program. For online learning (as with any form of distance education), initial planning should primarily center on two issues: identifying the educational goal of the program, and identifying the practical issues of implementation. Planners must recognize that while online learning is a technology-based activity, it must be organized around clear educational goals that are strongly aligned with one or more key areas for the institution. Although educational goals will be different for each institution, this chapter suggests common tools and strategies that can be used to help identify key goals. Once goals (and accompanying objectives) are identified, practical issues of implementation must also be carefully considered. These include determining the initial investment, deciding on profitability goals, putting strong program leadership in place, creating an effective program, and identifying support needs for faculty and students.

Introduction

If planned correctly, an online program can expand an institution's reach, enhance its stature, and satisfy needs for its traditional and non-traditional students. For online learning (as with any form of distance education), initial planning should primarily center on two issues: identifying the educational goal of the program, and identifying the practical issues of implementation.

This chapter makes the case that while online learning is a technological enterprise, it must be carried out with educational goals firmly at the forefront; these goals must be strongly aligned with one or more key areas specifically affecting the institution. Although such goals will be different for each institution, this chapter suggests common tools and strategies that can be used to help identify them.

Once goals are in place and objectives are derived from the goals, the distance learning program will need to address a number of practical implementation issues. As seen in case studies and retrospectives by others (cf., Bennett, 2001; Gibson & Herrera, 1999), many of the implementation issues are common among programs. This chapter suggests issues that should be considered by the planning group, including establishing the program's leadership, determining the program's initial budget, and identifying the program's support needs.

Keep the Focus on the Educational Goal

Perhaps you are reading this book because someone at your institution has said, "We need to have an online program." In that case, you may be off to a bad start.

Although your online learning program will be built on a technology infrastructure, it is not "about" the technology — it is about the ability to deliver *courses via technology*. An online program must always be fundamentally organized around an educational goal. While this may seem obvious, too often the initial goals for an online learning program are described through technology. When a program statement begins, "Our goal is to connect our three branch campuses with videoconferencing connections," this is not an educational goal; it is a technology *solution* that could be used to support an identifiable educational mission if one exists.

Listen carefully when attending your institution's planning meetings. Do the discussions about a potential online learning program focus more on the course delivery mechanisms than the courses themselves? Do colleagues justify the need for an online learning program by talking about the proliferation of the Internet and the speed of networks? If so, the program may simply be a technology in search of a problem (Meyer & Boone, 1995).

A distance education program may suffer the same fate as many of the dot.com startups if the institution focuses too much on the technological *possibility* of technology and the Internet to enable online courses, rather than on a real, articulated need. Research on communications technologies has shown that expectations for many technologies (including videotext, cable television, broadband to the home, and the World Wide Web) have often been driven by twin assumptions about the inevitability of the technology plus the assumed desirability of the services offered on it (Kyrish, 1994).

In other words, it seems obvious that offering something as desirable as learning and education through technology would be appealing to many people. The technology offers clear benefits of convenience and asynchronous access to knowledge and learning. Yet the *product* itself (a course or set of courses) is not a simple, replicable item such as an appliance. Individuals seek learning for a variety of reasons, including career advancement, personal enjoyment, or vocational necessity. Individuals are not all in search of the "same" learning; some seek full degree programs and a university diploma, while others seek certificate programs or even single classes (whether for personal or professional interest). And individuals often do not pursue learning even when it is freely available through public television telecourses or the Web.

There are many good reasons to offer courses online; these reasons will be presented in this chapter and in other chapters in this book. The bottom line of success for an online curriculum, however, will not be that it is technologically elegant or that it can be delivered across the world as easily as across the street. Instead, simply put, an online program will be successful when the college or university identifies one or more areas of interest for an *identifiable set of learners* that can be *effectively delivered via an online medium* to a group that *finds clear value in the courses offered.*

Defining the Goal

It is crucial to establish clear educational goals that will be of specific and definite interest to an identifiable population. An online learning program must be designed to address one or more identified *educational needs or opportunities that can be met by your institution*. It should never be designed to establish a "technology beachhead" or to respond to other institutions' programs.

Different institutions will have very different educational goals. This chapter cannot tell you what your goals should be; it can only help you clarify them. (If you are already clear about your educational goals, and you are looking to this book for guidance and ideas on implementation, you may wish to move to the section "Developing Objectives" later in this chapter).

To identify and clarify your goals, a group consisting of you and your colleagues will need to conduct interviews and discussions with the people who know the most about the institution's *educational priorities* and those who know the most about students' *individual issues*. You should begin your discussions by explaining your charge (e.g., a planning group is exploring the appropriateness of online learning for the institution), and that your group wants to understand key problems and possibilities at the institution to determine whether any of them can be addressed with an online solution.

You should *not* begin by asking, "What do you think would be appropriate for a distance learning program to offer?" This is still a technology-centered approach and guarantees that the conversation will be framed by participants who are thinking about what *could* be done rather than about what *should* or *might* be done. (Imagine if someone had asked you in the early 1980s what you could use a computer for. Since you likely would have thought about what was being done at the time, you probably would not have envisioned many of the tasks for which you now use a computer).

Leaving the technology *out* of the discussion is perhaps the hardest part of any technology planning enterprise, whether designing an online program or writing a grant application. Fundamentally, technology is a tool to carry out an activity. The best planning occurs by holding the technology solution away from the discussion as long as possible, to guarantee that the conversation stays focused on identifying the real problems and opportunities that need to be met.

Springboards for Discussion

One useful starting point is to use the discussions to identify *unmet needs*. What are the problems that students face in completing their degrees? What are the problems the institution has in offering appropriate courses at appropriate times to the students who need them? Insights on needs will often come from persons who have the closest contact with students, such as student advisors and department chairs. It is important at this stage not to jump specifically to the question of whether an online learning program can solve these needs — it will be more productive to simply outline the range of issues.

Another area to pursue is to think about academic *opportunities* — what could the institution do that it is not doing now? Is there interest in pursuing new groups of students or new certificate programs? This information is perhaps best gained from deans and other persons working at the university level. However, it may be quite useful to solicit information from external groups, including prominent regional employers and the alumni association.

But just as an online program should not be formed simply because others are doing so, educational opportunities should derive from legitimate indicators of need or demand, and not from amorphous or "blue-sky" possibilities. One risk of open-ended discussion is that the conversation may drift into "We should be doing…" Such conversations often capture a group's attention because they are interesting and thought-provoking. However, if you sense that a conversation has moved away from current institutional goals, work to re-focus it back to ideas and issues that are currently important to the institution. *It will be risky for an online program to be based on an educational opportunity that is not anchored in some way to the institution's existing strengths.* There will be enough challenges without having to develop and market a new area.

Often there is the temptation to skip the discussion of needs and opportunities, particularly if the planning group is already versed in the priorities of the institution. This approach is not recommended. Talking with key decision-makers about institutional priorities accomplishes several important things. It demonstrates the planning group's awareness and appreciation for educational goals over technology objectives. It also provides an opportunity for decision-makers to re-clarify what is important to the institution — it could even identify whether priorities have changed. These conversations will be worth the time invested. A single key insight can give the program a more successful direction.

Once the group has identified crucial needs and opportunities for the institution, the next step will be to honestly ask which of these can be effectively addressed by online learning methods. It is unlikely that all the issues that are identified can be addressed by online learning (e.g., the university identifies a strong opportunity to begin a sculpture program). However, it is likely that the group will have uncovered one or more valid educational *reasons* for an online program and will be able to identify a strategy for reaching a target audience or set of audiences for the institution's online classes. This is the crucial step, because identifying the focus will drive all other decisions, from budget to curriculum decisions to expansion opportunities.

Identify the Audience

There are many possible audiences that will be identified. Obviously, institutions will differ in size, in breadth of offerings, in location, and in general culture, but here are possible examples that could emerge from a set of discussions.

Attracting or Retaining Matriculated Students, Particularly Those Whose Schedules or Locations Make it Difficult to Attend Conventional Classes

This goal focuses on serving students who are already enrolled at the institution and who accumulate the majority of credit hours in face-to-face classes; online courses would be complementary to an existing curriculum. Many institutions already offer this "hybrid" model (Young, 2002).

Perhaps the institution has identified a significant number of students who would strongly prefer an alternative to coming to campus for class. These students can include: (1) persons who almost finished a degree but left the area before completion and need just a few courses to graduate; (2) persons who are still in the area but whose time commitments conflict with the requirements of coming to campus at a specified time for in-class meetings; (3) persons whose disabilities make it difficult to physically come to class; and (4) persons who want to get a head start on their degree before coming to campus for classes.

One difficulty of implementing this goal through an online strategy is that students fitting these general profiles may be pursuing very different degree programs. One answer is to offer core courses online, recognizing that this will effectively serve some of the above populations but will probably not help the nearly graduated students who have likely already taken these courses. A second answer is to offer specifically targeted online degrees or certificate programs, recognizing that these programs will serve only a particular set of students.

Strengthening the Readiness of Incoming or Matriculated Students for College-Level Work

This goal focuses on serving prospective students who may not be able to satisfy entrance requirements or incoming and current students who require additional learning and study skills to function successfully.

Perhaps the institution has identified a significant number of promising applicants (or accepted students) who either (1) lack necessary courses or (2) lack necessary skills to be admitted to the institution. Because high school students come from a variety of backgrounds, it is possible that a promising student will not have had access to the necessary mathematics, science, or language requirements for admittance to that particular institution. (Indeed, many successful distance learning courses at the secondary level are designed specifically to provide high school students in remote or rural areas with access to advanced level courses.)

Through an online curriculum, students could be offered the opportunity to take mathematics or science courses, for example, or could be offered courses that would strengthen their writing and comprehension. One concern, of course, is that if students lack these skills, it is also possible that they lack the technology tools or capabilities to work autonomously in an online learning environment.

Expanding the Institution's Reach to Non-Matriculated Students

This goal focuses on serving persons who may not want or need a four-year degree, but who do require professional certification or other educational accomplishments. This initiative would be useful for persons who do not live near the institution, hold full-time jobs, or simply are not interested in a campus atmosphere and would prefer to absorb the necessary knowledge in a private environment. Online courses would be either complementary to an existing curriculum or created solely for a new potential market.

Perhaps the institution has identified a critical mass of such persons and substantial reasons that an online degree program would be of interest to them, such as: (1) the institution offers the only certification program in a particular field for the state or a region; or (2) state or national laws have recently changed in a field, and regular re-certification is required for a particular group or groups. An online curriculum could serve such groups effectively; however, an issue underlying this strategy is that the institution must actively recruit this audience.

Developing Objectives

By first focusing on the institution's educational priorities — considering both its needs and opportunities — the goals for an online learning program can be directed toward that institution's unique educational mission. For example, a program plan might begin, "Our goal is to provide students on all three branch campuses with the ability to take upper-level business courses that are only available on the main campus, thus strengthening the degree programs at the branch campuses. We will accomplish this goal by connecting the branch and main campuses with videoconferencing connections."

This "purpose first, technology second" approach is particularly important when developing the written proposals that will be submitted to the administration for funds for the project.   It demonstrates that the planning group understands the issues that matter to the institution's well being, and it offers a practical means to address these issues. This approach establishes the true importance of the program to the institution in a way that is likely to resonate more strongly than a proposal that begins with a discussion of the needed hardware.

Whether identifying needs or opportunities, this last point about relevance cannot be emphasized enough. The value of any distance learning program (online or otherwise) will be judged relative to its value in *helping the institution achieve one or more goals that key decision-makers see as important.* This is not an issue of "politics," but of wise strategic planning that will guarantee the program's health and growth. An online program that offers seven courses could be judged more valuable than one offering seventy courses, depending on the importance of those courses to the university's mission.

The program proposal will need to demonstrate how the academic goal will be quantified into specific, measurable objectives. A three-year timeframe is a useful measure; it is difficult to accomplish much in one academic year, but no one wants to wait five years to decide if an investment is worthwhile. Three years should be enough time to develop a substantive program and to maintain enthusiasm about reaching performance targets.

Objectives should be based on such indicators as courses offered and degree programs available. The following is an example of a statement of objectives:

> *"By our third year, we will offer at least 40 courses per semester via online learning, focusing on students completing their first two years of a business degree through an online program. We will arrange online course sequences to enable students to complete at least one-third of the undergraduate core requirements and to take at least two courses in their major per semester via online learning. A student should be able to complete two full years of an undergraduate business, business law, or economics degree program, or to earn one of three continuing education certificate programs via online learning."*

Such objectives provide a clear roadmap of what the online program intends to provide, and of what needs to be done to get there. Objectives can be captured in a table that suggests yearly progress markers.

Determine the Initial Investment

Once a goal (or set of goals) has been established, and realistic performance objectives have been put in place, it is time for the group to turn its attention to the practical issues of launching an online program. Establishing the preliminary budget is a critical element.

Perhaps the institution has earmarked a specified amount of money for the program, and the budget must fit within this constraint. Or perhaps the budget is being built upon a new request for funds, either through the institution or through an application to an external funding agency. Providing specific guidelines and budget amounts is beyond the scope of this chapter; however, this section outlines some of the elements to consider for an initial investment.

Profitability and Sustainability

Before the program is launched, all involved decision-makers at the institution should be in agreement about the program's profit and sustainability goals. It would be disastrous for the program if profitability were assumed yet not planned for. Profit goals (or "lack of profit" goals) should be strongly related to educational goals. If the online program is seen as an essential support function for a changing student population, the institution's leaders may need to agree to cover its costs in the same way as covering the costs of equipping classrooms or providing library facilities. If, however, the online program is seen as a means to attract new students who would be unlikely to attend on-campus classes, then it may be appropriate to treat it as a revenue-generating enterprise, or at least an enterprise that fully covers its costs.

Regardless of the initial budget, it is important not to expect any form of distance learning program to become an immediate profit center for a college or university. Conservative, incremental targets should be designed into the three-year plan.

Personnel Costs

An online learning program will require some investment in staff and in faculty support. It is important not to underestimate the need for personnel, as there are a range of practical issues in introducing an online curriculum into existing University procedures — including development of degree completion pro-grams, recruitment of faculty, integration into academic advising, procedures for student registration, methods for listing courses in the university catalog, internal and external marketing, and other items. It would be a false economy to hamper the program's ability to be properly integrated into the institution by limiting the personnel available to work on it.

At a minimum, the program will need a director and some support staff time. The director could be a faculty member or an administrator; staff could be administrators or possibly graduate students. Putting leadership in place will be more fully discussed in the next section.

Faculty Support

Faculty may be compensated for aspects of course development, and they may also need student or staff assistants for help with the technology elements of their courses. Faculty may also require new or upgraded computers and software, peripheral equipment, and/or infrastructure improvements to their offices.

Technical Infrastructure

The technology requirements for online learning may integrate into the institution's existing infrastructure, or additional investments may be required. These investments could be charged to the online learning program budget or absorbed by the institution, but they must be identified. For courses delivered via the Web, a sufficient network infrastructure will be needed. Faculty and students would require access to password-protected, graphical Web pages, individual e-mail accounts, file transfer capabilities, and listserv and newsgroup capabilities. Instructors will need network connections in their offices and possibly in a secondary work laboratory. They will require access to a development server with sufficient disk storage space for creation and storage of course material.   Instructors will also need appropriate hardware and software to develop and conduct courses. For courses delivered via videoconferencing, there will be expenses associated with outfitting a conference room with appropriate equipment, furniture, and lighting, and with transmitting the videoconferencing signal between rooms.

Marketing

The budget for marketing will depend greatly on the target audience. An online program serving existing students may need few resources, since a stand-alone marketing campaign will not be necessary. (Promotion could be built into existing university methods, including broadcast e-mails, Web announcements, and inclusion in existing campus brochures.) An online learning program aimed at attracting a new audience may need to employ traditional marketing methods such as direct mail and print advertising.

Program Website

The website for the program will not only serve as a portal for courses and information, but will also act as a "calling card" for the program. An attractive and highly functional website will lend the program greater credibility and may even serve as a useful marketing tool. Although a sophisticated website will not likely require much physical expense (particularly since the institution should probably already have the storage and network capacity needed), it will definitely require a large initial investment of professional time and regular, ongoing investment in upkeep.

External Relations

Funds should also be allocated for external activities. Staff and faculty would benefit from attending professional conferences or symposia, or from subscribing to professional journals and trade publications.

Put Leadership in Place

Equally important to the goals and objectives outlined above is the establishment of good leadership for the distance learning program. A successful online learning program must be fundamentally driven by a clear educational purpose; yet it will need strong leadership from an individual who understands the academic mission, is technology savvy, and can rely on a reasonable amount of staff support.

A relatively straightforward way to begin an online program would be to provide sufficient course release to a faculty member to act as director. At least 50% of this person's time should be available for the directorship (which suggests naming a tenured faculty member to the position). Choosing a faculty member with appropriate administrative talents will have several advantages. The director will be familiar with the institution and its culture, and he or she will have credibility with other faculty members. The director will also already understand the pedagogical and practical issues of creating and teaching courses.

Using an existing faculty member also makes it easier for an institution to pilot a program without worrying about hiring a new, full-time employee into the system (or transferring an existing employee away from his or her duties). It is critical, however, that the faculty member fully understands and embraces the administrative tasks required of the job. (Typical responsibilities will be detailed later in this section.)

Alternatively, an institution may elect to assign an existing administrative employee to run the program. Again, at least 50% effort is recommended. This strategy also has the advantage of having a director who is familiar with the institution, and it enables the institution to select someone with particular administrative strengths (such as new program development).

Or the institution may open a new position, ideally with the intent of hiring an individual already experienced in online learning or another form of distance learning. All are legitimate alternatives; the decision will be based on the individual institution's situation.

Whether the director is new to the university or not, it will be crucial for him or her to have sufficient academic credentials for the program to be perceived as academically driven, not technologically driven. The ideal candidate will have a PhD or terminal degree, plus university teaching experience. Managerial and technological experience is also vital; the director will need management and communications skills, expertise in using computer-based communications technology, and knowledge of issues involved in online delivery of courses.

The director should be expected to carry out operational activities as well as strategic activities over a multi-year time frame. If the directorship is filled through internal means, such as by giving a faculty member course release or re-assigning an administrative employee, there may be the temptation to simply ask the person to "go to it" and figure out the details along the way. This should be avoided to reduce misunderstandings later on. The better approach is to formally prepare a job description to ensure that all parties involved understand the scope of roles and responsibilities. (This could be particularly important for an administrative employee who leaves a secure position to assume the online learning directorship, if the program is ultimately not successful due to factors beyond the director's control.) A detailed job description clarifies the "deliverables" for the director. It may also cause some re-thinking of assumptions about how many personnel will be required and at what level of effort, and about whether the budget will be too low or too high for the expected results. (Ideally, the job description will be prepared at the same time as the initial budget is conceived.)

A director can expect to address the following areas as the program is developed. Whether the individual is selected internally or externally, inter-viewers should be satisfied that the individual could succeed in these areas.

Developing Courses and Degree-Completion Programs

An online program will be significantly dependent upon good relationships with the academic leaders in the institution. The director must be able to work with the deans and associate deans in schools, colleges, and/or departments to encourage development of necessary courses and tracks, and to guarantee degree-completion objectives. He or she should also know (or be able to find out) who the other key players are — for example, it may be extremely beneficial to regularly brief the academic advising staffs of academic units.

The director should work with the schools and colleges within the university to help determine which faculty members should be recruited for online courses. There are many criteria that could be used for recruiting faculty, including selection by level of technological expertise, by teaching talent, by willingness to participate and interest in an online learning program, and by the appropri-ateness of the faculty member to the necessary courses that must be taught.

Mindful of the importance of keeping educational goals at the forefront, there are risks in hiring an excessively technology-oriented person who may not have significant higher education experience. The selection committee must ensure that the director will be able to understand curricular structure and effectively communicate with academic leaders.

Supporting the Distance Learning Students

Enrolling in an online learning class should not pose a technological challenge for any student. The director and staff will need to work with university and college personnel to carry out timely procedures for registration and to effectively list all available classes in the catalog. The program may need to provide students with remote access to research, library, and other online services and with a printed or electronic packet of essential technology-related information.

Supporting the Distance Learning Faculty

The director should exhibit strong interest in cultivating the distance learning faculty as a cohort. Regular communication is essential not only to clarify procedures and obligations, but also to share ideas and experiences. Faculty training and support will be needed for new or inexperienced online learning faculty members. Content and style guidelines should be developed and encouraged for Web-based courses to ensure whatever level of consistency the institution's leaders wish to promote for courses delivered to external audiences.

Developing Strong Administrative Procedures

Good administration usually goes unnoticed, but it is almost always a function of careful attention to detail and quick follow-through. The director and staff can expect to be involved in handling administrative procedures for any faculty stipends or course release; procuring approved faculty computers; building and maintaining databases of faculty and courses; issuing timely reminders to individuals and departments for deadlines of all sorts; and fielding telephone calls and e-mails from persons interested in the program.

Integrating Online Learning into the Institutional Culture

Online learning initiatives will both purposely and unintentionally raise conflicts and questions about various institutional procedures. The director must be able to ensure positive integration of online learning into the university culture by assisting in the framing and resolution of potentially sensitive issues. These include intellectual property issues relating to course ownership; effects of teaching online on promotion and tenure; and copyright and fair use issues regarding materials on class websites. (These are all major issues appropriate for a more detailed analysis.)

The sensitivity of different issues will be dependent on the particular institution's culture and its unique personalities; some may go without definitive resolution for years, while others will be flashpoints that may involve the faculty union or an ad hoc committee. The director will need to appreciate which issues demand careful attention within that institution's culture.

Marketing the Program Internally and Externally

The director must be able to represent the program effectively to university committees, officers, and faculty. The director should be attuned to the different groups' priorities and be able to "speak the language" of each group. As mentioned above, the resources (e.g., the budget) available for an online learning program will be largely dependent on how strongly it is seen by decision-makers as fulfilling one or more important goals. The director will need to communicate the value of the program in strategic terms, not simply cite the number of courses offered or the degree programs in place.

The director should also be willing to network with peers in other universities and professional associations to keep up with "best practices" and to promote the institution's image as a distance-learning provider. Similar to many schools' requirement that a faculty member must present a paper to receive travel funds for a conference, it is reasonable to expect the director to be an active participant at external events by either participating on a board or presenting information.

Developing and Monitoring an Annual Budget in Accordance with Program Goals and Objectives

The director must be able to forecast an annual operating budget, administer received funds within budget guidelines, and argue successfully for appropriate increases. The director should also be able to supplement the institutional budget with external funds, as noted below.

Developing Program Evaluation

The director should be able to design, or oversee the design of, quantitative and qualitative tools for individual and aggregate evaluation of online courses. The data should be provided on a yearly basis to demonstrate whether the program is effectively serving the students and the faculty. Ideally, the director (or the director and a co-author) should be able to publish results and case studies in academic and trade publications.

Securing External Funds and Grants

Few higher education institutions have generous funds for new initiatives. The online learning program should be expected — although not immediately — to raise funding from external sources, including state and federal grants and foundation awards. Again, the focus on educational goals will pay off. A program designed to provide continuing education for health care professionals living outside of urban areas, for example, may be eligible to compete for a variety of grants from agencies or foundations with an interest in rural education. A director who is aware of funding opportunities and who has experience competing for funds will contribute to the long-term viability of the program.

Along with the articulation of goals and objectives, the determination of a level of investment, and an understanding of the needed leadership, an online program requires a final essential cornerstone of planning — technology support.

Determine Support Requirements

An online learning program is an academic initiative, but its success is highly dependent on its technology support team. It is essential for a planning group to work with the institution's computer and information services department to outline technology support issues and agree on a level of service commitment. As with other aspects of the plan, it is important not to just "let it evolve." Technology support is a resource-intensive activity, and compromises will almost certainly have to be made in one or more areas.

Discussions in the initial planning stages will clarify expectations and responsibilities for both the online learning program and the information services group. As noted in the budget discussion, these conversations may also reveal hidden or unanticipated costs that must be dealt with — both in start-up and during ongoing operation. Increasing levels of support may also be built into the three-year plan, consistent with projected growth of courses or increased sophistication of delivery.

Although the program itself can be expected to grow incrementally, the learning curve for faculty and students involved in distance learning will still be steep and sudden. Faculty is likely to need assistance with the technology aspects of developing courses, and both students and faculty will have periodic technical problems or questions during the trajectory of a course.

Faculty Training and Support

If faculty members have been recruited based on their experience in particular courses they teach rather than their technological savvy, it is likely that some will have limited experience with developing Web-based courses and using advanced e-mail and listserv features. Faculty members may need a hands-on workshop for each software application (e.g., Web development tools, presentation software, electronic mail) used in development of computer-based courseware. Faculty members with adequate technology experience may also need some form of "advanced" workshop to ensure that they are aware of the latest applications and possibilities. Such workshops may need to be held regularly and include faculty presentations and discussions.

A faculty technology support center may be necessary (if one does not already exist) to provide faculty with ongoing support and technical assistance during the progress of courses. This issue also raises the question of evening and weekend support. If the institution maintains a technology support center, the decision must be made whether support consultants will be available by telephone 24/7 in the event an instructor has a technical problem that affects a class, for example, at midnight on Friday night.

On-site technical support will also be needed for videoconference facilities. Decisions will need to be made about whether a person trained in the basics of room operation and troubleshooting will be available for in-person or telephone consultation at each videoconferencing facility at all times that courses are being offered.

Student Training and Support

Students who have little or no experience with the Internet, World Wide Web, e-mail, listservs, and other tools used in the online course might also require training in these areas. Alternatively, such knowledge might be required as a prerequisite skill. Agreement on the level of knowledge required and on ways to deal with a lack of it will be essential in preventing instructors from being burdened with technology questions from their students.

If the institution currently offers Help Desk support for computer-related problems, there should be discussion on whether distance-learning students will receive any form of preferential access, and on whether the institution will commit to the expense of twenty-four-hour, seven-days-a-week support for distance learning students. Some amount of extended support may be needed, especially if courses are marketed as a means to enable students to complete coursework at their own convenience. Because many students will log on in the evening or at night, some amount of extended support might be needed to answer student or faculty questions related to technical, not courseware, issues.

Dial-In Accessibility and Internet Access

The University may need to provide dial-in and Internet-based access for remote students taking computer-based courses and for faculty conducting or developing courses from home. With the recent proliferation of commercial Internet Service Providers (ISPs), this may not be as critical an issue now as it was in the past; the institution may opt to provide a limited number of dial-in circuits and restrict their usage to a fixed number of hours per day.

Conclusion

This discussion of issues is not intended to discourage readers, although some may come away feeling overwhelmed by the array of items (and costs) that must be considered. Remember, however, that a program does not have to be developed and launched within a short time frame. Online learning is not a fad that must be quickly capitalized upon but an alternative method of course delivery that an institution can explore at any point in its history. Although it is possible that some advantage may be lost if an institution fails to act promptly on a promising market opportunity, in most cases there will be no harm and much benefit in investing a semester, or even a year, to working through the goals process, thinking through the implementation issues, and developing a clearer idea of the costs and support issues needed to launch such an endeavor.

A successful program will align its educational goals with the key strategic goals of the institution. It will follow a clearly defined roadmap of objectives designed to propel the program on a multi-year path of growth and expansion. It will be based on good leadership by an individual who understands technology implementation but gives highest priority to understanding and fulfilling academic goals and objectives. It will be founded on a realistic budget that acknowledges the need for sufficient personnel, technology infrastructure, and internal and external integration. And it will provide reasonable levels of technical support to the faculty and students who are the core of the program.

Acknowledgments

The author thanks Gisela Gil-Egui for her contributions to this chapter.

References

Bennett, C. (2001). Global business classroom — A team approach to online program development. *Technological Horizons in Education Journal, 28*, 42-6.

Gibson, J. W. & Herrera, J. (1999). How to go from classroom based to online delivery in eighteen months or less: A case study in online program development. *Technological Horizons in Education Journal, 26*, 57-60.

Kyrish, S. (1994). Here comes the revolution — Again. *Media Information Australia*, 74, 5-14.

Meyer, D. & Boone, M. (1995). *The Information Edge* (2nd ed.). Ridgefield, CT: NDMA Publishing.

Young, J. R. (2002). "Hybrid" teaching seeks to end the divide between traditional and online instruction. *Chronicle of Higher Education*, 48, A33.

Chapter II

Faculty Participation in Distance Education Programs: Practices and Plans

Catherine Schifter

Temple University, USA

Abstract

Universities around the globe are putting Distance Education (DE) in place, often through administrative choice. However, if a DE program is to be successful, faculty must be involved. This change is multidimensional in that established systems may need to change to support development and delivery of courses through DE technologies. This chapter presents results from two related studies that attempt to answer two questions that should be asked and answered before starting a DE program: (1) What factors are considered motivating or inhibiting to faculty for participating in DE? and (2) Which compensation models support DE make sense?

Introduction

As has been noted through out this book, distance education is not new to higher education. Correspondence programs have served higher education students since the nineteenth century. What makes distance education different today — to universities, colleges, and corporations — is the use of interactive, computer-mediated communication systems for Distance Education (DE). Indeed, universities and colleges around the globe are putting DE in place, and the decision to do so is often an administrative one with faculty consulted after the fact.

However, if a distance education program — asynchronous or synchronous — is to be successful, faculty members must be willingly involved; that is, they need to reconsider or redefine their perception of the teaching and learning process. This change is multidimensional in that established systems may need to change to support development and delivery of courses through distance education technologies. And faculty members will need to modify their teaching and to adopt innovative technologies and teaching strategies to take advantage of the resources afforded by technology-mediated pedagogy. Given the need for learning how to teach in a different environment (i.e., DE), there are two questions that arise for administrators to answer. First, what motivates faculty members to want to embrace this new teaching environment and to change their teaching strategies? And second, what assistance, incentives and compensation policies support faculty in this educational metamorphosis?

The literature on DE describes the students as older, mature, self-initiators interested in outcomes (Field, 1982; Hiltz, 1994; Knowles, 1970; Sewart, Keegan, & Holmberg, 1983) who are taking time away from family and careers to go back to school (Keegan, 1986; McIntosh, Woodley, & Morrison, 1980); less likely to be female (Blumenstyk, 1997; Canada & Brusca, 1991; Faith, 1988); and less likely to be from a minority population (DeVillar & Fallis, 1991; Gose, 1997; Sanchez & Gunawardena, 1998). There are articles on "how-to-do" distance education (Berge & Collins, 1995; Forsythe, 1996; Khan, 1998; Melton, 1997) addressing such issues as distance learning environments and course design (multimedia, CD-ROM, etc.), and case studies of successful DE courses similar to those described in this book. What is missing from this literature is a significant discussion of the faculty, full- or part-time, who teach the courses and why some faculty members participate while others do not. In addition, there is little discussion as to what DE program administrators are doing to encourage and support faculty participation in DE.

Taylor and White (1991) reported that faculty preferred conventional face-to-face courses over distance teaching due to the difference in the degree of interpersonal contact available in each mode. Fewer interactions with distance education students led to less faculty interest in participating. It should be noted, however, that the Taylor and White study was completed when computer-mediated communication was severely limited in scope (e.g., limited to e-mail, listservs, and/or bulletin boards). Clark (1993) showed within a national survey that faculty support for distance courses was tempered by concern for quality of interaction, administrative support, and rewards. And Olcott and Wright (1995) suggested that faculty are not enthusiastic about participating in distance education due to a lack of administrative support. Perhaps the required change in teaching methods and the teaching environment also led to this reported lack of enthusiasm for participating in distance education. Unfortunately, change does not come easily.

In some institutions of higher education, faculty participation in DE has been supported only through financial rewards and incentives. Wolcott (1997) discussed how teaching in distance education is not highly valued and is not related to tenure and promotion decisions. Dillon (1989) studied faculty rewards in telecourses and discovered faculty participated "for a variety of personal reasons, ranging from diversity of experience to altruism toward the non-traditional learner" (p. 42). Dillon and Walsh (1992) reviewed 225 articles and concluded that "... faculty motivation to teach at a distance results from intrinsic [prestige, self-esteem] rather than extrinsic incentives [monetary rewards]" (p. 16). This finding was further supported by Betts (1998) and Schifter (2000), who opposed the notion that financial incentives are the primary motivating factors for faculty to teach in DE programs.

Knowing what motivates and inhibits faculty participation will facilitate the implementation of new DE programs and the expansion of current programs. But even the best-designed program will be difficult to implement without faculty support. For instance, the faculty role in DE changes from a teacher-centered model to one that is more student-centered (Beaudoin, 1990; Beaudoin, 1998; Berge, 1998). This shift in roles means that successful teaching skills for distance education are different from those required in face-to-face teaching (Hackman & Walker, 1990; Strain, 1987); however, faculty training programs tend to focus on to how to use the computers or software, not on *how to teach* in DE environments (Merkley, Bozik, & Oakland, 1997). Administrators need to understand their faculty population if they are to support faculty participation in DE.

This chapter presents results from two studies related to the two questions posed to administrators that must be answered before establishing compensation and incentive policies to support faculty participation in DE: (1) What factors are considered to be motivating or inhibiting to faculty for participating in DE? and (2) Which compensation models are currently used nationwide to support DE? The first study consisted of an examination of the motivating and inhibiting factors at one large urban University. The second study presents findings from a national survey of compensation and incentive models for faculty participation in DE programs.

Motivating and Inhibiting Factors

This study used a modified version of a survey developed by Dr. K. S. Betts in 1998. With her permission, the survey was adapted for use at a large urban, research-extensive university. This university has over 25,000 students and 1,200 full-time faculty. At the time of the survey, courses had been offered by DE for four years. This survey was appropriate because it specifically addressed the issues of motivating and inhibiting factors for faculty participation in distance education.

The survey was distributed to all full-time faculty and 25 senior administrators, including all deans. After accounting for faculty on leave (paid or unpaid) from the university, the target faculty population totaled 1,312 individuals. Two hundred and sixty-three respondents completed and usable faculty surveys were returned for a response rate of 20%, and 11 administrators returned the survey for a 44% response rate. While the survey addressed many issues related to faculty use of instructional technology in general, this chapter discusses only a factor analysis of the motivating and inhibiting factors, and an analysis of variance between faculty responses (DE participators and DE non-participators) and administrator responses to the survey instrument.

Factor Analysis

A factor analysis of the 46 motivating (Appendix A) and inhibiting items (Appendix B) from the survey rendered four distinct and independent scales listed below with Alpha coefficients. It is important to note that all 46 items loaded into the four scales without any outliers or overlapping across scales.

Scale 1 was labeled "Intrinsic Motives" with an Alpha coefficient of .9123. The following factors were grouped into this scale:

- Intellectual challenge,
- Opportunity to diversify program offerings,
- Opportunity to develop new ideas,
- Overall job satisfaction,
- Opportunity to improve my teaching,
- Greater course flexibility for students,
- Personal motivation to use technology,
- Ability to reach new audiences that cannot attend classes on campus,
- Opportunity for scholarly pursuit,
- Opportunity to use personal research as a teaching tool.

Scale 2 was labeled "Personal Needs" with an Alpha coefficient of .8956. The following items were categorized as "Personal Needs":

- Release time,
- Credit toward promotion and tenure,
- Merit pay,
- Monetary support for participation (e.g., stipend, overload),
- Visibility for jobs at other institutions/organizations,
- Lack of credit toward tenure and promotion,
- Grants for materials/expenses,
- Reduced teaching load,
- Working conditions (e.g., hours, location),

- Professional prestige and status,
- Job security,
- Career exploration,
- Graduate training received.

Scale 3 was labeled "Inhibitors" with an Alpha coefficient of .8878. The following items were grouped into "Inhibitors":

- Lack of release time,
- Lack of support and encouragement from institution's administrators,
- Lack of merit pay,
- Lack of support and encouragement from departmental colleagues,
- Lack of monetary support for participation (e.g., stipend, overload),
- Lack of support and encouragement from dean or chair,
- Lack of grants for materials/expenses,
- Lack of technical support provided by the institution,
- Lack of salary increase,
- Lack of distance education training provided by the institution,
- Lack of professional prestige,
- Concern about faculty workload,
- Negative comments made by colleagues about distance education teaching experiences,
- Concern about quality of courses,
- Concern about quality of students.

Scale 4 was labeled "Extrinsic Motives" with an Alpha coefficient of .8440. The following items were categorized as "Extrinsic Motives":

- Expectation by university that faculty participate,
- Requirement by department,
- Support and encouragement from dean or chair,

- Support and encouragement from departmental colleagues,
- Distance education training provided by the institution,
- Support and encouragement from institution's administrators,
- Technical support provided by the institution,
- Lack of technical background.

The natural development of these four scales was interesting, especially in the order in which they loaded. The strongest scale related to factors that were interpreted as *intrinsic factors* — those that come from within the individual and benefit the program or students (e.g., "improve teaching," "greater flexibility for the students"). The second scale includes factors that are related to *personal needs* or gains for participation and cannot be interpreted as benefiting the program or students. The third scale contained all but two of the 17 *inhibiting items* (i.e., "lack of credit toward tenure and promotion" which loaded on Scale 2, and "lack of technical background" which loaded on Scale 4). The fourth and final scale included all factors relating to university administrative support and encouragement, or issues totally *extrinsic* to the faculty, programs and students.

Using the scales as a template, the ratings by both the faculty (participating and non-participating in DE course delivery) and administrators of the 29 motivating items were re-reviewed. The participating faculty rated highest (top seven) only items that loaded into Scale 1 (intrinsic motives). The non-participating faculty rated six out of the top seven items that loaded into Scale 1, but also rated second highest an item that loaded into Scale 4 (extrinsic motives). What is more interesting is that the administrators, while rating highly two items from Scale 1, rated three items from Scale 2 (personal needs [e.g., related to monetary support, credit toward promotion and tenure, and release time]) as highly motivating for faculty. It would appear that the administrators who responded to this survey believed that faculty are more motivated by things they could "get" by participating in distance education efforts (e.g., more money, personal credit, and reduced teaching load) than factors that might be more beneficial to the program and students (e.g., developing or diversifying ideas, improving teaching, and flexibility for students).

The means of each of the four scales and each set of items (motivating and inhibiting) were analyzed using an ANOVA to test for significant differences between the levels of faculty participation in distance education (participate, not participate). Significant differences were found for nine motivating (M) items and one inhibiting (I) item. Overall, faculty who participated in DE rated intrinsic motives higher, while non-participating faculty rated personal needs, inhibitors, and extrinsic motives higher. The same analysis was conducted for administrators' means. Significant differences were found for twelve motivating items, two inhibiting items, and personal needs.

Using the mean scores for faculty responses only, an ANOVA was calculated for differences by gender, age, position level, and tenure status in the individual item lists (motivating = M, inhibiting = I) and/or the four scales. While there were some differences found for each variable set, a Chi-square post-hoc analysis showed that the differences were not statistically significant. However, there were some findings that should be noted. Differences in responses were found for women, faculty under the age of 30 years, faculty at the assistant professor or instructor level, and non-tenured faculty. Women seemed to be more motivated by extrinsic factors having to do with administrative support and encouragement for participation. The scope and design of this study could not explain this finding. Differences that were found for three faculty groups fitting the "junior faculty" definition (e.g., age, position level, and tenure status) are not surprising. These three faculty groups are closely related and have the most to gain or lose from participating in DE, including the possibility of a negative effect on promotion and tenure at institutions that have promotion and tenure practices, or a positive impact on career exploration and job opportunities. In research-extensive universities, junior faculty are pressured to get grants, conduct research, and publish results. The process of preparing for and teaching a DE course can be very time-consuming, possibly taking away from precious research time. The time concern is more for the first-time teaching of a course than for subsequent offerings, but a concern nonetheless. Therefore, junior faculty members, who may be more adept at using technology and excited about distance education, may be dissuaded from participating due to competing demands.

This study showed that faculty who are participating in one DE program were much more likely to be motivated to participate by intrinsic motivators (i.e., overall job satisfaction), rather than personal needs (i.e., release time) or extrinsic motives (i.e., encouraged by department chair). Interestingly, the non-participating faculty members also indicated that they would be more motivated by intrinsic motivators over all other factors, with the additional factor of technical support having some import. Finally, although the administrators in this study did not seem to understand what motivates faculty to participate in distance education, they were very sure about what would inhibit participation.

Administrators must understand what motivates and inhibits faculty participation in distance education in order to maximize efforts to support such initiatives, yet this study suggests that administrators may not understand what motivates faculty to participate. This lack of understanding of motivating factors could negatively affect DE program development. It may skew compensation and incentive efforts toward the extrinsic scale (i.e., expectation by university) rather than concentrating on what really motivates faculty (i.e., opportunity to develop new ideas or reach new audiences).

These findings support those previously reported by Lonsdale (1993) and Dillon (1989) who found that faculty are influenced more by intrinsic rewards for participating in DE rather than other factors. Ironically, these findings also manifest a practice in higher education to focus on extrinsic motivations — an observation confirmed by Taylor and White (1991) and Wolcott and Haderlie (1996). We can further illuminate this practice by looking at DE program faculty and compensation policies nationwide.

Compensation and Incentives Policies

A national sample of convenience was used for this second study. Queries were sent to eight listservs (i.e., NUTN, the Urban 13/21 Provosts, UCEA, TAET, TDLA, FDLA, ITC, and DEOS) and were mailed to the membership of the National Association of State Universities and Land Grant Colleges asking for participation in a national survey regarding faculty compensation and incentives policy models for participating in DE programs. A total of 212 individuals from 160 identified institutions completed and submitted the survey. The respondents were from two-year institutions (27%), four-year institutions (56%), primarily graduate education institutions (10%), public institutions (79%), private institutions (10%), state-related institutions (21%), and both public- and state-related institutions (13%). They were from 45 states, Puerto Rico, Mexico, and three Canadian provinces (i.e., New Brunswick, New-foundland, and Quebec). Respondents indicated their institutions have been offering DE options for less than five years (39%), between five and ten years

(20%), and more than 10 years (39%). Also, respondents were from institutions where the faculty was unionized (34%), where participation in DE was applicable toward merit pay (37%), and where participation was applicable toward promotion and tenure (43%). According to respondents from institutions that have DE participation as part of promotion and tenure procedures, teaching a DE course is treated just like any other teaching assignment, service, or professional development. Only summary information about faculty compensation and incentives practices is presented.

Respondents were asked to respond to whether any of seven options were used at their institution for faculty compensation or incentives for faculty **developing** a DE course. The "most often" paid expense for faculty was Internet Service Provider (ISP) costs, while "least often" paid expenses were for graduate assistants (GAs) and faculty overload pay. The "sometimes" response related to many factors, including faculty status, availability of adjunct faculty, and departmental budget constraints.

Overload pay for faculty **developing** a DE course was the subject of a series of items. Responses showed the minimum overload pay for developing a DE course ranging from $0 - $5,000 with a mean of $1,885. The maximum overload pay ranged from $700 - $15,000 with a mean of $4,097. Differences in overload pay occurred based on school or department policies, faculty rank or level (e.g., full, associate, or assistant professor, instructor, adjunct or on contract), and/or union contract terms.

Regarding graduate or teaching assistants for all institutions represented, respondents were asked under what conditions graduate or teaching assistants were assigned to faculty when a distance course is being **developed**. For private schools, 10 schools (50%) indicated that they "sometimes" assign a teaching assistant (TA), while eight (40%) "never" assigned a TA. For public schools, 14 (8%) noted they "often" assign a TA, 75 (45%) "sometimes" assign a TA, and 64 (38%) "never" assign a TA. Graduate assistants (GAs) are more often assigned based on departmental policies, documented need, or the scope of the project. One specific function for GAs is technical assistance, so if the faculty member is comfortable with the technical environment or there is technical assistance available in other ways, a GA may not be requested.

The respondents were asked to answer whether any of seven options were used at their institution for faculty compensation or incentives for **teaching** a DE course. The "most often" paid expense was for ISP costs, while "least often" paid expenses were for teaching assistants and, interestingly enough, for

ISP costs. As with developing a DE course, the "sometimes" response related to faculty status, availability of adjunct faculty, and departmental budgets.

Overload pay for **teaching** a DE course was similar to that for developing a course. The minimum overload pay for teaching a DE course ranged again from $0 - $5,000 with a mean of $1,876. The maximum overload pay ranged from $1,200 - $8,000 with a mean of $3,341. As appeared with developing a DE course, differences in overload pay for teaching a DE course occurred based on university or department policies, faculty rank or level (e.g., full, associate, or assistant professor, instructor, adjunct, or on contract), and/or union contract terms.

The results of this study indicated there are no clear models of faculty compensation or incentives for participating in a DE initiative because compensation practices vary on many points, including whether the educational institution is public or private, two-year or four-year, the years of institutional experience with DE, the nature of union contracts, and more. According to these respondents, faculty compensation is slightly higher for developing a DE course than for teaching one. This finding is of interest given the anecdotal reports that teaching a DE course requires significantly more faculty time and energy than traditional courses and may be reflective of the "lack of institutional support" noted as a barrier to faculty participation by Olcott and Wright (1995).

Differences were found between non-compensation practices for faculty developing — versus teaching — a DE course. ISP costs appear to be the "most often" paid expense for developing and teaching a DE course and, in some cases, the "least often" paid expense. About one-third of the institutions represented were willing to support this expense, and about one-third were not. Faculty Internet access is fundamental for developing and/or teaching an Internet-based course, so paying for this cost shows institutional support for DE participation. The "least often" paid expenses for **developing** a DE course were for faculty release time and for a graduate assistant. For **teaching** the course, the "least often" paid expense was for teaching assistants.

Paying for faculty release time depends on access to replacement faculty, funding sources, or both. One solution is to provide summer pay for faculty rather than a course release for either the development or the teaching of a DE course when a replacement is not available. This may depend, however, on union rules or funding sources. While summer pay may be one option for administrators (and faculty may enjoy the additional income), it does not compensate for the additional work required in developing a DE course at institutions where the instructor does not have access to an instructional technologist or design team. These policies and practices are institutionally based, and often department-driven.

Graduate assistants (GAs) are not available at two-year institutions or colleges without graduate programs, but they are available at many four-year institutions where they are assigned to faculty based on availability and overall need. As for assigning teaching assistants (TA), schools and colleges have policies for TA assignments, which most often relate to course enrollment. The results of this study indicate that the average maximum number of DE students required for a course to run, after adjusting for outlying responses, was 26 students — a number that might be too low to qualify for traditional TA assignments. Perhaps policies that assign TAs to traditional classes should not be applied to DE courses. In addition, one could argue that if graduate students are being groomed to be the faculty of the future, they should experience the DE environment to be truly prepared to be educators in the 21st century.

Anecdotally, teaching a DE course is more demanding on faculty time, which is why 39 of these institutions capped enrollments in these courses to between 20 and 30 students. While enrollment levels may not seem an obvious incentive to faculty, online DE courses require an increase in faculty-student and student-student interaction; therefore, having a class size that facilitates required computer-mediated interactivity would be an incentive for faculty participation. Large class sizes for DE courses, although potentially eligible for TA support and favorable to economies of scale promoted by many supporters of DE (Green & Gilbert, 1995), would be a factor in the establishment of a pedagogical environment that is not conducive to group interaction — one hallmark of Distance Education.

Summary

The original questions asked in this chapter were: What motivates faculty to want to embrace teaching in a DE environment and change their teaching strategies? and What assistance and compensation policies support faculty in this enterprise? The two studies discussed have attempted to answer these two questions with limited, but applicable, outcomes.

As for why faculty participates in distance education, it is clear from the research that participating faculty members do so because of internal or intrinsic motives. They want to expand their teaching opportunities, reach out to new students, and see teaching at a distance as an intellectual challenge. They were not highly interested in release time, merit pay, or other monetary rewards. The problem is that administrators believe that faculty members must be compensated financially to entice them to participate in distance education, although that is not the most compelling motivating factor overall. To provide support for DE initiatives, administrators would be well served to learn more about what motivates and inhibits faculty participation.

The findings of the study on support and compensation that were discussed in this chapter indicate that financial rewards—more so than other support needs—are being used extensively across this country to encourage faculty participation in DE courses. Although extra pay as compensation for faculty participation may seem important from an administrative perspective, non-compensation support can be even more important. For example, faculty compensation in the form of support for ISP costs for at-home access and for the provision of graduate teaching assistants when possible should be considered.

Overall, distance education is here to stay on university and college campuses nationally and around the world. A successful DE program will capitalize upon what motivates faculty to participate and will provide the supports needed to ensure quality courses and student success. To accomplish these goals, the campus culture needs to be understood—what motivates faculty participation on one campus might not be appropriate on another. Once you understand what motivates faculty members to embrace the distance education teaching environment and what motivates them to change their teaching strategies to meet the demands of this new teaching environment, appropriate assistance and support practices can be delivered to sustain this educational metamorphosis.

References

Beaudoin, M. R. (1990). The instructor's changing role in distance education. *The American Journal of Distance Education*, 4(2), 21-29.

Beaudoin, M. R. (1998). A new professoriate for the new millennium. *DEOSNEWS,* 8(5), Doc. N. 98-00004. Retrieved from http://www.ed.psu.edu/acsde/deos/deosnews/deosnews8_5.asp.

Berge, Z. L. (1998). Changing roles of teachers and learners are transforming the online classroom. *Online-Ed*, (August 30). Doc N. 74. Retrieved October 22, 2002 from http://www.edfac.unimelb.edu.au/reserve/online-ed/mailouts/1998/aug30.html.

Berge, Z.L. & Collins, M.P. (1995). *Computer Mediated Communication and the Online Classroom.* Volumes I, II, & III. Cresskill, NJ: Hampton Press.

Berge. Z. L. & Muilenburg, L. Y. (2000). Barriers to distance education as perceived by managers and administrators: Results of a survey. In M. Clay (Ed.), *Distance Learning Administration Annual 2000.* Retrieved October 5, 2002 from http://userpages.umbc.edu/~berge/man_admin.html.

Betts, K. S. (1998). *Factors Influencing Faculty Participation in Distance Education in Postsecondary Education in the United States: An Institutional Study.* Unpublished doctoral dissertation, The George Washington University, Washington, DC.

Blumenstyk, G. (1997). A feminist scholar questions how women fare in distance education. *The Chronicle of Higher Education,* 44(10), A36.

Canada, K. & Brusca, F. (1991). The technological gender gap: Evidence and recommendation for educators and computer-based instruction designers. *Educational Technology, Research and Development,* 39(2), 43-51.

Clark, T. (1993). Attitudes of higher education faculty toward distance education: A national survey. *The American Journal of Distance Education* 7(2), 19-33.

DeVillar, R. A. & Fallis, C. J. (1991). *Computers and Cultural Diversity: Restructuring for School Success.* Albany, NY: Sunny Press.

Dillon, C. (1989). Faculty rewards and instructional telecommunications: A view from the telecourse faculty. *The American Journal of Distance Education,* 3(2), 35-43.

Dillon, C.L. & Walsh, S.M. (1992). Faculty: The neglected resource in distance education. *The American Journal of Distance Education,* 6(3), 5-21.

Faith, K. (ed.). (1988). *Toward New Horizons for Women in Distance Education: International Perspectives*. New York: Routledge.

Field, J. (1982). Characteristics of OU students. *Teaching at a Distance Supplement*, No 1. Milton Keynes: Open University.

Forsyth, I. (1996). *Teaching and Learning Materials and the Internet*. London: Kogan Page.

Gose, B. (1997). Morehouse's Trinidad connection provides a steady stream of top black students. *The Chronicle of Higher Education,* 44(17), A41-42.

Green, K. C. & Gilbert, S. W. (1995). Great expectations, content, communications, productivity and the role of information technology in higher education. *Change,* (March/April), 27(2), 8-19.

Hackman, M. Z. & Walker, K. B. (1990). Instructional communication in the televised classroom: The effects of system design and teacher immediacy on students learning and satisfaction. *Communication Education*, 39(3), 196-209.

Hiltz, S. R. (1994). *The Virtual Classroom*. Norwood, NJ: Ablex Publishing.

Keegan, D. (1986). *The Foundations of Distance Education*. London: Croom Helm.

Khan, B. J. (ed.) (1998). *Web-Based Instruction.* Englewood Cliffs, NJ: Educational Technology Publications.

Knowles, M. (1970). *The Modern Practice of Adult Education*. New York: Association Press.

Lonsdale, A. (1993). Changes in incentives, rewards and sanctions. *Higher Education Management*, 5, 223-35.

McIntosh, N. E., Woodley, A., & Morrison, V. (1980). Student demand and progress at the Open University: The first eight years. *Distance Education,* 1(1), 37-60.

Melton, R. (1997). *Objectives, Competencies and Learning Outcomes: Developing Instructional Materials in Open and Distance Learning*. Sterling, VA: Kogan Page Ltd.

Merkley, D.J., Bozik, M., & Oakland, K. (1997). Investigating support for teachers using distance learning in education: A case study. *DEOSNEWS,*

7(11). Doc. No. 97-00011. Retrieved from http://www.ed.psu.edu/ acsde/deos/deosnews/deosnews7_11.asp.

Olcott, D. & Wright, S. J. (1995). An institutional support framework for increasing faculty participation in postsecondary distance education. *The American Journal of Distance Education* 9(3), 5-17.

Sanchez, I. & Gunawardena, C. N. (1998). Understanding and supporting the culturally diverse distance learner. In Gibson, C.C. (Ed.*), Distance Learners in Higher Education,* (pp. 47-64). Madison, WI: Atwood Publishing.

Schifter, C. (2000). Factors influencing faculty participation in distance education: A factor analysis. *Education at a Distance*, 13(1). Retrieved from http://www.usdla.org/html/journal/JAN00_Issue/Factors.htm.

Sewart, D., Keegan, D., & Holmberg, B. (1983). *Distance Education: International Perspectives*. London: Croom Helm.

Strain, J. (1987). The role of the faculty member in distance education. *The American Journal of Distance Education*, 1(2), 61-65.

Taylor, J. C. & White, J. V. (1991). Faculty attitudes towards teaching in the distance education mode: An exploratory investigation. *Research in Distance Education,* (July), 7-11.

Wolcott, L. L. (1997). Tenure, promotion and distance education: Examining the culture of faculty rewards. *The American Journal of Distance Education*, 11(2), 3-18.

Wolcott, L.L. & Haderlie, S. (1996). Institutional support for distance teaching: A study of reward practices. *Distance Educator*, (Fall), 2-5.

Appendix A

Motivating Factors

1 Personal motivation to use technology

2 Graduate training received

3 Opportunity for scholarly pursuit

4 Reduced teaching load

5 Opportunity to use personal research as a teaching tool

6 Requirement by department

7 Support and encouragement from dean or chair

8 Working conditions (e.g., hours, location)

9 Job security

10 Monetary support for participation (e.g., stipend, overload)

11 Expectation by university that faculty participate

12 Opportunity to develop new ideas

13 Visibility for jobs at other institutions/organizations

14 Professional prestige and status

15 Grants for materials/expenses

16 Support and encouragement from departmental colleagues

17 Intellectual challenge

18 Overall job satisfaction

19 Technical support provided by the institution

20 Career exploration

21 Credit toward promotion and tenure

22 Release time

23 Distance education training provided by the institution

24 Merit pay

25   Greater course flexibility for students

26   Opportunity to diversify program offerings

27   Ability to reach new audiences that cannot attend classes on campus

28   Opportunity to improve my teaching

29   Support and encouragement from institutional administrators

Appendix B

Inhibiting Factors

1   Concern about faculty workload

2   Negative comments made by colleagues about distance education teaching experiences

3   Lack of distance education training provided by the institution

4   Lack of support and encouragement from departmental colleagues

5   Lack of release time

6   Lack of professional prestige

7   Lack of technical background

8   Lack of support and encouragement from dean or chair

9   Lack of grants for materials/expenses

10   Concern about quality of courses

11   Lack of technical support provided by the institution

12   Lack of merit pay

13   Lack of support and encouragement from institution administrators

14   Lack of monetary support for participation (e.g., stipend, overload)

15   Concern about quality of students

16   Lack of salary increase

17   Lack of credit toward promotion and tenure

Chapter III

Can a Viable DE Program Stay Behind the Technology "Wave"?

John A. Sorrentino

Temple University Ambler, USA

Abstract

Starting with a quote from Herbert Simon to that effect, this chapter questions whether distance education programs should strive to be on the cutting edge of information technology. The general perspective taken is that of the Value Net. A provider of distance education can be seen as a Firm linking Suppliers and Customers while interacting with Competitors and Complementors. The Supplier-Firm-Customer chain can be seen as education production, and the chapter briefly discusses the debate over whether quantitative production models can explain the education process. Theoretical generality is sacrificed in favor of a discussion of the actual mechanics of an online course taught to MBA students by the author. Mean numerical grades in face-to-face and online sections of the course are compared to show that educational outcomes face-to-face and online are not significantly different. Enrollments in the course are stable. Hence, the course is thought to be viable, as a program of such courses might be. The results of a survey of MBA students reveal that most students consider the professor more important than the technology in their learning and satisfaction. Taken together, the two results provide the beginnings of a case for Distance Education programs staying behind the technology wave.

> In the coming years, many new technologies will be proposed to you for use in your university, and you will have the task of raising difficult questions in order to decide when and how these technologies can contribute to the mission of the university. … we must resist the temptation to use technology just because it is available.

> *(Herbert Simon, Late Nobel Prize Winner in Economics, 2001, pp. 62-63)*

Introduction

Few reasonable people would disagree with the observation that the economies of the world are being influenced more and more by Information Technology (IT). Very few aspects of human life, at least in developed countries, are not affected by computer hardware, software, and appendages. The rapid pace of change in IT gives one the impression of riding on a technology *wave*, and staying on the crest of that wave is often perceived as integral to one's survival. Moore's Law for Intel CPUs informed us that processing power doubled every year and a half. Although the pace of growth in processing power may be decelerating (Markoff, 1999; Watson, 2000), "bang-for-the-buck" in processing is still increasing. Increasing bandwidth is allowing the expanded movement of data/information among expanding networks. Internet2 has 200 universities worldwide collaborating with industry and government on the Next Level. The consortium is working on developing and deploying advanced networking technologies, including high-quality collaborative and interactive technologies across the myriad of user platforms.

The education sector has not been exempt from IT influence. As education is the process of expanding knowledge and skill, what better milieu can it inhabit than the expanding universe of IT? Every past issue of *National Geographic* on one CD-ROM! Full medieval texts within a click's notice! Satellite teleconferencing with international academic superstars! Wireless everything!! What can be wrong with any of this? Does the "leading" edge *have* to be the "bleeding" edge?

Yes, there is a *Dark Side*, Luke. Norman (1993) warns that "… the technology that is intended to aid human cognition and enjoyment more often interferes and confuses than aids and clarifies" (p. 9) and "Technology is used much too often for dramatic effect, without worrying about content…" (p. 252). The seductive lure of technology must not blind us to a basic tenet of economics — for every *benefit* side of the ledger, there is a *cost* side. Because institutions have limited budgets, they must be careful to spend them on things that have the highest net benefit, i.e., [total benefits minus total costs]. Spending on IT is no exception. As John Oberlin (1994, 1996a, 1996b) points out, when obsolescence-induced replacement and burgeoning support requirements are factored in, the cost of educational IT will be *far from decreasing* over time. The dot.com shakeout and the retreat from many distance-education ventures by universities show the power of cost-benefit analysis.

Distance Education (DE) can be described as using one or more forms of communications technology to convey knowledge and skills to "clients" who are not in the same physical location as the "server" of this knowledge and these skills. Some say Distance Education dates back to the postal mailing of materials to those who took correspondence courses. Courses by closed circuit TV seemed to be the next to fit the description. In the modern portfolio of DE options are TV courses (broadcast/analog), courses videoconferenced in real-time (i.e., synchronous) over fiber-optic cables, and World Wide Web-based courses over broadband cable, networks, and phone lines (i.e., asynchronous). Each option uses infrastructure and has a set of inputs, outputs, and a technology that transforms inputs into outputs. The benefits of time- and space-flexibility, such as avoided travel costs, 24/7 communications options, and worldwide access to information vary over the portfolio.

For the purposes of this chapter, *viable* means capable of sustaining enroll-ments and achieving the same educational outcomes as traditional methods. It is thought that imposing the condition of breaking even or better financially would be unduly restrictive, as cost allocation would need to be extremely fine-tuned for this calculation to be made (Rumble, 1997). A *program* is a collection of courses the completion of which will lead to an academic credential, e.g., a

Master of Business Administration (MBA) diploma. Enrollments in MBA programs have been booming over the past decades, and many companies are more than willing to pick up the tab as their employees increase their *human capital*. That additional human capital often involves the ability to use IT and Information Systems (IS). Programs often compete on their capacities to instill such abilities in their students and on their use of IT/IS to increase access to their programs. They complement each other in providing a market for IT/IS vendors to sell their goods and services and in providing IT/IS-capable potential employees to those vendors. All this takes place in a "Value Net," a network of interrelationships among the principal agents in the market.

In this chapter, a Value Net perspective will be taken to discuss "education production." This is followed by a section that steps down from the theory pedestal, discusses a particular MBA course taught by the author, and sets up a comparison of grades in face-to-face and online sections of that course. Also found in that section is a discussion of a survey given to MBA students in general, assessing student perceptions and preferences regarding technology in their program. Next, the chapter has a section that contains the empirical results and inferences. Conclusions and suggestions for future research are then discussed.

The question in the title is addressed, *if not answered*, with the following logic: A *behind-the-wave* course is one that does not use the most current hardware and software in course delivery. It is shown that one online, behind-the-wave, MBA course sustains enrollments and achieves comparable educational outcomes to face-to-face sections. It has been ascertained by a survey of MBA students that the quality and availability of the professor exceed the input of technology in importance to self-assessed student learning and satisfaction. It can be reasonably assumed that with instructors similar to this author in their commitment to preserving face-to-face topic coverage and to paying careful attention to each student, a *program* that stays behind-the-wave can be viable. Such a program can provide most of the benefits that sustain enrollment and corporate subsidies, while avoiding the cost involved with staying on the edge.

The Teaching/Learning Enterprise

The art and science of conveying knowledge and skills by those who know to those who want or need to know appears to have evolved slowly except for occasional, innovative spurts. Some believe that among the spurts were the multi-person classroom, the printed book, and the lecture hall. The latest spurt is IT in the teaching/learning process. Those instructors who have included computer activities in their classrooms beginning in the 1980s, and who have taught online beginning in the 1990s, have had to deal with quite a few questions of instructional pedagogy (Sorrentino, 1997). Determining what content and which techniques would be amenable to face-to-face instruction and online computer-mediated instruction was no small task. IT infrastructure has now become a permanent fixture in both business and education, IT training is a frequent activity, and partnerships now exist between IT support staff and, heretofore, largely "independent" instructors. A useful way of putting the IT transformation into perspective is a "Value Net."

The Value Net

The notion of the "Value Net" (Brandenberger & Nalebuff, 1996) surrounding an individual or institution can be explained with the help of Figure 1. The boxes are generic types of individuals or institutions that interact with the primary generic player, the Firm. The components of the Value Net are defined as follows:

1. Firm: the primary product/service provider;
2. Suppliers: those that provide inputs to the Firm's production/provision;
3. Customers: those willing to buy the product/service of the firm;
4. Competitors: those sellers for whom Customers value the Firm's product/service LESS, and Suppliers find it LESS attractive to supply to the Firm, in their presence; and
5. Complementors: those sellers for whom Customers value the Firm's product/service MORE, and Suppliers find it MORE attractive to supply to the Firm, in their presence.

While (1) to (4) have been common in the economics/management literature, (5) is a new twist provided by the authors. As Brandenberger and Nalebuff (1996) were using a game-theory framework, they offered the notion that, in some dimensions, the Firm's enemies can simultaneously be its friends. They prescribe that the Firm's decision maker(s) play the role of each of the other components in the Value Net to gain insight into the Firm's relationship with each component, and to seek out fertile ground for *cooperation* (see Figure 1).

In the DE market, the "Firm" can be any for-profit or not-for-profit provider of courses to remote sites. The Firm in the following discussion is Temple University, which provides courses such as ECON403: Economic Analysis to MBA students. The "Suppliers" include those instructors (e.g., this author), administrators, and staff that combine to create the courses that the Firm sells or gives to its Customers. The "Customers" are those who have a demand for, and are the recipients of, the courses provided by the Firm. The students and their employers are the principal Customers. "Competitors" are institutions other than the Firm that provide *substitutes* to the courses provided by the Firm. For example, Drexel University is a crosstown Competitor to Temple University in Philadelphia. "Complementors" provide the products/services that are wanted or needed by the Firm and its Customers to *complement* the courses produced by the Firm or supplied to the Firm by Suppliers. Included as Complementors are Gateway2000 and Dell Computers that supply computer systems, Macromedia and Microsoft that provide website development tools, and Blackboard and WebCT that provide course management software to Temple University (and/or to its Customers).

Some of the Complementors to the Firm are producers and providers of "infrastructure." Various government institutions provide different levels of infrastructure by using public funds to purchase it, or its components, from

Figure 1: The Value Net (the Lines Designate Linkages or Interactions)

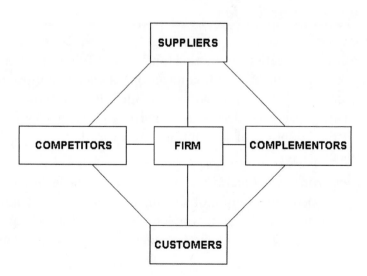

vendors. *IT infrastructure* consists of systems connecting end-users, local area networks (LANS), regional networks, and backbone networks (Choi, Stahl, & Whinston, 1997). Griffiths and McCord (2001) provide more detail on the levels of IT infrastructure and define the campus IT infrastructure as including the following components: physical infrastructure, facilities and operations, middleware and enabling technologies, and core applications.

The *physical* layer of IT infrastructure consists of physical telecommunications channels that connect end-users with campus computing resources. This includes wiring, fiber, routers, and switches. The *facilities and operations* layer includes classrooms and computer labs, central computing systems, voice services, video services, and operations management. The *middleware and enabling technologies* layer consists of directory, storage, and security services in campus networks. Finally, while Griffiths and McCord (2001) admit that the *core applications* layer may not be considered *true* infrastructure, they argue for including it. Their reason is that these applications have strong impacts on what the lower layers of IT must do. For example, a sophisticated optical image-processing program will, in general, require high levels of storage capacity. Except for paper-oriented correspondence programs, DE course providers would not be in business without this infrastructure. Also, many "hybrid" traditional instructors are using IT to digitize traditional class materials, and are themselves becoming more dependent on the IT infrastructure.

The process by which infrastructure is added to the mix of other educational inputs to create educational outputs is sometimes called education *production*.

Education Production

The literature on "education production functions" is filled with controversy. One may ask, "How can the simple connection between Suppliers, the Firm, and Customers in the Value Net be so problematic?" It should not be surprising that problems begin with the identification and measurement of the outputs and inputs, and the adoption of a functional form to depict the process of transformation.

An *education production function* is an expression of the technical relationship giving the *maximum* output of an education process for each level of various inputs to the process. Outputs include the levels of knowledge and skill achieved by students. Unlike widgets, however, students must actively participate in the production of their own knowledge and skills. Inputs are often categorized into land, labor, capital (physical, not $$), energy, and materials. As the categories of outputs and inputs are fairly broad, they must be made more concrete for researchers to perform numerical analysis on them.

Most economists are trained to model processes with inputs, outputs, and a technical recipe connecting them quantitatively. Production theory generally assumes that inputs and outputs can be expressed as real numbers, i.e., are perfectly divisible. At one extreme is the fixed-proportions recipe of input-output analysis that allows no substitution of inputs to produce the same level of output. At the other extreme is the typical "neo-classical" formulation that allows infinite substitutability among inputs to produce the same level of output. The function relating inputs to outputs is often a real-valued, continuous function, with continuous first and second derivatives, that is able to assign one (and only one) value of a single output to each level of input(s). The case of two or more outputs is significantly more complicated.

Production theory has given rise to certain functional forms that, given their attendant simplifying assumptions, can be used to estimate parameters in empirical production functions. The latter can be used to predict the approximate value of output given any reasonable values of input(s).

Becker and Walstad (1987) edited a collection of quantitative-modeling essays on the production of *economic* education. The authors in that volume chose observable and measurable dependent variables as measures of learning. Such measures included scores on standardized post-tests of economic knowledge (TUCE: Test of Understanding Economic Knowledge; TEL: Test of Economic Literacy; TEK: Test of Economic Knowledge; BET: Basic Economics Test), or the differences between pre-test and post-test scores. These outputs themselves do not distinguish between points gotten due to student inputs, teacher inputs, or technology. As inputs, they variably used the academic "program," student aptitude, student effort, student attitude, pre-test score, and technology. Notably missing are teacher-related inputs. Most of the discussion centered on what estimation techniques to use to avoid or offset error and bias.

Some authors (Okpala, Okpala & Ellis, 2000) unabashedly used the single-equation, "Cobb-Douglas," multiplicative/log-linear functional form with Ordinary Least-Squares estimation to explain learning outcomes in a macroeconomic principles course. Besides having the theoretical restriction that all inputs must be present for any output to occur, this functional form falls prey to the warnings of Intriligator (1978) and several authors in Becker and Walstad (1987) that the estimates resulting from such a process may be highly unreliable. To some, however, these nit-picking considerations are far from important.

Practitioners in the field of education are familiar with the nuts and bolts of everyday operation of schools (and school districts), colleges, and universities. There are those in this group who reject the use of educational production functions altogether. Hodas (1993), in a critique of Monk's (1992) critique, suggests:

> ...that the production-function model and its corollary, efficiency, as with much else in economics, are based on the quintessentially 19th century tenets of materiality, scarcity and non-simultaneity of ownership...It looks to discover a direct connection...between what goes in and what comes out...Taylorism applied to schools as factories. (p.6)

This means, in effect, that the requirements of mathematical/statistical rigor irreparably distort the real picture. The author of the present chapter speculates that this attitude may be closely related to the quantitative (left brain)/qualitative (right brain) bifurcation of approaches to education in general.

Monk (1992) had written a survey of education productivity research techniques in terms of their relative usefulness as a basis for educational finance reform. He found production function research inadequate, but Hodas (1993) apparently thought that Monk should have gone so far as to *condemn* that body of thought. Monk (1992) reviewed studies involving purchased inputs (e.g., computers and supplies), non-purchased inputs (e.g., peer and parental influence), and "configurations" of inputs (e.g., organizational attributes) that used deductive math/stat methods or inductive experiments down to the classroom level. His general conclusion was that the studies done by that time had almost no consistent results, and the variables almost no explanatory significance. Monk (1993) responded to Hodas' critique by calling it an "intemperate outburst" that "...spreads misinformation...", but his own work expressed the frustration of those in education with the deductive methods of economists. In the years since Monk's (1992) review, many of the same problems have lingered.

Gauging the Effects of Technology: Discussion

Having enunciated a list of complications and frustrations involving the process of estimating relationships between educational inputs and output, this author prefers two simple approaches to assessing the viability of online courses that remain behind the technology wave. The first approach is that of comparing output in face-to-face and online sections of a single course taught by the same instructor with the same textbook and roughly the same materials over comparable periods of time. The second approach is to analyze the results of a survey of Temple University MBA students taken during June 2002. The rationale for the two approaches is that the case study and the survey avoid the serious controversy surrounding efforts to characterize educational production using secondary data.

ECON403: Description of Course

The Temple University School of Business and Management (SBM) had been offering videoconferencing of MBA courses to a campus 100 miles away (Harrisburg, PA) before any course was offered online. The first web-based MBA course in the School was ECON403: Economic Analysis, a course developed by this author for the Spring 1997 semester. It was subsequently offered in the Fall 1997 semester and each spring semester from 1998 to 2002. Since then, SBM has been offering many other MBA courses online and via videoconferencing. Many of these more recent offerings are making significant use of the course-management tool, *Blackboard*.

It is the philosophy of this author to put *content before technology* in both ECON403 and another online course (ECON500: Economic Decision Making in the Firm, offered in Spring 2002). This approach makes the technology serve the content. ECON403: Economic Analysis, is currently at http://astro.temple.edu/ECON403/. The original version of the course was written in html, and these files are modified each semester to update material and links, and to change media readings and assignments. Some content is created with web development tools such as Macromedia's *Dreamweaver*. Students are given passwords to the course site to access the weekly topics modules, available one at a time, each at least a week before the assignment deadlines. The text reading, media readings and other links, and assignments and their deadlines are embedded in the modules. Assignments are submitted as e-mail and e-mail attachments, or are uploaded to the Digital Drop Box in *Blackboard*. Communication takes place either by phone (rarely) or through private e-mail, the class listserv, or the class Discussion Board in *Blackboard*. Peer discussion-assignments are posted by the students in various Forums created on the class Discussion Board. Grading spreadsheets are posted for download so that students may keep track of their grade status. This education production process, then, involves teacher inputs, student inputs, infrastructure, and applications. One teacher input that has generated considerable controversy is teaching time with Distance Education courses.

The conventional wisdom (National Education Association, NEA, 2000) about the commitment of faculty time to online teaching compared to face-to-face teaching is that it is *more labor intensive*. Visser (2000) has endorsed this view via an "experiential case study" of a master's-level course in Public Administration. While the savings in delivery time for Visser did not make up for the additional development time, he admitted that repeated performances of the course and increased institutional support would relieve some of the additional load. DiBiase (2000) debunked the conventional wisdom (National Education Association, 2000) by recording his time and having support personnel record theirs when teaching a geographical information systems course online and face-to-face. Like the grade comparison later in this chapter, his study was not a controlled experiment. DiBiase concluded that the number of hours per student spent teaching the distance course was *lower* than the face-to-face version. He made one admission that is important to this author's endorsement of the conventional wisdom. Commenting on the NEA study (2000), he noted that "Interviewees who took the most hands-on approach to distance teaching — including developing and managing their own online content — tended to spend more time than others. *How one teaches online, it seems, is more pertinent than the number of students*" (DiBiase, 2000, pp. 7-8; emphasis added). He reported that he had had a support team and used *WebCT* course-management software for the online course. The author of this chapter estimates that he spends from 25% to 50% more time with online students to handle the increased grading and the communications that keep the students "involved." This occurs even with some help from *Blackboard*.

Students' numerical grades on the midterm (micro) and the final (macro) exams in both face-to-face and online sections are used here as educational output.

Though Becker and Walstad (1987) argue for the superiority of standardized tests, none was available for this comparison. Five course sections of face-to-face and four and one-half (no final exam data found for Spring 1999) sections of online provided the sampling frame of grades. The face-to-face sections spanned from the Fall 1997 to the Spring 2000 semester. The online sections ranged from the Spring 1997 to the Spring 2002. The teacher (this author) and text (Schiller, 2000) were the same, except that there were small revisions in the text during the period. Materials differed slightly between the face-to-face and online sections. The online course had more assignments to "hand in," as the instructor thinks that remote students need more work and attention. The nearly constant digital exchange is a substitute for the human interaction that takes place in the physical classroom. The conceptual content of the face-to-face and online versions of the course have been kept virtually identical. Until Spring 2002, exams in the online class took place in person in computer labs proctored by the instructor. In that semester, exams were conducted online.

Student Preferences

The 30-question survey queried current and recently graduated MBA students in the School of Business and Management of Temple University about how technology affected their learning and satisfaction in MBA courses. It was written for the most part by Ms. B. Erin McCormick, a graduate assistant on this project from the Temple University Economics Department. A copy of the web-form of the survey created by Mr. Greg Szczepanek, an instructional support specialist in the Temple University Computer Services Department, is given as Appendix A.

The responses vary over the nominal, ordinal, interval, ratio, and absolute scales. In the *nominal* category are questions that asked whether students are female or male, and whether students are excited about using the latest technology in a course. On the *ordinal* scale are questions asking students to rank various alternatives. This type of question, for example, asked for a ranking of the importance of course characteristics. The *interval* scale is represented by asking for an expression of how students value the option of taking courses online on a scale of one (very much) to five (hardly at all). The "don't know" option makes such a question a hybrid with nominal. The *ratio* scale shows itself in the question on willingness to pay for the online option. The *absolute* scale is represented by asking how many online courses students had taken.

The survey questions basically cover what students have experienced, how they perceive their learning under certain circumstances, how satisfied they are with what they experienced, what can be done in the future to improve things, and student demographics.

Gauging the Effects of Technology: Empirical Results

The empirical results from the two-sample comparison of grades and from the survey on the effect of technology on student learning and satisfaction are displayed below. Some inferences are drawn about the relationship between the two outcomes.

ECON403 Student Grades: Results

Random samples of 30 and 50 were generated in MINITAB from the students' midterm and final numerical grades in five face-to-face sections and four and one-half online sections of the course. It must be emphasized that this comparison is *not the result of a controlled experiment*. Though the same teacher purports to be using the same standards, "noise" is not filtered out of the grading process. For example, the fact that more assignments are handed in and graded in the online course may cause grades to differ from the face-to-face course. Nevertheless, two-sample z-tests for means were performed. The data that went into the z-calculations are given in Table 1. The raw sample data are given in Appendix B.

Table 1: Data for Z-Test Computations

Sample Size		Face-to-Face		Online	
		Midterm	Final	Midterm	Final
30	Mean	78.90	81.86	79.17	85.33
30	S.D.	11.35	10.48	17.17	14.66
30	Variance	128.78	109.77	294.9	214.92
50	Mean	77.90	77.1	81.58	83.82
50	S.D.	13.83	15.95	14.97	16.25
50	Variance	191.23	254.5	224.04	264.07

The computed z-statistics for independent samples of size 30 of midterm (mid) and final (fin) grades were $z_{mid}(30) = -0.07$ and $z_{fin}(30) = -1.05$. For sample size 50, $z_{mid}(50) = -0.4$ and $z_{fin}(50) = -.09$. These computed values are less (in absolute value) than the critical values of z for the 10% level of significance and higher, for both the one-tailed and two-tailed tests. The *null hypotheses that the means of the grades in the face-to-face and online sections are not significantly different from each other cannot be rejected.* Hence, it can be inferred that the educational outcomes of the face-to-face and online methods of instruction are not significantly different. This is one indicator of what has been previously defined as the viability of a Distance Education course. The other component is that of sustaining enrollments. The enrollments in ECON403 have been 8, 7 (given twice in 1997), 18, 21, 15 and 17, even as the Harrisburg students have largely dropped out. They were given a face-to-face section of Economics 403 starting in 2000.

Student Preferences: Results

There were 86 responses out of a respondent pool of approximately 1,000. According to the dean's office staff, the students were surveyed quite frequently in the 2001-2002 academic year. With regard to student demographics, it is somewhat noteworthy that the gender split was almost even, most respondents had 10 or more courses in the program (more experienced), and most had grade point averages in the highest two ranges (smarter?). Thirty-five percent had online experience. Most of those who thought they knew about what salary increase to expect from completing the MBA forecasted a double-digit raise.

The following general inferences can be made:

1. In rankings of the importance to students' perceived learning and satisfaction, the *professor* options are invariably *more important than the technology* options.

2. The *traditional* lecture course with technology assistance is still the *most popular form of course.*

3. *Technology*, if bundled with other forms of interaction, is a *generally positive* attribute that should not be carried to excess.

4. Though the number of respondents is questionable (39, with 30 answering "Yes" on Question 3), *students* who had taken at least one online course

valued the option fairly highly but *would not be willing to pay much* additional tuition *for* the *online* option.

Any MBA program dedicated in the Value Net to the needs of its Customers should pay attention to their preferences and expressed wishes. All MBA programs are not created equal (Haksever & Muragishi, 1998; Hamlen & Southwick, 1989), and those that want to be competitive have to meet Customer needs while being responsible on the cost side.

Conclusions

Brandenberger and Nalebuff (1996) suggest that universities should think more like for-profit businesses in the Value Net context. The "privatization wave" implies that governments should as well. This implies that a "business case" must be made in the non-profit sectors for all investment options, including IT. Oberlin (1994, 1996a, 1996b) outlined the format for universities, and there is a growing movement for governments to evaluate IT with respect to expected returns to the money spent (City of Philadelphia, 2001).

Applying cost-benefit analysis can be a sobering process. "Geeks and gizmos" get put into a "Do we *really* need them?" light. As Norman (1993) points out, they often cannot make it past this type of scrutiny when resources are tight. What can come to their rescue are alliances with the "technology wave" Complementor companies (e.g., the IBM Laptop University) and Complementor governments (e.g., accelerated tax write-offs) in the Value Net. These help "seed" the future with the techno-transformation of the present. Economists warn, however, that at any point in time, the subsidization of goods and services can generate *deadweight losses*. Future gains, at an appropriate discount rate, must exceed those losses for efficiency to be achieved over time.

The true answer to "Can a Viable Distance Education Program Stay Behind the Technology 'Wave'?" must entail detailed cost-benefit analyses of actual programs. These analyses should critically evaluate the goals of the programs (Kaufman, Watkins, & Guerra, 2001), the internal means of achieving these goals, and the relationships to external Value Net components, especially Customers. The roles of IT and IS in each dimension should provide fertile ground for research, as will estimation of the benefits of space-time flexibility.

The single-course and single-program perspectives used above need to be generalized into a generic program-evaluation template. The road to future Distance Education (Collis & Gommer, 2001a, 2001b) should be paved with *reason*. Staying *slightly* behind the wave may be the best policy for programs viable in the above sense to also generate positive net benefits. Only time and careful evaluation will tell.

References

Becker, W.E. & Walstad, W.B. (1987). *Econometric modeling in economic education research.* Boston, MA: Kluwer-Nijhoff Publishing.

Brandenberger, A.M. & Nalebuff, B.J. (1996). *Co-opetition.* New York: Doubleday.

Choi, S.Y., Stahl, D.O., & Whinston, A.B. (1997). *The economics of electronic commerce.* Indianapolis, IN: Macmillan Technical Publishing.

Collis, B. & Gommer, L. (2001a). Stretching the mold or a new economy? Part I: Scenarios for the university in 2005. *Educational Technology*, XLI, (May-June), 5-18.

Collis, B. & Gommer, L. (2001b). Stretching the mold or a new economy? Part II: Realizing the scenarios for the university in 2005. *Educational Technology*, XLI, (July-August), 5-14.

DiBiase, D. (2000). Is distance teaching more work or less work? *American Journal of Distance Education*, 14, 6-20.

Griffiths, J.M. & McCord, A. (2001). The art and science of infrastructure. In Goodman, P.S. (Ed.), T*echnology Enhanced Learning.* Mahwah, NJ: Lawrence Erlbaum Associates.

Haksever, C. & Muragishi, Y. (1998). Measuring value in MBA programmes. *Education Economics*, 6, 11-25.

Hamlen, Jr., W. & Southwick, L. (1989). Quality in the MBA program: Inputs, outputs or value added? *Journal of Economic and Social Measurement*, 15, 1-25.

Hodas, S. (1993). Is water an input to a fish? Problems with the production-function model in education. *Education Policy Analysis Archives*, 1. Retrieved from http://olam.ed.asu.edu/epaa/v1n12.html.

Intriligator, M.D. (1978). *Econometric models, techniques, and applications*. Englewood Cliffs, NJ: Prentice-Hall.

Kaufman, R., Watkins, R., & Guerra, I. (2001). The future of distance learning: Defining and sustaining useful results. *Educational Technology*, XLI (May-June), 19-26.

Markoff, J. (1999). Chip progress may soon be hitting barrier. *New York Times*. Retrieved on October 9, 2002 from http://www.nytimes.com/library/tech/99/10/biztech/articles/09chip.html.

Monk, D.H. (1992). Education productivity research: An update and assessment of its role in education finance reform. *Educational Evaluation and Policy Analysis,* 14, 307-32.

Monk, D.H. (1993). A reply to Mr. Hodas. *Education Policy Analysis Archives*, 1. Retrieved from http://olam.ed.asu.edu/epaa/v1n15.html.

National Educational Association. (2000). *A survey of traditional and distance learning higher education members*. Retrieved on July 8, 2002 from http://www.nea.org/he/abouthe/dlstudy.pdf.

Norman, D.A. (1993). *Things that make us smart*. Reading, MA: Addison-Wesley.

Oberlin, J.L. (1994). Departmental budgeting for information technology: A life-cycle approach. *CAUSE/EFFECT*, (Summer), 37-46.

Oberlin, J.L. (1996a). The financial mythology of information technology: The new economics. *CAUSE/EFFECT*, (Spring), 19-35.

Oberlin, J.L. (1996b). The financial mythology of information technology: Developing a new game plan. *CAUSE/EFFECT*, (Summer), 10-17.

Okpala, A.O., Okpala, C.O., & Ellis, R. (2000). Academic efforts and study habits among students in a principles of macroeconomics course. *Journal of Education for Business*, 75, 219-24.

Philadelphia, City of (2001). Information technology project business case and project evaluation process. Department of Water Resources, Unpublished (July).

Rumble, G. (1997). *The costs and economics of open and distance learning*. Sterling, VA: Kogan Page.

Schiller, B. (2000). *Essentials of economics* (4th ed.) New York: McGraw-Hill.

Simon, H. (2001). Cooperation between educational technology and learning theory to advance higher education. In Goodman, P.S. (Ed.), *Technology Enhanced Learning.* Mahwah, NJ: Lawrence Erlbaum Associates.

Sorrentino, J.A. (1997). Going virtual: What to bring along from the F-2-F classroom and LAN computer lab? In Morrison, J.M. (Ed.), *Technology Tools for Today's Campuses,* a CD-ROM. Retrieved on October 9, 2002 from http://horizon.unc.edu/projects/monograph/CD/.

Visser, J.A. (2000). Faculty work in developing and teaching web-based distance courses: A case study of time and effort. *American Journal of Distance Education*, 14, 21-32.

Watson. G. (2000). *Silicon, circuits, and the digital revolution SCEN103.* October 9, 2002 from the University of Delaware, Department of Physics and Astronomy website: http://www.physics.udel.edu/wwwusers/watson/scen103/intel.html.

Appendix A

The Survey Instrument

The survey is available at http://island.temple.edu/MBAsurvey/index.asp.

1. When selecting a business school to pursue your MBA, the Fox School's level of technology use was:

20.9%	A vital part of the decision-making process
52.3%	A marginal concern
09.3%	An unimportant concern
16.3%	Not an issue at all
01.2%	Don't know

2. Please rank the following factors in terms of their importance in providing you with a positive MBA course experience (one being the most important; number can be used more than once):

3rd	A professor who is available to help
2nd	Challenging coursework
5th	Comprehensible textbook
4th	Latest technology
1st	Knowledgeable professor

3. Have you taken a course online in the MBA program?

34.9%	Yes
65.1%	No

4. Which of the following type of course is most appealing to you?

02.3%	One that uses technology as the only mode of communication
26.7%	One that uses technology as primary mode of communication
62.8%	One that uses technology as an alternative mode of communication
05.8%	One that uses technology rarely as a mode of communication
02.3%	One that never uses technology as a mode of communication

5. When choosing an MBA class to take, assuming all else is equal, would you choose to take a class that uses technology?

38.4% A lot
48.8% Sometimes
05.8% Rarely
02.3% Never
04.7% Don't know

6. In your MBA experience so far, you have used technology (choose more than one if relevant):

07.0% Only as a mode of communication
96.5% As a mode of communication and information gathering
05.8% Only as a mode of information gathering
02.3% Not at all
04.7% Don't know

7. With regard to its influence on learning, technology as a mode of communication and information gathering is:

72.1% Very positive
23.3% Somewhat positive
03.5% Neutral
01.2% Somewhat negative
00.0% Very negative

8. Looking back over the MBA classes that you have taken, indicate the number of courses in which the impact of technology on your satisfaction was:

30.6% Very positive
28.5% Somewhat positive
30.8% Neutral
06.1% Somewhat negative
04.0% Very negative

9. Which of the following levels of technology use would most likely persuade you to enroll in a course?

08.2% "Online" course, with all materials and communication on the Internet

14.1%   "Online" course that also welcomes communication via telephone, and has specified office hours for face-to-face contact
69.4%   Traditional lecture class that uses the Internet for class notes and e-mail communication
07.1%   Traditional lecture class that uses e-mail as a secondary mode of communication
01.2%   Traditional lecture class with no technology use

10. Rank the following as important factors regarding how you learn at the MBA level. (one being the most important; number may be used more than once)

3rd   A professor who is available to help
2nd   Challenging coursework
4th   Comprehensible textbook
5th   Latest technology
1st   Knowledgeable professor

11. To maximize your learning, which of the following statements is most correct?

07.0%   I must use the latest technology
62.8%   The latest technology is very helpful
25.6%   The latest technology is somewhat helpful
04.7%   The latest technology does not affect me
00.0%   The latest technology just confuses me

12. When a professor relies on the latest technology to teach a course, you feel:

27.9%   Excited, you enjoy using the latest technology
50.0%   Somewhat happy, as any additional way to gather information or communicate is helpful
14.0%   Indifferent
07.0%   Apprehensive, but decide to take the course anyway
01.2%   Very unhappy, you drop the course and seek a more traditional approach

13. Which of the following best describes what you think about the current emphasis on technology use in Temple's MBA program?

    09.3%   I would be more satisfied if my classes were much more techno-centric.

    40.7%   I would be more satisfied if my classes were somewhat more techno-centric

    45.3%   My satisfaction is independent of the emphasis on technology.

    04.7%   I would be more satisfied if my classes were somewhat less techno-centric.

    00.0%   I would be more satisfied if my classes were much less techno-centric.

14. Recall the MBA class in which you had the most positive experience. That class used technology:

    05.9%   Exclusively
    48.2%   A lot
    30.6%   A little
    10.6%   Rarely
    04.7%   Never

15. Would you say that the latest technology (e.g., streaming video) helps you to learn?

    10.6%   Much more
    50.6%   Somewhat more
    38.8%   No effect
    00.0%   Somewhat less
    00.0%   Much less

16. Which of the following statements do you think is the most correct?

    04.7%   Temple's MBA program uses too much of the latest technology.

    43.5%   Temple's MBA program uses just the right amount of the latest technology.

    32.9%   Temple's MBA program does not use enough of the latest technology.

    00.0%   Temple's MBA program does not use any of the latest technology.

    18.8%   Don't know

17. Rank the following in terms of how they would lead you to learn more in Temple's MBA program. (one being the most important; number can be used more than once)

- 2nd   Better textbooks
- 1st   Better professors
- 5th   Better classrooms
- 3rd   Better technology
- 4th   Other

18. Recall the MBA course in which you think that you learned the least in so far. Rank the following in terms of which had a negative influence on your learning the material. (one being the most negative; number may be used more than once)

- 2nd   The material was too unchallenging and/or uninteresting
- 1st   The professor was not helpful and/or understandable
- 5th   The latest technology was not used
- 3rd   The textbook was incomprehensible
- 4th   Other

19. Which of the following statements best describes your overall Temple MBA experience so far?

- 28.2%   I am very satisfied
- 58.8%   I am somewhat satisfied
- 08.2%   Indifferent
- 04.7%   I am somewhat dissatisfied
- 00.0%   I am very dissatisfied

20. Recall the MBA course in which you think you learned the most from so far. That class used technology:

- 06.0%   Exclusively
- 48.8%   A lot
- 29.8%   A little
- 11.9%   Rarely
- 03.6%   Never

21. If Temple's MBA program were to invest more money in acquiring the latest technology, which of the following do you think would be true for you?

    09.4%   I would learn a lot more
    54.1%   I would learn somewhat more
    36.5%   My learning would be unaffected
    00.0%   I would learn somewhat less
    00.0%   I would learn much less

22. What is your gender?

    52.3%   Male
    47.7%   Female

23. How many courses have you completed in the program?

    10.6%   Less than three
    27.1%   At least three, but not more that six
    18.8%   At least seven, but not more than nine
    42.4%   Ten or more
    01.2%   Don't know

24. In what range is your approximate grade point average in the program?

    69.4%   4.0 to 3.51
    28.2%   3.5 to 3.01
    01.2%   3.0 to 2.51
    01.2%   2.5 and below
    00.0%   Don't know

25. In what range is the percent salary increase you expect when you finish your MBA program, in the same company or another company?

    15.3%   0 to 4.99
    05.9%   5.0 to 9.99
    21.2%   10.0 to 14.99
    27.1%   15 or above
    30.6%   Don't know

PLEASE ANSWER THE REMAINING QUESTIONS **ONLY IF YOU HAVE HAD AN ONLINE COURSE**.

26. How many courses have you had online in the Fox School MBA program?

39.3%   One
25.0%   Two
10.7%   Three
10.7%   Four
14.3%   Five
00.0%   Don't know

27. Recall your online course(s). Rank in order the importance of the following technologies in those courses. (one being the most important; number may be used more than once)

1st   E-mail
4th   Listserv
3rd   Discussion Board
2nd   Course Management Software (e.g., Blackboard)
6th   Videoconferencing
5th   Other

28. Did you ever feel that the technology was being used for its own sake, and not because it meaningfully added to the teaching/learning process?

50.0%   Yes
50.0%   No

29. How would you express the degree to which you valued the convenience of being able to take the course online? (one = very much; five = hardly at all)

46.2%   One
41.0%   Two
10.3%   Three
0.0%   Four
2.6%   Five
0.0%   Don't know

30. In what range is your willingness to pay extra tuition to be able to take a course online as opposed to in class?

72.4% $10 - $50
03.4% $51- $100
13.8% $101 - $150
03.4% $151 - $200
06.9% More than $200

Appendix B

The Sample Grades Data (All on 100 Points)

Legend: Sam: Sample; Mi: Midterm Face-to-Face; Fi: Final Face-to-Face; Mo: Midterm Online; Fo: Final Online

30-sample			
sam-mi	sam-fi	sam-mo	sam-fo
68	77	76	95
81	95	66	63
83	81	93	92
66	85	102	92
62	69	98	91
70	64	47	75
95	94	89	95
88	91	42	63
92	85	96	98
91	82	68	100
76	87	92	80
92	66	60	50
53	61	63	70
81	89	95	83
78	77	91	94
79	86	73	50
88	86	65	98
74	88	83	67
71	82	96	98
87	84	50	81
91	93	66	91
78	96	79	85
74	89	94	100
73	70	99	100
68	66	71	81
56	63	87	90
93	79	92	96
93	95	100	95
79	86	62	100
87	90	80	87

50-sample

sam2-mi	sam2-fi	sam2-mo	sam2-fo
100	74	73	80
68	70	93	95
98	82	96	75
52	91	90	50
92	87	95	50
80	70	66	96
93	49	87	80
79	82	85	92
53	66	71	95
55	64	98	50
90	34	50	89
81	63	52	81
64	87	84	77
97	85	80	87
92	84	76	98
92	84	92	92
75	93	79	98
59	88	89	70
88	95	42	83
80	52	89	89
64	25	96	63
86	90	56	65
95	82	66	96
77	63	69	100
73	96	72	93

50-Sample

90	88	47	80
79	95	94	85
78	85	91	50
68	86	92	94
63	82	75	79
78	70	90	95
42	67	95	95
61	51	85	98
94	75	91	95
92	100	87	98
82	89	84	81
85	80	79	88
93	95	102	100
79	69	76	80
93	77	98	100
83	89	92	87
79	93	97	94
72	70	98	100
69	88	63	32
56	66	89	100
89	57	56	75
70	92	92	63
69	76	89	82
78	82	82	100
70	77	89	96

Chapter IV

Universal Design for Online Education: Access for All

Rosangela K. Boyd

Temple University

Bonnie Moulton

Temple University

Abstract

This chapter will discuss accessibility issues related to online education. It will provide rationale for designing online courses that cater to different levels of functional ability. It will also present an overview of the challenges faced by students with disabilities in accessing and interacting with online course materials and activities. In order to address the potential barriers to full participation, national and international guidelines will be examined, with particular emphasis on their implications for specific course components. In addition, mechanisms for validation of web accessibility will be suggested and resources will be listed for those interested in obtaining further information on the topic.

Introduction

Universal design calls for the development of information systems flexible enough to accommodate the needs of the broadest range of users of computers and telecommunications equipment, regardless of age or disability (Campbell & Waddell, 1997, p. 4).

In terms of learning, universal design means the design of instructional materials and activities that makes the learning goals achievable by individuals with wide differences in their abilities to hear, see, speak, move, read, write, understand English, attend, organize, engage, and remember. Universal design for learning is achieved by means of flexible curricular materials and activities that provide alternatives for students with differing abilities. These alternatives are built into instructional design and operating systems — they are not added on after-the-fact (Danielson, 1999, pp. 2-3).

At a recent faculty workshop on inclusive education, an experienced professor raised his hand and commented "Good teaching is good teaching." After a pause and a few puzzled looks from the other participants, he explained his statement in greater detail. He claimed that if teachers use effective pedagogical strategies in their teaching, they automatically reach out to diverse populations, including persons with disabilities.

In fact, a review of the Theory of Multiple Intelligences developed by Gardner (2000) points to a similar conclusion. This theory postulates eight different pathways to learning (linguistic, logical-mathematical, spatial, musical, bodily-kinesthetic, naturalistic, intrapersonal, interpersonal). Learners use different channels to acquire information; therefore, an effective teacher should ensure that his or her teaching is not based on only one mode of instruction. By utilizing a variety of ways to present course materials, the teacher will increase the likelihood that a broader range of students will access and process the information. Consequently, students with disabilities will benefit from teaching approaches that integrate various sensory, physical, cognitive, and social experiences.

Such a concept parallels the notion of "universal design." According to Bergman and Johnson (1995), universal design has gained visibility as the concept of accessibility[1] has expanded to encompass more than accommodations for people with disabilities. The Center for Universal Design defines this term as "the design of products and environments to be usable by all people, to the greatest extent possible, without the need for adaptation or specialized design" (2002a, p. 1). As the word "universal" implies, the emphasis is on designing for everyone, not just for persons with disabilities. It recognizes that there is no such entity as the "average" consumer and that good design should aim to fit the broadest range of user abilities possible. As a consequence of well-planned design, many individuals benefit. Experts in this area admit that to design any item to be universally usable is a great challenge. But it is the goal that matters, the effort to strive for products that can be useful to as many consumers as possible (Mace, 1998). This idea has gained momentum. It is possible to see examples of it everywhere around us. A walk along the aisles of a store selling household items will show items such a utensils with handles built up for improved grip, soda bottle and milk carton holders, jar openers, etc. These products could be considered assistive technology[2] for persons with disabilities who have difficulty with fine motor skills; for the rest of the buyers, they add to convenience and efficiency. And who nowadays would consider a remote control anything less than a daily necessity? Such a device allows a non-disabled person to perform several functions without lifting more than a finger; it also increases the amount of control an individual with a physical disability has over his or her environment.

Another very popular example that illustrates universal design is the use of "curb cuts" on sidewalks. Although currently mandated by accessibility related laws, curb cuts benefit not only wheelchair users, but also mothers with baby carriages, older adults with canes, and small children who have not learned how to climb steps yet. As a spin off of this easily understood term, the expression "electronic (or virtual) curb cuts" was born (WebAIM, 2002b). It communicates a similar idea for those interested in computer access. If we envision the Internet as an information highway traveled by millions of users, virtual curb cuts are ways to equalize access, thus offering persons with disabilities the same opportunities to use the Web independently as everyone else. And in the process, these virtual curb cuts benefit other groups of people who may have temporary limitations or who process information in less traditional ways. As defined by Cynthia D. Waddell, JD, ADA (1998), Coordinator of the San Jose, California region, web accessibility refers "to the design of a web page that embraces the requirements of Universal Design in order to ensure that all users can access the information on the page" (p. 2).

The use of the Internet is fundamental for the delivery of online courses. Faculty committed to online education must be informed on the challenges faced by students with disabilities and on the solutions available to overcome access barriers. In addition, we should keep in mind that other modalities utilized in online education (e.g., print materials, video and audio conferences) also need to adhere to accessibility guidelines.

The Market

It is estimated that one out of ten individuals in the world has a disability (Paciello, 2000). In the United States, 20% of the population has some kind of disability, and that 10% have severe disabilities that limit use of the Internet (WebAIM, 2002c, p. 2). Based on population trends, the fastest segment of the population is age 65 years old and above. Functional limitations such as motor and sensory disabilities increase with age. If by age 30, only about 10% of us have a disability, by age 65, the percentage increases to approximately 50% (American Association for Retired Persons, 2001; Henry, 2002; Vanderheiden, 1990). Considering that the typical online student is more likely an adult leaner (Schwitzer, Ancis & Brown, 2001), it is expected that faculty will encounter students with functional limitations in their courses. Persons with disabilities already represent 10% of Internet users (Henry, 2002). Unfortunately, only 21.6% of people with disabilities have access to the Internet, compared to 42.1% of those without disabilities (Abramson, 2000). This gap is likely to change as barriers for computer purchase and usage are eliminated in the future. For persons with disabilities, the ability to use the Internet for educational purposes opens a door to greater independence. Students with disabilities feel empowered to access information without having to travel long distances or make use of attendant services in order to take notes or participate in a group discussion. A deaf student can communicate with her professor via e-mail independently; a blind student can read the computer screen while utilizing specialized software; a student with learning disabilities may download information and go over it at his own pace. Anyone can participate in a listserv without the need to self-identify as a person with a disability. Ironically, the same mode of instruction that can offer greater freedom to persons with disabilities may also pose severe obstacles if access considerations are not part of the course design process.

In addition to consumers with disabilities, accessible design also favors other groups. For instance, a number of students do not have fast Internet connections at home. Complex sites may become very frustrating to navigate due to the time it takes to follow links and open certain elements such as video clips. It is also quite possible that some students still carry older versions of a particular browser, which makes it more difficult—and sometimes impossible —to access state of the art technology. Students may also have lifestyle issues that require accommodations, even though they may not have a disability. Imagine for a second that one of your students was involved in a car accident right before the beginning of the academic semester and will have to wear a body cast, making a trip to the university an impossibility. This student may be able to follow an online course, but may have to find alternate ways to use the computer if access to the mouse or keyboard is not feasible. And how about the computer programmer who is taking your course for professional development and has been diagnosed with Carpal Tunnel Syndrome? Will he still be able to navigate the website without straining his wrist by using the mouse? If your student shares the office with three other persons, she may not be able to listen to an audio recording posted on the course site; without a text transcript, she may not be able to access course information during her lunch time. In a reverse situation, the mother of a young child who has very little time to attend to coursework may find it helpful to listen to a audio recording of a presentation rather than reading it while she watches her child play safely next to her. These are only a few examples of situations for which planfull course development that meets accessibility guidelines for individuals with disabilities may eventually reach out to other segments of the educational market.

Legislative Forces Guiding Accessibility

Perhaps the most compelling reason to utilize principles of universal design in online education is that access to an appropriate education for all students is a moral and ethical imperative. "Moral and ethical imperatives" make for resounding rhetoric, but have little impact on the lived experience of marginalized individuals unless backed by the force of law. In the case of educational opportunities for people with disabilities, Federal statutes do exist and should not be ignored by those involved in online education.

Federal laws designed to protect the civil rights of people with disabilities provide them with the best opportunity to engage in every arena of life and to achieve educationally, vocationally and socially. These laws permit free and active participation across multiple environments, including the virtual environment of the World Wide Web. This section of the chapter will provide an overview of Federal law regarding access to assistive technology and information technology. Particular attention will be given to the following statutes:

- The Individuals with Disabilities Education Act of 1990 (as amended 1997) (P.L. 101-476 and P.L. 105-17). (Originally known as The Education for All Handicapped Children Act passed in 1975 (P.L. 94-142);

- The Rehabilitation Act of 1973 as amended in 1992 and 1998 – Sections 504 and 508 (P.L. 102-569 and P.L. 105-220);

- The Americans with Disabilities Act (1990) (P.L. 101-336);

- The Telecommunications Act of 1996 – Section 255 (P.L. 104-104);

- The Assistive Technology Act of 1998 (P.L. 105-394); and

- The Technology Related Assistance for Individuals with Disabilities Act ("The Tech Act") of 1988 and its amendments of 1994 (P.L.100-407 and P.L. 103-218).

Each of these laws share a common focus – the provision of civil rights to individuals with disabilities, and the provision of necessary supports and services to make it possible for them to exercise those rights. In addition, many of the laws share common language that can be traced back to the Rehabilitation Act of 1973, the first of a set of sweeping civil rights laws that, in the relatively short span of just under thirty years, have begun to mitigate centuries of oppression and have allowed people with disabilities access to schools, work environments, public accommodations, and information technologies. This increased access can only serve to further enhance their abilities to take their rightful place as productive and informed citizens.

We will return to a discussion of the impact of the Rehabilitation Act following a brief discussion of the Individuals with Disabilities Education Act. The discussion of each statute will address the following issues:

- the key points of the law — using the language of the law itself as space permits;

- a brief explanation of what the law means in the daily lives of people with disabilities; and

- the manner in which the law has been (or can be) used to provide increased access to online education for students with disabilities.

Key themes will be repeated throughout this analysis. The reader is encouraged to recall these points so as to achieve a holistic understanding of the social and legislative history of the movement toward civil rights by people with disabilities. The purpose of this section is to provide an overview of the legislative mandates relating to the use of technology in educational settings. If a detailed analysis is preferred, the reader is referred to the section on resources at the close of the chapter.

The Individuals with Disabilities Education Act (IDEA) of 1990 as Amended in 1997 (P.L. 101-476 and P.L. 105-17); Originally Known as The Education for All Handicapped Children Act of 1975 (P.L. 94-142)

P.L. 94-142 was enacted in 1975 in an effort to address the failure of education systems at the state level to meet the educational needs of millions of children with disabilities who were underserved or completely unserved at the local level. Briefly, the law exists to:

> *(a) assure that all children with disabilities have available to them...a free appropriate public education which emphasizes special education and related services designed to meet their unique needs, to assure that the rights of children with disabilities and their parents or guardians are protected, to assist states and localities to provide for the education of all children with disabilities, and to assess and assure the effectiveness of efforts to educate children with disabilities (Tucker, 1988, p. 331).*

The law guarantees the right to a free and appropriate public education (FAPE) based on an individualized education plan (IEP) and mandates that education be provided in the least restrictive environment (LRE). The IEP is a written document that provides a "blueprint" for the determination of the FAPE; any requirement for the use of "related services" such as assistive or information technology is written into the IEP. The law also outlines various policies to safeguard the rights of the student and his or her guardians. IDEA currently provides protections to students with educationally based disabilities from birth to age 21.

Given the explosive growth in the use of online education as well as other instructional technologies starting at the elementary level, knowledge of the protections afforded by IDEA is of increasing importance to educators at all levels. Early exposure and access to instructional technologies is increasingly important for all children but access to assistive technology is of particular importance for children with severe disabilities as technologies such as voice-output communication devices, word processors, and screen readers not only facilitate learning, but also mastery of the environment and the development of social relationships.

The Vocational Rehabilitation Act of 1973 as Amended in 1992 and 1998, Sections 504 and 508 (P.L. 93-112, P.L. 102-569 and P.L. 105-166).

Section 504 states:

> *No otherwise qualified individual with a disability in the United States...shall, solely by reason of her or his disability, be excluded from participation in, be denied the benefits of, or subjected to discrimination under any program or activity receiving Federal financial assistance or under any program or activity conducted by any Executive agency...(Tucker, 1998, pp. 30-31).*

Section 504 of the Rehabilitation Act specifically prohibits recipients of federal financial assistance from discriminating on the basis of disability in numerous areas of endeavor, including employment, education, physical access to the built environment, and social service programs. Section 504 is, in effect, the first national declaration of the rights of people with disabilities, serving to establish the rights of Americans with disabilities to the dignity and respect owed to them as equal and contributing members of society and to permit them access to every sphere of American society. The Act specifically pertains to entities that receive federal funds, the services of federal personnel, or property from the federal government.

Because Section 504 guaranteed access to federally funded programs and activities, including educational programs and activities, Section 504 foreshadowed IDEA in providing access to FAPE in an appropriate educational setting with appropriate procedural safeguards. Even now, Section 504 provides protections to students who, for a variety of reasons, are not covered under IDEA; for example, students in post-secondary education who fall outside of the age limits outlined in IDEA, and students who have a limitation in one or more major life activities who nonetheless do not meet the definition of "disability" under IDEA (Alexander & Alexander, 1995).

The 1998 amendments to the Vocational Rehabilitation Act — Section 508 — recognized the increasing importance of information technology in American society. The amendments require the Federal government to make the technology it uses accessible to people with disabilities. The degree of access must be equivalent to the degree of access enjoyed by those without disabilities, unless the provision of such access would result in "undue burden." The 508 amendments apply to technology developed, procured, maintained, or used by the Federal government. Thus, hardware and software used by Federal entities or those receiving Federal funds must be accessible (FCC, 2002a). This would include any web page developed by the Federal government or web pages for online courses sponsored by educational entities receiving Federal funds.

The Americans with Disabilities Act – Title III (1990) (P.L. 101-336)

The Americans with Disabilities Act (ADA) is known as the civil rights law for people with disabilities. The language of the ADA echoes both the language and the intent of Section 504. Various Titles provide legal protections across a variety of situations. Title I prohibits discrimination in employment, Title II mandates access to state and local government programs and access to public transportation, Title III, access to places of public accommodation, Title IV requires that all common carriers provide functionally equivalent telecommunications equipment for use by individuals with communication deficits.

Since passage of the ADA in 1990, legal arguments have been successfully developed using the language in Titles I, through IV to provide access to information technologies to individuals with disabilities. Title I with its emphasis on non-discrimination in employment, calls for the provision of "reasonable accommodations" and accessible environments to permit "qualified individuals with disabilities" to be maximally effective in the work setting. The reader is reminded that accessible online environments can be considered a "reasonable accommodation" and may, therefore, have as much potential to benefit instructors with disabilities as they do students with disabilities (Tucker, 1998).

Legal arguments also exist regarding provision of access under Title II and Title III. The reasoning is as follows: Title II, in providing access to state and local government entities is reminiscent of the language of Section 504 and provides the right to access websites and other information technologies maintained by state and local governments and by organizations receiving funding from state and federal sources. The language of Title II is significant in that there is recognition of the power of "effective communication" by way of access to information technology. Simply put, "access to technology" is not enough. People with disabilities must be provided a means of communication that is *as effective* as that provided to individuals who do not have disabilities. Finally, Title II clearly stipulates the requirement to design electronic media that is accessible at first use—that it is a violation of the law to wait to modify existing technology until a request is made (Waddell, 2002).

In a similar manner, Title III, that portion of the ADA relating to access to public accommodations, requires that public accommodations that utilize electronic communication modalities must make those modalities accessible to and usable by people with disabilities. The rationale used in this instance was that accessibility in the virtual environment of the World Wide Web was *not* just an extension of the guarantees of accessibility in the physical environment envisioned with the passage of the ADA, but that the virtual environment had become more and more *real* with increased opportunities for e-education, e-commerce, e-banking and e-government. And because these sites were designed to be used by the public, the fact that they were not accessible to people with disabilities was analogous to a denial of access to a public accommodation in the built environment (Waddell, 2002).

Title IV of the ADA is specifically concerned with the provision of telecommunications relay services to those with hearing or speech disabilities. Specifically, the law says that all "common carriers" (telephone companies) must provide "telecommunications relay services." These services may be provided "through designees, through a competitively selected vendor, or in concert with other carriers" (Tucker, 1998, pp. 283-284). Again, these services must be functionally equivalent to telecommunication services provided to consumers without disabilities. Title IV is specific to telecommunications relay services and does not speak to the use of modems or other telecommunications equipment more closely related to the use of electronic and information technologies. However, the implicit acknowledgment that current telecommunications systems were inadequate to meet the needs of a significant number of citizens may have foreshadowed the explicit mandates of Section 255 of the Telecommunications Act of 1996.

The Telecommunications Act of 1996 –
Section 255 (P.L. 104-104)

Section 255 of the Telecommunications Act of 1996 mandates that all telecommunications equipment **must** be accessible to people with disabilities. Key portions of the statute follow.

A *manufacturer* of telecommunications equipment or customer premises equipment (CPE) shall insure that the equipment is designed, developed, and fabricated to be accessible to and useable by individuals with disabilities, if readily achievable.

A *provider* of telecommunication services shall insure that the service is accessible to and useable by individuals with disabilities, if readily achievable (Waddell, 2002, p. 36).

CPE includes equipment used in the home, office or elsewhere "to originate, route, or terminate telecommunications" (FCC, 2002b, p. 2). Examples include modems, fax machines, pagers, and telephones. If access is not readily achievable, Section 255 stipulates that manufacturers and providers should make devices and services that are compatible with peripherals and any specialized customer premises equipment that are commonly used by people with disabilities, if compatibility is readily achievable.

The Assistive Technology (AT) Act of 1998 (P.L. 105-394)
and The Technology Related Assistance for Individuals with
Disabilities Act ("The Tech Act") of 1988 and Its Amendments
of 1994 (P.L.100-407 and P.L. 103-218)

These two laws are particularly significant in that they provide financial supports to the states to enable the design and implementation of consumer-responsive programs to provide statewide education and training related to assistive technology supports and services. The language of the Assistive Technology Act emphasizes the increasing importance of technology in all aspects of life. For both people with disabilities and those without, technology has become an increasingly important facet of daily life. If technology represents convenience for people *without* disabilities, it means greater independence and productivity for people *with* disabilities.

Computer Challenges Faced by Different Disability Groups

Individuals with disabilities are in no way a homogeneous group, not even those who share the same type of disabling condition. This section will present generic information on various disability groups regarding the access issues involved in participating in online learning (Bergman & Johnson, 1995; Brummel, 1994; Burgstahler, 2002; Chancellor's Office at California Community College, 1999; Coombs, 2002a; Paciello, 2000; WebAIM, 2000b). Future sections will discuss national and international guidelines and suggest accessibility solutions. The underlying assumption is that faculty will use this information as a starting point in designing course materials, but will keep in mind that each student should be asked about reasonable individual accommodations that may facilitate learning.

Visual Impairments

Approximately 4% of the U.S. population (10.4 million) is visually impaired or blind. Three subcategories will be discussed below: blindness, low vision, and color blindness.

Blindness

It is estimated that .5% of the population (1.3 million) is legally blind.[3] Typically, students who are blind access print materials displayed on their computer screen through screen readers. A screen reader is a software program that can be used in conjunction with a speech synthesizer[4] or a Braille refreshable display.[5] Screen readers are capable of reading text, punctuation, control buttons, and menus, but they do not read graphics. They also work in a linear way, going left to right and top to button. They allow the user to interface with the computer by pressing certain commands from the keyboard;

they do not work with the mouse. Many documents, especially those on websites, make use of images to enhance the aesthetics of the pages, to stress a point made in the text, or to direct a user to take some action (e.g., go to a linked page, scroll down, enter information). Many web pages are also organized with graphical elements such as tables, frames, and navigation bars. Some may also contain embedded video clips or multimedia objects. A sighted person is able to process images and changes in text colors and move around the screen with a mouse, skipping irrelevant information after quickly scanning the page contents. In contrast, a blind person may miss important information from graphics, color highlighted text, or videos, and get confused while tediously tabbing through menus of links, visiting frames separately, and encountering other graphical features in a page that is not organized in a linear fashion. When encountering a house icon with the words "click here" highlighted, a sighted person may deduce that clicking it will produce the action of returning to the homepage. If text information is embedded into images, if words indicate the need to perform an action that is not clearly described, or if complex tables are used to convey information, the blind user may be quite frustrated unless the html code is written in a clear and descriptive way that facilitates navigation and understanding of visual content. Another modality being increasingly adopted by online courses is synchronous communication via chat sessions. A blind person may not be able to follow the fast moving text and changing frames associated with some programs. They will have no problem, however, with programs that use audio input and output for group dialogue. They will not benefit from a camera, but as long as no crucial information is conveyed through this device, other sighted students participating in the chat session can make use of it to communicate with classmates and faculty.

Low Vision

Approximately 3.5% of the population (9.2 million) has significantly impaired sight. In general, low vision[6] is associated with poor acuity or vision deficits in different areas of the visual field (e.g., central, edges). A student with low vision may choose to use screen magnification in order to enlarge a portion of the screen. This type of software can magnify text and graphics, while allowing the user to track position on the screen. By increasing the size of text, this technology improves readability; however, it also limits the amount of information that can be displayed at one time. The user may need to scroll frequently to get to different sections of the page. Like blind students, low-vision students may have trouble with pages organized in nonlinear formats, interspersed with frames and graphics. In addition, when enlarging pictures, it may make them pixilated and harder to interpret. Another strategy a person with low vision may use to improve visibility is to change contrast settings on the screen. Using low contrast between text and background or creating patterned backgrounds may hinder accessibility for these individuals. The same comments made about blind students regarding video and audio conferencing apply to low-vision students.

Color Blindness

As a genetic, sex-linked trait, color deficiency is experienced by approximately 10% of the male population and .5% of the female population. There are different kinds and degrees of color blindness. Individuals born with this condition, frequently have difficulty distinguishing colors such as those in the red, green, orange, and yellow.

Spectrums. If color blindness is severe, other colors may also be hard to see. Dark and muted tones present a greater challenge. There is no device or software that will correct this deficiency, although users may choose to adjust the color contrast in their monitors. When confronted with the use of colors to code information or direct specific actions on a web page, students who are color blind may not perceive the message as intended and ignore important commands. As with students with low vision, color-blind students will have trouble with pages that use juxtaposing colors of similar contrast.

Hearing Impairments

Approximately 8.2% of the population (22 million) report some level of hearing loss; near 10% of these individuals have severe loss (2.4 million). Because a great portion of online course content is delivered visually, individuals who are deaf or hard of hearing do not require much assistive technology to access information or participate in online activities such as listserv, e-mail, or typed chat session. If born deaf and trained in sign language, they may process language less rapidly and require more time to read information and respond to it. In this case, a fast chat discussion may be problematic; nevertheless, a much greater barrier will come from audio conferencing or from the use of videotapes or audio recordings. In face-to-face situations, some hearing-impaired individuals will resort to reading lips in order to communicate with others or simply absorb information. It is usually difficult to read lips of characters in a video or television broadcast because of the shifting angles; it is nearly impossible to use lip reading for videos delivered over the Web due to screen size and resolution.

Physical Disabilities

Approximately 10% of the population has a physical condition resulting in motor impairment. Examples of such conditions include spinal cord injuries, cerebral palsy, multiple sclerosis, muscular dystrophy, limb amputation, etc. If the disability does not restrict keyboard and mouse use, the user is not likely to encounter access barriers (provided other sensory conditions are not present). If the motor deficit limits controlled manipulation of the mouse, keyboard access is still possible with applications such as MouseKeys.[7] Because using the keyboard keys is a time consuming process, keyboard accelerators that combine keystrokes (e.g., "control" + "s" for saving a file) may be helpful. If direct access to both mouse and keyboard is impossible, pointing devices (such as a head wand or mouth stick) or switches may be used. Anytime direct access is not feasible, speed is compromised. Some key combinations such as a "Shift" +"Alt"+ "PrtSc" (used to freeze and save a particular screen) may be more challenging than others because of the distance between each key. Another task that may result in fatigue and muscle strain is that of tabbing from link to link in order to access new information. Some users may also choose to use voice recognition systems.[8] This technology has the advantage of being hands-free, but is sensitive to deviations in speech patterns. Students with physical disabilities may be able to participate in phone conferences through the use of speaker phones. Chats may be more challenging. A text-input type of chat may be too fast for someone who types slowly or accesses the keyboard through pointers or switches. A video or audio chat may be easier, but some persons may require assistance in setting up the headphone and/or camera. Individuals with upper limb functional limitations may prefer to have text available online rather than in print since page manipulation may be an issue in independent reading.

Cognitive Disabilities

Although it is unlikely that persons with severe cognitive disabilities will be found in post-secondary education, the trend towards inclusion and the fact that online courses may provide an opportunity to pace one's learning process may bring more focus to this group in the future. Currently, there are already students in our colleges and universities who have learning disabilities and residual effects of head injury. Although very capable of acquiring an education, some of these students may require increased time in processing information, as well as organized and logical set ups. Web pages containing a lot of different types of information (colors, audio, moving objects) may be very distracting. The same can be said for information presented in inconsistent formats. For these students, a courseware platform that organizes information and requires consistent actions for input and output may be helpful, as long as information is provided on a routine basis as to what tasks are due and where to go to access specific course materials.

Other Disabilities

Some seizure disorders may be severe enough to cause functional limitations. Usually, such disorders are easily accommodated in online education. One issue regarding Web access, however, is the flickering rate of web pages. Intensive flashing or flickering may induce seizures.

At times, disabilities include limitation in more than one area of functioning. An example of this is *deaf-blindness*. A student with these characteristics will have difficulty with both audio and visual information. The more likely computer interface access technology would be a screen reader with a Braille refreshable device. If information displayed on the screen is complex, this can become a time-consuming process. Like the blind student, a deaf-blind student will have trouble with graphical elements and color-coded content.

Another functional combination is that of *speech and motor* disabilities. In severe cases of cerebral palsy, for example, an individual may experience physical limitations that impair both movement of limbs and/or speech muscles. These students are sometimes not recognized for their average or above average cognitive abilities because of their difficulty in expressive communication. Those who reach college will probably make use of augmentative communication devices,[9] which, depending on the level of motor impairment, may require interface with computers. Even the fastest augmentative communication users will require additional time to compose messages during phone or audio chat conversations, and the synthesized voices of the devices may be hard to understand in busy environments. They may also require similar accommodations to those of individuals with other physical disabilities, because direct mouse and keyboard access will be not be possible.

Guidelines for Accessible Design in Online Education

After reading about the challenges faced by students with different disabilities, it may seem that designing accessible online courses is an insurmountable task or that the only solutions are to design plain and unattractive web pages and avoid state of the art technologies for synchronous communication. Some faculty faced with these access barriers may try to discourage students with disabilities from participating in their courses or create independent learning sessions to accommodate them. They may also decide to wait to make necessary design adjustments until a student with a disability, who has already registered for their course, forces them to examine their materials and activities in light of that student's or her particular needs. More often, though, faculty is simply unaware of the solutions available to increase accessibility.

Ethical and committed faculty members are invested in facilitating learning and teaching every student. Becoming informed about available guidelines is the first step to building courses that can be accessed by all.

Before engaging in a detailed discussion of the two most recognized and adopted sets of guidelines for Web Accessibility, it may be helpful to review some universal design and usability principles. The Center for Universal Design has issued seven principles to guide designers of products in variety of disciplines. They are:

1. Equitable Use: The design is useful and marketable to people of diverse abilities (equality or equivalency in access methods, safety, and privacy).

2. Flexibility in Use: The design accommodates a wide range of individual preferences and abilities (choices are provided, user's pace is accommodated, etc.).

3. Simple and Intuitive: Use of a design that is easy to understand, regardless of the user's experience, knowledge, language, and/or concentration level, and consistent with user expectations. The design should be low in complexity, arranged according to importance, and include effective prompting and feedback.

4. Perceptible Information: The design communicates necessary information effectively to the user, regardless of ambient conditions or the user's sensory abilities (different modes for presenting information are offered,

legibility is maximized, compatible with devices used by persons with sensory limitations).

5.   Tolerance for Errors: The design minimizes hazards and adverse consequences of accidental or unintended actions (warnings are provided, safety features included, elements organized to reduce error or hazards).

6.   Low Physical Effort: The design can be used efficiently and comfortably and with a minimum of fatigue (avoiding use of excessive force, repetitive actions and unnatural body positions).

7.   Size and Space for Approach and Use: Appropriate size and space is provided for approach, reach, manipulation, and use, regardless of a user's body size, posture, or mobility (components can be easily reached, space dimensions allow for interface with assistive devices, variations in body positioning or grip size are accommodated). (Center for Universal Design, 2002b, pp. 5-11).

When these principles are applied to online education, some common sense strategies emerge. For example, in organizing instructional materials on a website, an infrastructure should be created to allow for fast mastering of navigational procedures. One of the reasons why courseware platforms have penetrated the academic market so rapidly is their "consumer-friendly" structure, facilitating usage by individuals of different levels of technological sophistication. Users appreciate visiting sites that are organized in ways that make quick scanning possible and clearly mark structural elements that guide actions such as following a link or skipping low-priority information. They get frustrated if they cannot find information in an expedient way and if there is an overwhelming amount of stimuli provided at once. A site that keeps referring users to other pages in order to get to particular content may confuse an user as to where he or she is after a number of links, which makes returning to other useful information identified on the way difficult, to say the least. Given the speed issues discussed above and the different ways in which assistive technology interfaces with computers and Internet-based application, following these universal design principles may greatly enhance accessibility.

Referring specifically to web accessibility, Henry (2002, pp. 7-8) states that "accessibility is a subset of a more general pursuit: usability." Because of the synergy between the two concepts, the distinction between them is often blurred. According to Henry, usability can be achieved if the following five elements are present:

1. Learnability: Can visitors use the website effectively the first time they visit it without becoming frustrated?

2. Memorability: Will visitors remember to use the website the next time?

3. Effectiveness: Can visitors easily navigate through the website, determine what to do next, and understand the content? Is the design consistent and predictable?

4. Efficiency: Can visitors find what they need and accomplish their goal is a reasonable amount of time?

5. Satisfaction: Do visitors have a good feeling about using the website? Will they use it again? Is the content presented effectively?

In many ways, these elements reinforce the principles of universal design. If faculty members are able to respond affirmatively to the above questions, they are probably already addressing some of the accessibility guidelines to be discussed in the following sections.

Techniques for Web Content Accessibility (WACG) 1.0 by the World Wide Web Consortium

The World Wide Web Consortium *(W3C)* is an international industry consortium composed of over 500 member organizations (W3C, 1999a). W3C was founded by Tim Berners-Lee, the inventor of the World Wide Web. In 1997, W3C created the Web Accessibility Initiative (WAI) Interest Group to work on web accessibility. In 1999, this workgroup released a set of recommendations for web content accessibility (Paciello, 2000; W3C, 1999b). Fourteen guidelines are included in this set of specifications. They are:

1. Provide equivalent alternatives to auditory and visual content.

2. Don't rely on color alone.

3. Use markup and style sheets and do so properly.

4. Clarify natural language usage

5. Create tables that transform gracefully.

6. Ensure that pages featuring new technologies transform gracefully.

7. Ensure user control of time-sensitive content changes.

8.   Ensure direct accessibility of embedded user interfaces.

9.   Design for device-independence.

10. Use interim solutions.

11. Use W3C technologies and guidelines.

12. Provide context and orientation information.

13. Provide clear navigational mechanisms.

14. Ensure that documents are clear and simple. (W3C, 1999c)

For each of the above guidelines, the Consortium also released several checkpoints that describe in greater detail how to implement the guideline under consideration. A detailed explanation of these checkpoints is available at http://www.w3.org/TR/1999/WAI-WEBCONTENT-19990505/checkpoint-list.html. Understanding that the task of putting such guidelines into practice may seem overwhelming for those not familiar with accessibility requirements, the working group decided to prioritize the checkpoints. Three priority levels were created:

- Priority 1: A Web content developer **must** satisfy these checkpoints, otherwise, one or more groups will find it impossible to access information in the document. Satisfying these checkpoints is a basic requirement for some groups to be able to use Web documents (17 checkpoints).

- Priority 2: A Web content developer **should** satisfy these checkpoints; otherwise, one or more groups will find it difficult to access information in the document. Satisfying these checkpoints will remove significant barriers to accessing Web documents (33 checkpoints).

- Priority 3: A Web content developer **may** address these checkpoints, otherwise, one or more groups will find it somewhat difficult to access information in the document. Satisfying this checkpoint will improve access to Web documents (16 checkpoints).

Since Priority 1 checkpoints are considered the benchmark for accessibility compliance, they are highlighted below, with numbers in parenthesis representing the guideline with which each checkpoint is associated (W3C, 1999e):

- Provide a text equivalent for every non-text element (e.g., via "alt," "longdesc," or in element content). *This includes*: images, graphical representations of text (including symbols), image map regions, animations (e.g., animated GIFs), applets and programmatic objects, ascii art, frames, scripts, images used as list bullets, spacers, graphical buttons, sounds (played with or without user interaction), stand-alone audio files, audio tracks of video, and video (1.1).

- Provide redundant text links for each active region of a server-side image map (1.2).

- Until user agents can automatically read aloud the text equivalent of a visual track, provide an auditory description of the important information of the visual track of a multimedia presentation (1.3).

- For any time-based multimedia presentation (e.g., a movie or animation), synchronize equivalent alternatives (e.g., captions or auditory descriptions of the visual track) with the presentation (1.4).

- Ensure that all information conveyed with color is also available without color, for example, from context or markup (2.1).

- Clearly identify changes in the natural language of a document's text and any text equivalents (e.g., captions) (4.1).

- For data tables, identify row and column headers (5.1).

- For data tables that have two or more logical levels of row or column headers, use markup to associate data cells and header cells (5.2).

- Organize documents so they may be read without style sheets. For example, when an html document is rendered without associated style sheets, it must still be possible to read the document (6.1).

- Ensure that equivalents for dynamic content are updated when the dynamic content changes (6.2).

- Ensure that pages are usable when scripts, applets, or other programmatic objects are turned off or not supported. If this is not possible, provide equivalent information on an alternative accessible page (6.3).

- Until user agents allow users to control flickering, avoid causing the screen to flicker (7.1).

- Make programmatic elements such as scripts and applets directly accessible or compatible with assistive technologies (8.1).

- Provide client-side image maps instead of server-side image maps except where the regions cannot be defined with an available geometric shape (9.1).

- If, after best efforts, you cannot create an accessible page, provide a link to an alternative page that uses W3C technologies, is accessible, has equivalent information (or functionality), and is updated as often as the inaccessible (original) page (11.4).

- Title each frame to facilitate frame identification and navigation (12.1).

- Use the clearest and simplest language appropriate for a site's content (14.1).

As suggested by Nielsen (1999), these priority levels should be used in developing a plan for accessibility compliance. New web pages should be designed in accordance with both Priority 1 and two checkpoints. Existing high-traffic pages and pages deemed crucial to performing essential tasks should, at a minimum, be redesigned to follow Priority 1 checkpoints. Other, less crucial pages should be gradually redesigned to meet Priority 1 checkpoints. As progress is made, all priority levels should be eventually included in the updating of the site.

Section 508 § 1194.22 Guidelines

As mentioned under the legislation section above, Section 508 of the Rehabilitation Act requires that federal agencies provide the same access to their electronic and information technology to persons with disabilities as to persons without disabilities. To facilitate compliance, a number of guidelines were issued. Section 508 guidelines are in many ways similar to those recommended by the Web Accessibility Initiative (U.S. Architectural and Transportation Barriers Compliance Board, 2000). They are:

(a) A text equivalent for every non-text element shall be provided (e.g., via "alt," "longdesc," or in element content).

(b) Equivalent alternatives for any multimedia presentation shall be synchronized with the presentation.

(c) Web pages shall be designed so that all information conveyed with color is also available without color, for example, from context or markup.

(d)   Documents shall be organized so they are readable without requiring an associated style sheet.

(e)   Redundant text links shall be provided for each active region of a server-side image map.

(f)   Client-side image maps shall be provided instead of server-side image maps except where the regions cannot be defined with an available geometric shape.

(g)   Row and column headers shall be identified for data tables.

(h)   Markup shall be used to associate data cells and header cells for data tables that have two or more logical levels of row or column headers.

(i)   Frames shall be titled with text that facilitates frame identification and navigation.

(j)   Pages shall be designed to avoid causing the screen to flicker with a frequency greater than 2 Hz and lower than 55 Hz.

(k)   A text-only page, with equivalent information or functionality, shall be provided to make a website comply with the provisions of this part, when compliance cannot be accomplished in any other way. The content of the text-only page shall be updated whenever the primary page changes.

(l)   When pages utilize scripting languages to display content or to create interface elements, the information provided by the script shall be identified with functional text that can be read by assistive technology.

(m)   When a web page requires that an applet, plug-in, or other application be present on the client system to interpret page content, the page must provide a link to a plug-in or applet that complies with §1194.21(a) through (l).

(n)   When electronic forms are designed to be completed online, the form shall allow people using assistive technology to access the information, field elements, and functionality required for completion and submission of the form, including all directions and cues.

(o)   A method shall be provided that permits users to skip repetitive navigational links.

Implications for Online Education

By examining both WAI and Section 508 guidelines, it is evident that the great majority of accommodations are related to visual components of websites. This has great meaning to faculty teaching online courses, given the predominance of visual content in such courses. This section will organize the major points from the accessibility guidelines into elements of online education conveyed through website design (Paccielo, 2000; Thatcher, 2002a, 2002b, 2002c; WebAIM, 2002a). A later section will comment on additional elements combined with web instruction in current online education.

Images

There are several applications for images in an academic site. They may be present to make the site more pleasant to look at, by providing a break from text. They may be present to emphasize or further illustrate a point made by the instructor. They may also contain links to other pages in the site or in the WWW.

Some users may choose to turn graphics off and access the text-only version of a page. This may be a choice based on speed of connection or the fact that the user cannot see the images or finds them distracting. One of the first questions a faculty member should ask in developing online content is "If I could not see, would I still be able to understand the information contained in this web page?"

Often, the temptation to use the latest technology available or to customize one's site in order to make it more appealing visually may limit access to potential users. The number one concern for faculty should be the content, with technology becoming the tool to communicate it. This is not to say that we should forget about using graphics. Text-only pages can be very dull and not constitute "good teaching" practices for students who learn better visually. In addition, relying on alternative text-only pages for students with visual impairments does not automatically lead to compliance with accessibility guidelines. If images are used to communicate messages on the regular page, individuals directed to text-only pages may miss important information. The trick is to find equivalent ways to provide the same information to everyone. As some of the guidelines indicate, html language already contains solutions for enhanced accessibility. An easy but often neglected solution is the use of "alt tags." An "alt tag" can be inserted in the html code to make it easier for a screen reader to identify a given image by its function. For example, suppose you want to use the logo of your university on your homepage, and that this image was imported from the university site as "logo3.gif." How descriptive is this title? If you really wanted to the student to know that the name of the university was written on this image, you could add an alt tag that in html code would look like this: < *img src="logo3.gif" alt="Temple University owl logo">*.

The adoption of alt tags may be a quick solution for the use of decorative graphics or graphics that emphasize a point. Some experts also suggest that if an image is not relevant to someone receiving the information auditorily, a null alt tag should be provided to tell the user that this image is not relevant to the content. An example of this would be a separator line. In this case the code might read as: *<img src="line05.gif" alt="">*.

One important use of alt tags is to describe a link embedded within an image. For example, if a house is used at the bottom of the page to indicate a link to the homepage, the alt tag should indicate the purpose of the image. Just writing something such as "link" or "click here" is not descriptive enough. The reader may not know the path for this link. A more descriptive tag would say "link to homepage."

When an image is too complex to be described by an alt tag, it is recommended that a "longdesc" attribute also be attached to the html code. For example, in an assistive technology course in which the photograph of a bowl on top of a shelf-lining square is used to convey the message that low cost and low tech solutions — such as a shelf-lining sheet as opposed to specialized materials such as dycem — may be available to enhance stability for persons with motor impairments. In this case, a tag that just says "bowl and shelf lining" may make not make enough sense to the student. Unless a text description of the image is provided below it, it is important to add a "longdesc" attribute. The html code might read: *<img src="lowtech4.gif" width="250" height="130" alt="bowl on top of shelf lining" longdesc="shelflining.html">*. The shelf-lining page could then be opened by the user for a more detailed description of the image. This same procedure can be used to further describe charts, graphs, photographs of people and places, etc.

An important alert to web designers, however, is that, at this point, the longdesc attribute is not fully supported by all types of assistive technology, so an additional convention is needed to ensure access; it is referred to as the "D-link." In simple terms, when activated, the D-link directs the user to the page containing the detailed information. In the example above, an the designer would add to the code already containing the alt tag and the longdesc attribute:

<A href="shelflining.html">D</A>. Next to the picture of the bowl, an underlined capital D would appear, indicating a link to the page with additional descriptive information, which the student could choose to read or ignore.

Size and resolution are also an important issues when planning to include images in the website. Because the disk space required by graphic images often slows the process of downloading web pages, images should not be very large in size. A student with low vision might have difficulty with small images, which could become distorted when going through screen magnification, especially if resolution of the original image is low. If a given image is considered crucial to the comprehension of specific content, the instructor may consider linking the smaller image to a page where a bigger version of it can be seen.

Colored Text

Like images, color can enhance the aesthetic of a website. If used correctly, it will pose no problems to persons with disabilities. If used in excess, it may be distracting. If used as the only means of conveying information, it can be a big obstacle to navigation. We often rely on color to indicate links, highlight information, or to organize content into categories. A student who is color blind may not see the red color indicating a link to another page, for example. A simple question to be posed while planning the structure for content display would be "If I could only see a black and white version of this page, could I still understand all the information and navigate all the controls?" It is not a crime to use color, as long as it is not the only way to communicate. There are other ways to emphasize certain points, such as making text bold. Text links could be underlined. Preferably, however, if a number of text links are to be included in a page, a better solution might be to repeat the information at the bottom of the page, under a title such as "Links to Additional Information."

Link

Aside from what has already been said about using images and color to indicate links, there are other conventions that facilitate usability and accessibility. For example, providing the user with the possibility to skip navigational links is very useful to persons utilizing a screen reader. As previously mentioned, it may be very time-consuming for a blind person to navigate a page that includes menus with links at the top. While a sighted person can focus directly on the main content of a page, a person using a screen reader will have to listen to all the items on the menu before being able to go to other sections of the page. Although this may facilitate orientation the first time someone accesses a given site, it becomes a waste of time on repeated visits. A solution to this problem is the use of an anchor (also known as "bookmark" in FrontPage®) that allows the user to skip navigational links and go directly to the main content of the page. This anchor can be displayed on the very top of the page (with the target immediately before the main content section) or can be hidden from sighted users by a picture or background colors containing html code that the screen reader identifies as the anchor command.

Tables

It is not advisable to use tables (i.e., lay-out tables) simply to format information that does not need to be read as a table. When thinking about using a table, faculty should ask how the information would read after being "linearized" (read from top to bottom, left to right). When tables are necessary (i.e., data tables), certain conventions should be followed to make sure that the person relying on auditory output can integrate the information displayed on each row and column. The most important features are the header element $<th>$ and the *scope* attribute, which indicate to the reader which cells are intended as headings and which ones are row or column headers. For more complex tables, where information is not aligned simply at the intersection of one main column header and row header, the header attribute should also be considered. Two other attributes that can greatly enhance understanding of tables are the caption and the summary attributes. As the term indicates, a caption attribute briefly describes the contents of the table. For example, the caption of a table might read "Increase in the Older Population in the United States by Cohort in the Twentieth Century." Similarly, the summary attribute would provide an idea of the purpose and organization of the table contents. Such a summary might say "This is a three columns and three rows table, depicting the numbers of older adults in the United States, ages 65 to 74, 75 to 84, and 85 plus, in 1900, 1950, and 1999." Because specific coded examples of these features would take more space than what is available for this chapter, readers interested in specific html coding for these attributes can refer to the books on web accessibility listed under Resources or visit websites from organizations such as the W3C (www.w3c.org) or WebAIM (www.webain.org).

Frames

As previously mentioned, frames are not always interpreted correctly by software packages used by students with disabilities. The same may be true for a student using a text only browser. Most experts suggest that designers find alternatives to the frame layout; if this is not feasible, the noframes attribute should be added to the html code so that the user can access the same information in an alternate format. A caution often associated with advice about the noframes attribute is to ensure that the content in alternative noframes pages and the content of the regular pages are updated simultaneously to avoid discrepancies in information. Frames should be given titles that help the user understand their purpose and decide whether or not to read its contents.

Forms

When interactive forms are used, it is important to make sure that the user is able to control input even if not using a regular mouse to point and click. If a file cannot be accessed by the arrow keys, some students with physical limitations may not be able to enter the required information. Forms are also tricky for individuals using screen readers, particularly if they use a variety of elements such as radio buttons, pull-down menus, and cells for entering text information. Often these elements are images, and some readers may have a difficult time identifying them if a text descriptor is not used to define the expected commands for data entry and submission. Labeling the input type as text, checkboxes, or buttons, identifying text areas for data entry, or indicating which options are available to be checked can make desired actions much easier for a screen reader user to grasp. Like tables, forms can be a complex component for faculty not experienced in writing programming code, so it is recommended that resources providing step-by-step design instructions and examples be consulted prior to engaging in this task.

Multimedia

Academic sites are increasingly making use of features such as animation and video and audio recordings to appeal to different learning preferences. It would be contrary to good pedagogical practices to ask faculty to ignore the benefits of such features. A student who learns more effectively through auditory channels may find a course much more enjoyable if sound is used to enhance learning. The reverse may apply to a student who prefers visual input. When additional sensory input is incorporated into a website, instructors need to make sure equivalent alternatives are given to students with sensory limitations. A common problem to avoid is the use of animations or elements that blink or flicker merely to produce a visual effect. These should be avoided if possible, particularly if elements flicker at a rate of 2 to 55 cycles per second, which can induce seizures. When necessary to convey a message, animations should also have descriptive information associated with them.

Let us consider the example of narrated PowerPoint presentations. A deaf student may miss important information if the slides have only brief outlines of what the professor says while narrating each slide in greater detail. The same is true for video or audio recordings inserted into the website. To accommodate students with hearing impairments, two options are available: captioning and transcriptions. Before uploading the video recording, faculty may ask technical support staff for help with captioning. By doing this, students may read the text while watching the video. A concern, aside from the time need to captioned videos, is the fact that videos opened through programs such as Quicktime or Real Player often open as much smaller images than what would be seen if shown on a television monitor. A simpler solution may be to provide a text transcript of the auditory content. Transcripts are not only beneficial to persons who cannot hear, but also to those who do not possess the plugs-ins needed to access media or to those who simply want a faster way to look at the information. Screen reader users, for example, may prefer to open a transcript of an interview, knowing that their software will read the contents much faster than the time it would take for them to listen to the original recording.

For persons with visual impairments, video recording may also be problematic because of the visual cues that are missed when only the auditory contents can be accessed. In this case, a transcript may not be sufficient. Audio descriptions are recommended for videos that contain a large amount of information delivered only in a visual format. For example, if the video is used to demonstrate a technique that is not described verbally by the narrator, it may be necessary to add an audio description. If this seems too time-consuming and hard to combine with the existing sound version of the video, it may be better to provide such description within the text transcript provided.

These alternate versions should be provided as optional links so as not to clutter any given page. Faculty members should not perceive these accommodations as a burden, but as ways to cater to individuals with various learning styles and technology resources. By having to provide these alternatives, faculty are led to examine more carefully what types of multimedia are truly effective and meaningful to their courses. These accommodations are no different from what is already required for face-to-face courses. Although a bit more time-consuming to tackle once a course is already being taught, they can be easily accomplished when planned from the very beginning and implemented gradually.

Another potential problem with multimedia is the need for plug-ins or specific software to open files. It is recommended that faculty assume that not all students will have the necessary technology to open such files. A good practice is to tell students in the beginning of the semester what types of programs they need to download to be able to access all course information. Accessibility guidelines also recommend that links should be provided to a disability-accessible page from which the programs and plug-ins can be downloaded.

Does Using Courseware to Build Online Courses Already Provide for Accessibility?

There are many examples of educational courseware packages in the market. Academic institutions typically adopt a commercial courseware package or develop one in-house. Courseware packages organize information in sections, so it is easier for instructors to upload their own documents and to interact with students. Some of the leading companies, such as Blackboard and WebCT, have made a concerted effort to comply with accessibility guidelines. On its website, Blackboard explains how its web designers have implemented Section 508 (see http://products.blackboard.com/cp/bb5/access/section508.cgi). For example, they have added row and column headers to tables within its platform. Because they have added a description field, complex images or media can receive a more detailed description when uploaded onto the platform. WebCT has also done considerable work on the first priority level of WAI guidelines. They have also created help files on accessibility for their online help (Harrison, 2000). However, there are still issues to be resolved before these platforms will be in total compliance. For example, Blackboard alerts users that the chat tool in Version five is not yet in compliance. Although students can go back to read the archives of any given chat, they may not be able to participate in one with other students if they are using a screen reader. These advances are exciting and show commitment from some of the courseware companies in developing truly useable products.

But even if these companies fully comply with all accessibility guidelines, there are issues that are beyond their control. For example, although they can make sure their courseware pages are in compliance, they cannot automatically transform a page added by the instructor to the "documents" or "links" sections of the courseware package. If an instructor creates word documents with pictures or tables, he or she should not assume that the platform has the power to add markups to the html code to provide for accessibility. The html code from the original document will transfer onto the platform. It would be unreasonable to expect that the courseware developers would add mechanisms for the product to "guess" what the instructor wishes to say with a given picture, math equation, music notation, or video clip. It is very important, therefore, for instructors to check the pages they develop *before* uploading them.

If web-authoring software such as FrontPage® or Dreamweaver® are used, it is possible to go into the html code to include alt tags or other accessibility markups. Increasingly, web-authoring software includes features that check accessibility. The following statement was taken from the University of Iowa site, referring to Dreamweaver's® accessibility extension:

This new Dreamweaver evaluation tool allows web pages to be "accessibility-checked" much in the same way as you "spell-check" a Word document. The extension covers Section 508 and level 1 W3C guidelines and a report can be run on one page, a complete website, selected section or any folder. The user can select sub-groups of the guidelines to customize tests to run on different web pages. The extension allows the user to collect answers to manual tests and includes content that explains how to perform tests, why the problems found could be accessibility issues and explains with examples how the problem can be fixed. In addition to the free extension, the user can link through to LIFT Online a service from UsableNet that allows tests to be automatically scheduled on live public websites (University of Iowa, 2002, p. 4).

This extension can be downloaded from the Macromedia site by down clicking on "accessibility" and then on "508 Accessibility Suite" (http://dynamic.macromedia.com/bin/MM/exchange/main.jsp?product=dreamweaver)

Similarly, FrontPage® can be checked for accessibility through a new tool called AccVerify® SE™. Microsoft and HiSoftware have partnered to develop this tool. According to HiSoftware (2002), this tool provides verification and reports all errors /non-compliance with accessibility policy and standards for websites under the WCAG 1.0 P1-P3 Guidelines and the Section 508 standards." This software also provides a complete checklist for standards that the website designer has to verify manually in order to achieve complete accessibility. This checklist is available on the HiSoftware's website (http://www.hisoftware.com/msacc/).

One of the advantages of using authoring software such as FrontPage® is the existence of built-in features that facilitate compliance with accessibility guidelines. For instance, it is possible to import a file into FrontPage® and manually insert alt tags without having to go into the html code. By right clicking on an image and going to "image properties," it is possible to fill in the blank tag for text under alternative representations. By doing so a brief description of the image is created and added to the html code as an alt tag. Those using a screen reader can read the description, but sighted viewers can also see it when the mouse is on the image.

Similarly, a PowerPoint presentation may be edited to include alternative descriptors. However, according to WebAIM (2002b), the html code generated is not accessible to screen readers. Saving the file as a web page does not assure accessibility either. Some web technicians suggest that the outline version be used as a solution; however, the outline does not include features such as textbox, graphs, pictures, or multimedia. If used in the presentation, instructors still need to describe them along with the rest of the text. A new plug-in is being tested at this time and can be downloaded from the Division of Rehabilitation, Education Services of the University of Illinois at Urbana/Champaign. According to its website:

This PowerPoint Accessibility Wizard offers an alternative to PowerPoint's Web Publishing feature. The standard Power Point Web Publishing option creates XML-based web content that can only be used by Microsoft Internet Explorer. Even if non-XML options are selected, users cannot easily add information that is required for accessibility. This PowerPoint Accessibility Wizard simplifies the task of converting PowerPoint presentations to text pure html through an easy-to-use user interface, and automates much of the conversion of PowerPoint Presentations to an html format that includes required accessibility information (Division of Rehabilitation, UI, 2002, p. 1).

Accessibility of Other Components of Online Courses

Online courses do not solely rely on web pages. They use other channels for conveying information and for faculty-student interactions. One of the most frequent modes of interaction is e-mail. It is a fairly expedient way for faculty to communicate with each student individually and answer questions. One of the greatest advantages of e-mail is that a student can pose a question at any time, which the instructor can also read and answer a convenient time. E-mail is often quite accessible to all students. One word of caution concerns checking for errors in spelling when we reply to questions or send out announcements. A screen reader reads words as they are spelled. If a letter is missing or an acronym is being used, the output may not make much sense to the student. A similar caution applies to listservs.

Another interactive technique gaining more popularity among online instructors is that of synchronized chat sessions. Before requiring them, instructors should be sure that their students can access the technology. This is especially true for text chats that do not use html-coded text. Norman Coombs from Equal Access to Software and Information (EASI), a provider of online training on accessible information technology for persons with disabilities, makes the following remarks regarding text chats:

In the old DOS days they worked rather well with a screen reader. When someone posted a new item, the screen reader read the new material. Worked nicely. Most chats in Windows do one of two things, neither very good: (1) What is new on the screen is not automatically spoken. I have to guess maybe something might have happened and use the Jaws cursor to explore the screen to find out if anything new happened. (2) The other is that the software redraws the entire screen whenever anything new happens and the screen reader reads the entire screen each time over and over and over and over and over and over … (August 21, 2002b, Listserv ACT@MAELSTROM.STJOHNS.EDU).

Instant messenger chats such as those provided by AOL, MSN, and Yahoo are somewhat better for screen readers, although the user must still make adjustments to settings in order to increase accessibility. As awareness increases, chat features should become increasingly more accessible. Companies such as HorizonLive have been working to achieve 508 compliance. Its 3.0 version released in the Fall of 2002 has added features to accommodate users with disabilities, such as an html messaging system, the ability to display text-only versions of slides, and keyboard shortcuts (HorizonLive, 2002).

WebAIM (2002c, p. 16) recommends that the following questions be investigated before adopting a chat program:

1   Is the interface accessible through the keyboard only?

2.   Does the program work with common screen readers?

3.   Can the user control the scrolling and/or refreshing of messages?

4.   Does sound alone convey important information?

5.   Are the controls easy to use and clear?

6.   If Java is being used, is it designed to work with Jaws and other screen readers?

For students with visual disabilities, perhaps the best solution is an audio chat (using a microphone and speakers) or a phone conference. This may also facilitate access for those with physical disabilities who may find it hard to type fast enough to follow the pace of an online text chat.

Needless to say, hearing-impaired students will not be able to participate in such chats without proper accommodations. For the deaf student, the text chat may work well, but an audio chat or phone conference may also be possible with the appropriate accommodations. For instance, for a brief phone conference, the Telecommunication Relay Service (a toll-free service) may be contacted so that an operator links the student and faculty though a TTY (a combination of telephone, keyboard, and display used for text-based communication). This way, the student will be able to get the messages the operator types and sends to his TTY phone and can type his replies so that the operator reads it aloud. In case of a chat, it may be necessary to have someone doing live captioning for the student. For example, if a live presentation is being broadcast through the Internet, the deaf student may be connected to a text chat system so that he or she can read the content being typed by the transcriptionist (the person providing the captioning services) and send back questions to the instructor or guest speaker as needed. The instructor following the chat transcripts can then relay questions or comments from the student to the rest of the audience. Similarly, if a video camera is available, an interpreter could be asked to provide sign language interpretation while the presentation takes place. This may be challenging, however, because most cameras that are compatible with computers do not have the range to show both the speaker and the sign language interpreter. If the institution has video-conferencing class-rooms equipped for distance-learning events, it may be a better solution to use that equipment for such events (Chancellor's Office of California Community Colleges, 1999).

In the case of video conferencing, it is important to keep in mind that although a blind student will be able to listen to the content, he or she may miss important non-verbal information. The use of PowerPoint slides or any other visual input should be accompanied by a narration of what is being shown, similar to what would happen in a face-to-face classroom. If an instructor makes frequent reference to text-based materials, such materials should be posted or sent in advance via e-mail so that the student has an opportunity to review them.

It is unlikely that multiple disabilities will be represented in one course; therefore, as long as the instructor understands the needs of different students, a decision about the technology and accommodations necessary for access can be made after discussing the issue with the student. Unlike a website, which is hard to change once developed, modes of interaction offer more flexibility. Knowing what options are available, faculty can experiment with different types of accommodation before deciding what method is the most efficient and effective for *all* students in the course. In addition, academic institutions are already mandated to offer services to disabled students such as interpreters and captioning for live events, so the instructor can contact the office in charge of providing such services and make arrangements for the online course the same way in which it is done for face-to-face courses.

Conclusion

This chapter provided some basic information on how to design online courses that accommodate individuals with diverse functional abilities. Instructors interested in evaluating their existing online courses for accessibility — or courses under construction — may consult Appendix A for suggestions on how to perform such evaluation.

When limitations are identified, it is important not to become overwhelmed with the potential amount of work required. Instructors who do not possess the expertise needed to make more sophisticated changes to their course sites are not likely to have created complex accessibility problems to begin with. Often, hard-to-fix accessibility infractions are a result of new technology, not yet modified to include accessibility options. Testing technology for access not only by persons with disabilities, but also by individuals with slower connections, older computers, or different browsers is always a wise idea. If the modifications seem to exceed the faculty member's technical capabilities, support staff available either though online education or computer services programs should be consulted. Not all support staff members will be aware of accessibility requirements, but they will have the skills to produce the necessary modifications if the instructor is able to communicate his or her needs to them. Faculty members can become advocates for greater technical support by educating university administration to the legal, ethical, and practical reasons for compliance with accessibility guidelines.

Finally, recognizing that space is limited for the vast amount of information available on the topic of accessibility, the authors have prepared a list of resources that include print and online materials on the issues identified throughout this chapter. As technology moves increasingly faster, many other resources are likely to become available by the time this chapter is published. Readers are encouraged to consult the major websites listed in Appendix B in order to acquire state-of-the-art information and to bookmark those sites that appear the most useful for ongoing technical assistance.

Endnotes

[1]   Removing barriers that present persons with disabilities from engaging in substantial life activities and from using services, products and information in everyday life (Bergman & Johnson, 1995).

[2]   The Assistive Technology Act of 1988 (PL 100-407) defined assistive technology devices as any device, piece of equipment, or product system that is used to increase, maintain, or improve functional capabilities of individuals with disabilities. It also emphasized the importance of services to assist consumers in the selection, acquisition, or use of assistive technology devices (Wallace, Flippo, Barcus, & Behrmann, 1995).

[3]   Legal blindness is defined as central vision accuracy of 200/20 or less in the better eye, after best correction. If central visual acuity is better than 20/200, it must be accompanied by a limit to the field of vision to such a degree that its widest diameter allows an angle of no greater than 20 degrees (Oregon Commission for the Blind, 2000).

[4]   Uses a synthesized voice to "speak" the information on the screen (The Alliance for Technology Access, 2000).

[5]   Provides tactile output by forming Braille characters, that can be "refreshed" after the user reads each line (The Alliance for Technology Access, 2000).

[6]   Denotes significant reduction in visual function. Clear vision is not achieved by the use of eyeglasses, contact lenses, or intraocular lens implants. Differs from blindness because visual devices can improve vision to some extent (The Center for the Partially Sighted, 2001).

[7]   This keyboard enhancement provides keyboard control of cursor and button functions by pressing the numeric keyboard and other key combinations (Bergman & Johnson, 1995).

[8]   Voice recognition software allows the user to speak to the computer to control data input or to control functions such as e-mail, Internet, and other applications (Bergman & Johnson, 1995).

[9]   Augmentative and Alternative Communication (AAC) is defined as the integration of a variety of strategies and techniques, other than speech, that enhance independent and interactive communication. AAC communication aids range from low-tech communication boards to high-tech electronic devices (Tanchak & Sawyer, 1995).

References

Abramson (2000). *Digital Divide Widens*. Retrieved from http://www.thestandard.com/article/display/0,1151,19429,00.html.

Alexander, K. & Alexander, M.D. (1995). *The Law of Schools, Students and Teachers*. Saint Paul, MN: West Group.

The Alliance for Technology Access. (2000). *Computer and Web resources for people with disabilities: A guide to exploring today's assistive technology* (3rd ed.) Alameda, CA: Hunter House Publishers.

Amazon.com. (2002). Home page. Retrieved from http://www.amazon.com.

American Association or Retired Persons. (2001). Profile of older adults. Administration on Aging, *U.S. Department of Health and Human Services.*

Bergman, E. & Johnson, E. (1995). Towards accessible human-computer interaction. In J. Nielsen (Ed.), *Advances in Human-Computer Interaction.* Norwood, NJ: Ablex Publishing. Retrieved from http://www.sun.com/access/developers/updt.HCI.advance.html.

Blackboard. (2002). *Accessibility – Section 508.* Retrieved from http://products.blackboard.com/cp/bb5/access/section508.cgi.

Bobby (2002). Home page. Retrieved from http://www.cast.org/bobby/.

Brummel, S. (1994). *White Paper - National Information Infrastructure — People with Disabilities and the NII: Breaking Down Barriers, Building Choice.* Retrieved from http://www.gsa.gov/attachments/ GSA_PUBLICATIONS/pub/People%20with%20Disabilities %20and%20the%20National%20Information%20Infrastructure. doc.

Burgstahler, S. (2002). Universal design of distance learning. *Information Technology and Disabilities.* Retrieved from http://www.rit.edu/~easi/ itd/itdv08n1/burgstahler.htm.

Campbell, L. & Waddell, C. (1997). *Electronic curbcuts: How to build accessible web sites.* Retrieved from The International Center for Disability Resources on the Internet http://www.icdri.org/CynthiaW/ecc.htm.

The Center for the Partially Sighted. (2001). *About low vision.* Retrieved from http://www.low-vision.org/low-vision.html.

The Center for Universal Design. (2002a). *What is universal design?* Retrieved from http://www.design.ncsu.edu/cud/univ_design/ud.htm.

The Center for Universal Design. (2002b). *Principles of universal design.* Retrieved from http://www.design.ncsu.edu/cud/univ_design/ princ_overview.htm.

Chancellor's Office of California Community Colleges. (1999). *Distance education: Access guidelines for students with disabilities.* Developed by the High Tech Center Training Unit in collaboration with the

Distance Education Accessibility Workgroup. Retrieved from http://www.catsca.org/articles/dis_guidelines.html.

Coombs, N. (2002a). *Barrier-free e-learning*. Online course offered by EASI (Equal Access to Software and Information). Retrieved from http://easi.cc/workshops/bfel.htm.

Coombs, N. (2002b). Comments on text chat posted on the ACT@MAELSTROM.STJOHNS.EDU listserv on August 21, 2002.

Danielson, L. (1999, Fall). Universal design: Ensuring access to the general education curriculum. *Research Connections*, 5, 2-3. Retrieved from http://www.rit.edu/~easi/law/weblaw1.html.

Division of Rehabilitation, Education Services, University of Illinois at Urbana-Champaign. (2002). *Microsoft Power Point WWW Publishing Accessibility Wizard*. Retrieved from http://www.rehab.uiuc.edu/ppt/overview.html.

Federal Communications Commission (FCC). (2002a). *About section 508*. Retrieved from http://ftp.fcc.gov/cgb/dro/ab508.html.

Federal Communications Commission (FCC). (2002b). *Section 225. Telecommunications access for people with disabilities*. Retrieved from http://www.fcc.gov/cgb/consumerfacts/section255.html.

Gardner, H. (2000). *Intelligence reframed: Multiple intelligences for the 21st century*. New York: Basic.

Harrison, L. (2000). *Accessible web design and curriculum adaptive technology*. Colorado Conference on Assistive Technology in Higher Education, EASI roundtable discussions, Colorado, November. Retrieved from http://easi.cc/colconf/trans/laurie7.htm.

Henry, S. (2002). Accessibility-usability synergy. In J. Tacher, P Bohman, M. Burks, S.

Henry, B., Regan, S., Swierenga, M., Urban, & C. Wandell (Eds.), *Constructing accessible web sites*. Birmingham, UK: Glasshaus.

HiSoftware. (2002a). *Frequently asked questions (AccVerify)*. Retrieved from http://www.hisoftware.com/access/faqs.html.

HiSoftware. (2002b). *AccVerify® SE™ for FrontPage*. Retrieved from http://www.hisoftware.com/msacc/.

HorizonLive. (2002). *Web's 1ˢᵗ conferencing solution fully accessible to people with disabilities*. Retrieved from http://www.horizonlive.com/aboutus/pr_102402.html.

Mace, R. (1998, Summer). A perspective on universal design. *UD Newsline*, 1(4).

Maromedia. (2002). *Macromedia exchange for Dreamweaver*. Retrieved from http://dynamic.macromedia.com/bin/MM/exchange/main.jsp?product=dreamweaver.

Nielsen, J. (1999, June). Disabled accessibility: The Pragmatic approach. *Alertbox*. Retrieved from http://www.useit.com/alertbox/990613.html.

Oregon Commission for the Blind. (2000) *Frequently asked questions*. Retrieved from http://www.cfb.state.or.us/faq.htm.

Paciello, M. (2000). *WEB accessibility for people with disabilities*. Lawrence, KS: CMP Books.

Schwitzer, A., Ancis, J. & Brown, N. (2001). *Promoting student learning and student development at a distance*. Lanham, MD: American College Personnel Association.

Tanchak, T. & Sawyer, S. (1995). Assistive technology. In K.F. Flippo, K.J. Inge & J. Michael Barcus (Eds.), *Assistive technology: A resource for school, work, and community*. Baltimore, MD: Paul H. Brookes.

Thatcher, J. (2002a). Accessible data input. In P. Bohmnan, M. Burks, S. Henry, B. Regan, S. Swierenga, M. Urban, & C. Waddel (Eds.), *Constructing accessible web sites*. Birmingham, UK: Glasshaus.

Thatcher, J. (2002b). Accessible navigation. In P. Bohmnan, M. Burks, S. Henry, B. Regan, S. Swierenga, M. Urban, & C. Waddell (Eds.), *Constructing accessible web sites*. Birmingham, UK: Glasshaus.

Thatcher, J. (2002c). Creating accessible content. In P. Bohmnan, M. Burks, S. Henry, B. Regan, S. Swierenga, M. Urban, & C. Waddell (Eds.), *Constructing accessible web sites*. Birmingham, UK: Glasshaus.

Tucker, B. (1998). Federal disability law. Saint Paul, MN: West Group.

University of Iowa. (2002). Dreamweaver resources. *nTITLE—New Technology in the Learning Environments*. Retrieved from http://www.uiowa.edu/~ntitle/resources/dreamweaver.shtml.

U.S. Architectural and Transportation Barriers Compliance Board. (2000). *Electronic and information technology accessibility standards.* Retrieved from http://www.access-board.gov/sec508/508standards.htm.

Vanderheiden, G. (1990). Thirty-something million: should they be exceptions? *Human Factors*, 32 (4), 383-396.

Waddell, C. (1998) *Applying the ADA to the Internet: A Web accessibility standard.* Retrieved from http://www.rit.edu/~easi/law/weblaw1.htm.

Waddell, C. (2002). U.S. Web accessibility law in depth. In P. Bohmnan, M. Burks, S. Henry, B. Regan, S. Swierenga, M. Urban, & C. Waddel (Eds.), *Constructing accessible web sites.* Birmingham, UK: Glasshaus.

Wallace, J., Flippo, K., Barcus, M., & Behrmann, M. (1995). Legislative foundation of assistive technology policy in the United States. In K. Flippo, K. Inge, & M. Barcus (Eds), *Assistive technology: A resource for school, work and community.* Baltimore, MD: Paul H. Brooks.

WAVE. Retrieved from. http://www.temple.edu/inst_disabilities/piat/wave.

WebAIM. (2002a). *Introduction to web accessibility.* Retrieved from http://www.webaim.org/intro/.

WebAIM (2002b). *Accessibility Training CD-ROM.* Retrieved from www.webaim.org.

WebAIM (2002c). *Accessibility of online chat programs.* Retrieved from http://www.webaim.org/articles/chats.

World Wide Web Consortium (W3C). (1999a). *About the World Wide Web Consortium (W3C).* Retrieved from http://www.w3.org/Consortium/.

World Wide Consortium (W3c). (1999b). *Fact sheet for "Web content accessibility guidelines 1.0."* Retrieved from http://www.w3.org/1999/05/WCAG-REC-fact.html.

World Wide Consortium (W3C). (1999c). *Web content accessibility guidelines 1.0: W3C Recommendations* (Latest version). Retrieved from http://www.w3.org/TR/WAI-WEBCONTENT/#Guidelines.

World Wide Web Consortium (W3C). (1999d). *List of checkpoints for web accessibility guidelines.* Retrieved from http://www.w3.org/TR/1999/WAI-WEBCONTENT-19990505/checkpoint-list.html.

World Wide Web Consortium (W3C). (1999e). *Priorities.* Retrieved from http://www.w3.org/TR/WAI-WEBCONTENT/#priorities.

World Wide Consortium. (2000a). *W3C Techniques for Web content accessibility guidelines*. Retrieved from http://www.w3.org/TR/WCAG10-TECHS/#gl-own-interface.

World Wide Consortium. (2000b). *Curriculum for Web accessibility guidelines*. Retrieved from http://www.w3.org/WAI/wcag~curric/intl-0.htm.

APPENDIX A

Validation Issues

How can you insure that, if you follow the recommendations in this chapter, your site is actually accessible? Following are three basic steps that will assist you in validating the accessibility of your site.

Step 1: Make Every Effort to Do Things "Right" the First Time

Part of what makes for good design is attention to design issues from the outset of the project, not as an afterthought when problems have already become apparent. A good first step that also offers an inexpensive and enlightening way to check your site is the following "quick tip" available on the WEBAim homepage (http://www.webaim.org):

Quick Tip # 9

What happens when you *use only your keyboard* to access your site (no mouse)? Can you get to all of the links? Is it easy to navigate?

What happens when you *turn off all images*? Is your site understandable (even if it isn't as "pretty")?

What if you *turn off the volume* on the computer? Is your multimedia still usable? These simple tests are a good starting point for anyone who wants to gauge the accessibility of their site.

Another key question to keep in mind is "What do I want the site to do or teach?" — as opposed to "How do I want the site to look?" This question will help to keep the emphasis on "good teaching," which is the issue that drives the design.

Step 2: Checking Your Site Throughout the Design Process with Tools Marketed Specifically to Help with Design Issues

Many of these tools are based on the Section 508 Standards and/or the W3C and WIA guidelines. Some of these tools are available for free or at a minimal cost. They will point out design flaws and suggest possible remedial activities.

"Bobby" (http://www.cast.org/bobby/) and *"WAVE"* (http://www.temple.edu/inst_disabilities/piat/wave) are two such tools specifically designed to help a designer locate potential elements of a web page that may cause some users to have difficulty accessing all or part of a site. There are other tools available as well, and you will find a selection listed in Appendix B of this chapter.

It is important to consider all of the elements of your site as you do a design check. Many validation tools have been constructed for specific purposes, for example, to check html code or to provide a developer with alternatives to the use of common site elements like the use of color, pictures, tables, and text placement. Other elements of your site, such as a PowerPoint® presentation, an audio file, or the use of specific programs, might require that you utilize specific techniques to insure compliance with accessibility standards. Do not be put off by the need to put in a little more work "up front." There are specific evaluation tools, tutorials, and free downloads available to help to maximize compliance with 508 Standards even when using software like PowerPoint®, Dreamweaver®, and FrontPage®. Remember, having a site that is accessible does not mean having a site that is only text-based. "Accessibility is about designing so that **more people** can use your web site **effectively** in **more situations"** (http://WEBAim.org). **Accessibility is not about being boring or having to forgo common instructional methodologies.** Also remember that if you make changes to your site, perhaps starting with simple elements and then adding more complexity as your own skill level increases, you should run a "validity check" each time you modify your site.

Step 3: Get Input from "Experts" Who Are Available to You

Experts include staff from computer services and instructional support. Other faculty members who are experienced in designing online education and user-friendly sites may also be willing to serve as resources. But most importantly, actively solicit input from students with disabilities. Many students would much rather be asked what they need and how it can best be provided before the fact, rather than being faced with the frustration of sometimes less than adequate adjustments that are made later on.

You should solicit input from students with a range of disabilities, including visual, auditory, motor, cognitive, and visual-perceptual conditions. Make a special effort to recruit students with hidden disabilities such as epilepsy or learning disabilities that can impact the ability to use online modalities. Act on the input you receive, and remember to ask your audience to review your revised site.

Appendix B

Resources

Websites
General Sites: These are extensive websites on the topic of web accessibility. Although it may take some time, it is worthwhile to explore these sites in detail.

CAST: The Center for Applied Special Technology

(http://www.cast.org) CAST is a "not-for-profit organization that uses technology to expand opportunities for all people, especially those with disabilities." This is an extensive site with multiple pages containing a variety of resources for educators, web designer, and other individuals with an interest in making the Web accessible to all. Note the pages on Universal Design for Learning and The National Center on Accessing the General Curriculum. CAST is also the home of "Bobby," a free tool that can be used to check the accessibility of any website.

The International Center For Disability Resources on the Internet

(http://www.icdri.org) This site contains the collected works of Cynthia Waddell, noted expert on accessible web design. There is also a searchable database of other assistive technology and information technology resources at this site.

WebABLE!

(http://www.webable.org) The WebABLE! library is "a collection of books, press releases, white papers, articles, plans, standards, reference guidelines, and journals that focus on accessibility, assistive and adaptive technology for people with disabilities." The homepage also contains a link, "Tools and Utilities," that will direct the user to many sites that describe and provide access to software, guidelines, and other tools to maximize web site accessibility.

Web Accessibility Initiative (WIA)

(http://www.w3.org/WAI) WAI, in coordination with organizations around the world, pursues accessibility of the Web through five primary areas of work: technology, guidelines, tools, education and outreach, and research and development. The website includes page-authoring guidelines to maximize the accessibility of a website.

WebAIM Web Accessibility in Mind Homepage

(http://www.webaim.org) This page offers "web accessibility information and solutions." There is something here for the novice as well as the experienced web designer. Includes a "Tip of the Day," a "508 Checklist," and a Discussion Group on accessible web design and a searchable list of resources on web site accessibility, as well as a variety of other resources.

Sites on Specific Aspects of Accessible Web Design
Adobe and PDF Accessibility

(http://access.adobe.com) This site provides information on Adobe accessibility and free tools such as Acrobat Reader to assist in making portable document files accessible.

Macromedia

(http://www.macromedia.com/macromedia/accessibility) This is a site describing accessible Macromedia tools. Plug-ins for Flash and Shockwave are featured, as are extensions designed to enhance the accessibility of Dreamweaver. Free templates for designing accessible websites are also available.

Section 508 Homepage

(http://www.section508.gov) The U.S. Government site designed to provide information about Section 508.

Applying the ADA to the Internet: A Web Accessibility Standard

by Cynthia D. Waddell, JD, ADA, Coordinator, City of San Jose, CA, USA

(http://www.rit.edu/~easi/law/weblaw1.html)

The Growing Digital Divide in Access for People with Disabilities: Overcoming Barriers to Participation by Cynthia D. Waddell, JD

(http://www.aasa.dshs.wa.gov/access/waddell.html)

Web Accessibility Initiative Policy Page

(http://www.w3.org/WAI/Policy) The WAI keeps an updated overview of laws pertaining to web accessibility on its site.

THOMAS — Legislative Information on the Internet

(http://thomas.loc.gov) If you wish to review the actual text of U.S. legislation, THOMAS is the definitive source. To read the text of the laws cited in this chapter, simply search by Public Law number (P.L. xxx-xxx).

Website Evaluation Tools
Bobby

(http://bobby.watchfire.com/bobby/html/en/index.jsp) *"Bobby"* software was first introduced in 1996 and was the first tool created to assist in implementing Web accessibility guidelines. Bobby will check your site one page at a time for free. To check an extensive site, a commercial version of the software is available.

WAVE

(http://www.temple.edu/inst_disabilities/piat/wave) WAVE is a tool that provides feedback for web developers. It uses an iconic system to convey information about potential problems with accessibility. A user can create a bookmark in a preferred web browser, then simply open a page in the browser and click on the bookmark to have it checked by WAVE.

A-Prompt

(http://aprompt.snow.utoronto.ca) A-Prompt is another accessibility check developed at the University of Toronto. It can be used at no cost.

A variety of products are available commercially. These include the commercial version of Bobby and the others listed here.

InFocus

(http://www.ssbtechnologies.com/products/InFocus.php) *Page Screamer* and *Accessibility Monitor* — Page Screamer will evaluate single pages, multipage sites, and complex multi-layer sites. Accessibility Monitor provides the designer with information specific to 508 guidelines.

Verify

(http://www.hisoftware.com/access/Index.html) AccVerify™ specifically checks for section 508 compliance. AccRepair™ assists a user in making changes to maximize accessibility. AccVerify™ Server, spiders entire sites and flags Section 508 violations. AccRepair™ Plugin for AccVerify Server, allows for repair of pages across a server. AccRepair™ and for AccVerify™ for FrontPage®, work within FrontPage.

AccessEnable

(http://www.retroaccess.com) RetroAccess provides a web-based accessibility checker that will crawl through a website and report on the errors that it finds. The evaluation is based on Section 508 Guidelines. AccessEnable "provides site-wide automatic and interactive fixes for a number of accessibility and syntax violations."

WebABLE Accessibility Monitor

(http://www.accessibilitymonitor.com) The WebABLE Accessibility Monitor is a fee-based online service. It provides scheduling of monitor services, customizable reports, e-mail alerts, W3C WAI, and Section 508 reporting and other features. It can monitor entire sites.

Books

Note: All publisher comments and reviews are quoted from the Amazon web site—http://www.amazon.com.

Homepage Usability: 50 Websites Deconstructed

by Jakob Nielsen and Marie Tahir, New Riders, Indianapolis, IN, 2001

While there is a plethora of books available that provide tips on Web design, most authors leave a significant gap between the theory and practice—a gap that is left up to the reader to fill. *Homepage Usability: 50 Websites Deconstructed* boldly steps into that gap with specific observations and suggestions backed with solid quantitative analysis. This book focuses only on home page design as the most important point of presence for any website.

Web Accessibility for People With Disabilities

by Michael G. Paciello, CMP Books, Lawrence, KS, 2000

Paciello's book is a critical resource for removing barriers to effective communication and commerce and should be on everyone's bookshelf.

Teaching Every Student in the Digital Age: Universal Design for Learning

David H. Rose and Anne Meyer, Association for Supervision and Curriculum Development, 2002

Discusses and illustrates Universal Design for Learning as a framework for understanding the needs of diverse learners and educating them. Drs. Anne Meyer and David Rose and contributing writers present case studies of diverse students, illustrations of teacher practice, demonstrations of software tools and learner technologies, and research from neuroscience and psychology.

Maximum Accessibility: Making Your Web site More Useable By Everyone

John M. Slatin and Sharon Rush, Addison Wesley Professional, 2002

This book by is described as "a comprehensive resource for creating websites that comply with new U.S. accessibility standards and conform to the World Wide Web Consortium's Web Content Accessibility Guidelines 1.0. This book offers an overview of key issues, discusses the standards in depth, and presents practical design techniques, up-to-date technologies, and testing methods to implement these standards for maximum accessibility."

Constructing Accessible Web sites

Thacher, Waddell, Swierenga, Urban, Burks, Regan, Bohman, Glasshaus, 2002

Accessibility is about making web sites that do not exclude people with visual, aural, or physical disabilities. This book will enable web professionals to create or retrofit accessible websites quickly and easily. It is a practical book; the accessibility techniques outlined within are illustrated with real world examples from live sites, demonstrating that accessibility is not the enemy of great visual design.

Chapter V

Certain about Uncertainty: Strategies and Practices for Virtual Teamwork in Online Classrooms

Stella F. Shields
Indiana University, USA

Gisela Gil-Egui
Temple University, USA

Concetta M. Stewart
Temple University, USA

Abstract

Many students face the prospect of working in teams with apprehension. This feeling is further magnified when most or all of the sensory cues are removed in the virtual environment. We argue that by adopting specific structural and situational strategies, instructors can substantially reduce the levels of uncertainty that usually surround the idea of virtual teamwork in students' minds. Such strategies are drawn from an exploration of the notion of trust as a key element for the successful performance of teams, as well as on a discussion of the concepts of swift trust, community of practice, and control as guiding principles for the establishment of practices that help build mutual reliance among virtual team members in an online classroom. We conclude with some suggestions that can be implemented at the micro level of the course and the macro level of the institution hosting distance and online learning experiences.

Introduction

> *"We believe we are experiencing the most dramatic change in the nature of the small group since humans acquired the capacity to talk to one another — the explosion of virtual teams"*
> (Lipnack & Stamps, 1997, Chapter 2, ¶ 5).

Small human groups have existed for thousands upon thousands of years. These groups were key to the existence of humankind beginning with the Nomadic Age. Their acquisition of food depended on group work. This reality of pre-civilized life becomes especially evident when one considers the mastodon. Mastodons were rather formidable creatures, yet we know that in distant millennia, our predecessors stalked, hunted, and killed them. Among the sites containing evidence of this practice is the Taima-Taima site in coastal Venezuela. Fragments of tools and bones uncovered here revealed that groups were formed to hunt these wooly behemoths, and that they were butchered down to the bone. Facing an animal weighing five tons that towered over them, hunters must have experienced the twin rushes of hope and fear. Yet the reward — food — was greater than the fear of death or the fear of being maimed by a potential repast. The passage from childhood to becoming a hunter must have had moments of terror, but also feelings of kinship and trust for fellow hunters.

Today, the students' passage from adolescence to adulthood is far more prolonged; moreover, the complexity of their lives has often precluded the need to work in a group. Or, if they have been members of a group, their experience might have been negative. Many students, therefore, face the prospect of working in groups or teams with great trepidation when they enter our classes. This apprehension exists in the traditional classroom, but it is further magnified when most or all of the sensory cues are removed in the virtual environment. Albert Mehrabian's (1971) formula for the communication of feelings explains that 93% of the impact of a message in face-to-face interaction is made by nonverbal cues. Kezbom (2000) noted:

> *Non-verbal communication can account for as much as 60% of the message an individual conveys. This can entail the furtive glance, a reddening neck, or twitching face ... clues that often convey a plethora of important emotions. Team members who are in separate locations are deprived of these clues that indicate their colleagues' opinions, attitudes, and emotions. Even in the best videoconferencing, facial expressions can be difficult to pick up if the transmission is poor, is someone is off camera, or when the mute button is pressed (p. 33).*

If so many students have such an innate dislike of working in groups or teams, then why impose such a requirement? And if we impose it, how can we lead them to understand the importance of cooperative, knowledge-constructing, behaviors as well as did those young people who lived well over ten thousand years ago? Although today the risks and rewards of cooperative behavior are different (e.g., failure to master technologies that enable team members to work together does not increase risk of death, but it supposes lost opportunities for efficient work), there are still gains and losses. So is there anything that we can learn from our past to help our students today?

Most importantly, we need to recognize that from our students' perspective, their fears are as real as those of youth millennia ago who feared loss of life or limb. And although our students no longer face hunger, injury, or death if they fail to perform, they find the prospect of working in a team threatening nonetheless. To them, their only reward is a grade, which many feel is actually threatened by working in groups or teams.   Fear, uncertainty, lack of experience in learning and working cooperatively are all accentuated by a strong belief in success as an attribute of the individual. Can our students overcome these barriers to virtual teaming?

We argue that by adopting specific structural and situational strategies, instructors and facilitators of online courses can substantially reduce the levels of uncertainty that usually surround the idea of virtual teamwork in students' minds. Through measures aimed at building trust and a sense of community, students can not only benefit from the immediate social and practical gains of collaborating with others in performing tasks, but also from valuable processes of participatory learning and collective elicitation of knowledge.

Still, adopting such strategies requires much investment of time, resources, and creativity, and many faculty might question the extent to which establishing virtual teams in academic environments is worth the effort. Once again, one could ask why make group or team work a requirement?   The quote by Lipnack and Stamps (1997) that opens this chapter suggests that we are experiencing one of the greatest changes in the "nature of small groups" to happen in thousands of years. Virtual teams will continue to increase, almost exponentially, as they become major components of organizational structures in our Network Age. They might become the dominant organizational form as we move from this age to the next.

In the following section, we will provide further justification for the incorporation of teamwork as a major component of online learning. Next, we will provide some conceptual clarifications regarding the notions of group, teams, and contributors. We will then explore the notion of trust as a key element for the successful performance of teams. And, finally, we will discuss the concepts of *swift trust, community of practice,* and *control* as guiding principles for the establishment of short-term and long-term practices that build trust among virtual team members in an online classroom. We conclude our chapter with some practical suggestions that can be implemented at the micro level of the course and the macro level of the institution hosting distance and online learning experiences.

The Network Age

The 2001 United Nations Development Programme Report describes the Networked age as a creation of the intertwining of "technological transformations and globalization" (UNDP, 2001, p.15). One characteristic of this age is the tremendous growth in distance learning classes and programs, as well as the development of completely virtual educational institutions. Even traditional, small, post-secondary educational institutions — whose strength lies in the relationships between faculty and students, and between students and other students — are beginning to integrate Information and Communication Technologies (ICTs) into their "bricks and mortar" classrooms.

Meanwhile, online courses and educational institutions that develop and offer these courses are ever increasing. A survey by the National Center for Education Statistics (2000) found a significant rise in the number of distance learning programs in recent years. Today, according to The International Distance Learning Course Finder (International WHERE+HOW, 2002), there are at least 55,000 organizations in over 130 countries developing and offering distance courses, many of them based on new ICTs. Furthermore, there are several annual international conferences for online and distance learning practitioners, with at least one of them attracting close to 1,000 participants from more than 50 countries (see, for example, http://www.online-educa.com). And, finally, a growing number of journals addressing education in a virtual, networked, environment have emerged (e.g., *Virtual University Journal*).

Virtual teams are familiar organizational structures outside academia, where they are already working together to develop and share knowledge, while simultaneously building knowledge structures. These structures reside within the individual group or team members, within the groups or teams, and ultimately within a network of organizations. Although there are still populations around the globe — including many in the U.S. — who are excluded from participation in this Network Age, we now have the possibility and responsibility of seeing that our students fully participate. Our students live in an age where virtual teams are an increasingly important reality of everyday life. This is where our students and our educational institutions need to be situated.

As educators, our mission is to prepare our students for the society in which we live and to which they will be expected to contribute. However, there is a dearth of research on virtual teams and groups in academic institutions. Although they are common in commercial, administrative, and some non-governmental organizations (NGOs), we do not know if they are being generally embraced in higher education. Anecdotally, we are hearing of their adoption in business schools, where most of the existing academic research on the subject seems to be located. We need, however, to conduct more broad-based research to better understand the process and outcomes of student virtual teams, so that our students are able to function in the institutions for which we are putatively preparing them.

We believe that the virtual teaming process itself determines individual and team outcomes, for it is this process that determines the ability of individual members to participate as well as the development path of the team itself. The degree of success or failure in setting goals, completing tasks, and ultimately finishing the projects we give groups and teams reflects on the processes that are employed. Consequently, learning the processes of virtual collaboration is crucial to both individual and team achievement.

In industry, the importance of group processes is borne out by the research of Lurey and Raisinghani (2001), who collected and analyzed data from 67 individuals who were members of 12 virtual teams working in eight companies. These individuals belonged to the high technology, agriculture, and professional services industries. Results of this study suggest "teams' processes and team members' relations presented the strongest relationships to team performance and team member satisfaction" (Lurey & Raisinghani, 2001, p.524). Our experience leads us to believe these same findings could also be borne out in research on virtual student teams.

Clarifying Concepts

Groups or Teams?

Let us again imagine we can observe our young mastodon hunters across the millennia. We might think of them as banding together with a common purpose and a common knowledge structure based on common experiences and teachings that adults transmitted to them from birth. This culture of collaboration greatly simplifies the process of teaming and, over time, increasingly contributes to positive outcomes for the teams.

Today, we attempt to define common purpose and goals in our syllabi. We work to build some sort of community in our class — be it traditional or virtual — so that our students feel a sort of common identity. But, unlike the case of the mastodon hunters, there is no shared understanding of reality that older members of the community can transmit to the younger ones. Instructors and students are lacking in many common knowledge structures and experiences of the virtual environment. So when we refer to our students working in groups or teams, we do so without reflecting upon the validity of the terms.

In 2001, we asked 93 students in three traditional classes to describe differences between teams and groups in classroom discussions.[1] Their answers could be categorized according to purposes, relationships, and processes. First, with regard to purposes they stated: "Teams have a common goal, to win" *versus* "Groups don't really have goals." Second, they described group relationships as follows: "Members of the team stay together," and "Team members hang together outside of practice and games," *versus* "People in groups join and drop out," and "Groups are large." Finally, they described the process: "In teams, each member does his best," *versus* "In groups, each person might do something."

Our students implicitly defined teams as important and as having a common goal — to win. Individual responsibility was also quite important because each individual contributed to or took away from the goal of the team, and were held accountable for their contribution to the team's performance. They could be "benched" or "penalized" based on reports of their poor performance made available to the instructor by other team's members. This decision was sometimes accompanied by a sense of letting down the team and their friends. Team members were supposed to be friends. They were supposed to like being together.

These students also defined group membership as a bit amorphous, and group activities were also unclear. In their class discussions, it seemed that while some individuals in groups might be friends, group members did not socialize as a group. (It should be noted, however, that the students participating in this particular discussion were a rather homogenous population with gender about evenly divided, so cultural differences did not play a role in their definitions.)

Defining Real and Virtual Teams

We frequently hear "team" applied to any work group, and many times it is used interchangeably with the term "group." Katzenbach and Smith (2001) provide a more precise definition of a team as: " A small number of people with complementary skills who are committed to a common purpose, set of performance goals, and approach for which they *hold themselves mutually accountable*" [emphasis added] (¶ 5). Conversely, they define working groups as hierarchical entities with one strong leader. And, in this case, accountability is individual, though the group may work together on issues.

According to some researchers, purpose is a distinctive feature of teams. Lipnack (as cited by Cantu, 1997) notes that:

When the exercise of writing a purpose statement becomes the basis [for teamwork], it is a powerful source of energy. The importance of a virtual team going through a process to make its purpose tangible cannot be overstated...Ultimately, this means writing down the purpose statement of intent that answers the question "Why are we doing this?" Make explicit the team's mission — its top-most goal and motivation to action. Although it may be difficult, it is essential that the virtual team gets the purpose right and makes it clear to everyone (p. 35).

Team leadership *shifts*. Team members work together to solve a problem and then they implement the solution. Katzenbach and Smith (2001, ¶ 7) further argue that if performance goals can be achieved through "the sum of individual assignments and achievements, then you should *not* use a team approach."

According to Gould (1999), virtual team characteristics are:

- "Members are mutually accountable for team results.

- Members are dispersed geographically (nationally or internationally).

- Members work apart more time than in the same location.

- The team solves problems and makes decisions jointly.

- The team usually has fewer than 20 members." (Gould, 1999, ¶ 14, citing Henry & Hartzler, 1997)

Lipnack and Stamps (1997, Ch. 1, ¶ 4) define the virtual team as working "...across space, time, and organizational boundaries with links strengthened by webs of communication technologies." Recognizing the unique challenges of virtual teamwork, these authors have identified some principles that allow virtual teams to form quickly and solve complex problems:

- **People:** Virtual teams are composed of independent members with significant autonomy and self-reliance. Leadership is informal, and shared. Most members are leaders at some point in the process.

- **Purpose:** The virtual team creates cooperative goals, undertakes independent tasks and reaches for concrete results.

- **Links:** The explosion in communication technologies allows for the creation of virtual teams. Multiple, constantly enhanced modes of communication are possible, providing access to vast amounts of information and interaction. Virtual teams operate on Internet time" (Lipnack & Stamps, 1997, Ch. 1, ¶ 5).

Individual Member Contributions

How do individuals contribute to teams? Once again, we turn to research conducted in industry. And according to Bandow (2001):

The difference between success and failure may no longer lie in technology or methods, but in how individuals contribute to teams. Team members have discovered that poor working relationships and lack of trust within the group may interfere with how effectively individuals contribute to teams, reduce overall team performance, increase cycle time, create higher costs and potentially impact product quality (p.41).

Students who work in virtual teams face many of the same problems faced by members of virtual teams in industry. However, the basis for selection of team members is very different in the academic environment. In building cross-functional teams, members of teams in industry are selected for their respective skills or expertise. It is expected that each member's contribution relates to these skills and expertise. Allocation of responsibility in student teams is not usually based on special skills or expertise. Team membership is more often than not a matter of happenstance, and all of the members are all expected to equally learn the content of the course.

Bonding Beyond the Task

Mutual knowledge seems to be a common assumption of both faculty and students in the creation and process of team activities. However, Cramton (2001, p. 2) identified five kinds of problems constituting failures of mutual knowledge. They are "failure to communicate and retain contextual information, unevenly distributed information, difficulty communicating and understanding the salience of information, differences in speed of access to information, and difficulty interpreting the meaning of silence" (Cramton, 2001, ¶ 2).

Any of the failures mentioned above could lead to distrust and the breakdown of social bonds among the team members. At issue is the fact that mutual knowledge is at the core of successful virtual teaming, but its actual development relies on that very same process.

Many researchers emphasize the need for trust in virtual teams. It is seen to increase team interaction and collaboration, healthy discussions involving conflict, and the equitable distribution of power and respect within the team. Lipnack and Stamps (1997, Ch. 9, ¶ 4) state that "[b]uilding trust is a key factor in building an effective virtual team.". Bandow (2001) argues that working relationships are built on trust. Information flows freely, there is no concealment, agreements are honored, and there is acceptance and collaboration. Work becomes the focus rather than the "politics, assumptions and innuendo found in human behavior" (Bandow, 2001, p.44).

Trust is closely related to the notion of social capital. "Task success (is) the value of the results" and "Social success (is) the value of the relationships" (Lipnack & Stamps, 1997, Ch. 9, ¶ 6). When both factors are combined, they form "Social Capital, the community of wealth that co-evolves when people work together" (Lipnack & Stamps, 1997, Ch. 9, ¶ 8). We have long known the importance of the socialization process of members into organizations. However, we still do not know enough about it in virtual teams. This process of socialization is undoubtedly related to trust and warrants closer examination.

Trust: A Multidimensional Concept

Departing from positions that attributed a deterministic role to technology as the enabler of tele-collaboration, researchers are now paying greater attention to complex socio-psychological factors involved in the performance of virtual teams. A review of relevant literature on the new cooperative paradigm that is gaining strength in organizations worldwide reveals that trust is increasingly recognized as a key factor for the success of teamwork, especially when team members are physically distant from one another.

However, this same scholarly work also reveals absence of a commonly accepted definition of trust. Mayer, Davis, and Schoorman (1995), for example, consider trust to be a function of both attitudinal and situational factors. On the one hand, an individual's propensity to trust is a personality trait that "is assumed to be stable during the relationship as well as from one situation to another, and is influenced by a trustor's cultural, social, developmental experiences, and personality type" (Jarvenpaa, Knoll & Leidner, 1998, p.31, citing Mayer et al., 1995). On the other hand, situation-related trust will be determined by perceived attributes of the trustee with regard to his or her ability (that is, competence to deal with an issue), benevolence (disposition to care for others beyond egoistic motives), and integrity (discipline, professionalism, work/study ethics).

As McKnight and Chervany (2001) observe, "[t]rust conceptualizations have ranged from a personality construct, to a rational choice, to an interpersonal relationship, to a social structure construct" (p. 30). According to these authors, trust is a multidimensional notion. Therefore, after exploring definitions from different disciplines and approaches, they propose a categorization of the term that comprehends the following factors:

- *Disposition* (tendency to rely on others in general, regardless of the person or situation);

- *Intention* (willingness to depend on a specific person, regardless of the situation);

- *Belief/Expectation* (conviction that the trustee is competent, benevolent, predictable, and/or has integrity, in light of a specific situations);

- *Behavior* (voluntary act of reliance on other person, such as that taking place when two parties share information or cooperate); and

- *Context* (structural and/or situational conditions are considered both normal and adequate to reduce risks involved in depending on others).

By arguing that trust is a complex concept and proposing the trust typology described above, McKnight and Chervany (2001) seek to provide constructs that are both comprehensive enough to be meaningful for different disciplines and specific enough to allow operationalizations and empirical measures. As we shall explain later, all the dimensions of trust considered above are relevant for academic environments, because performance of virtual teams in online classrooms involves individual, interpersonal, group, and institutional task.

Unfortunately, most of the literature available on trust and virtual teams focuses on non-academic contexts, with few exceptions (e.g., Bitter-Rijpkema, Martens, & Jochems, 2002; Crisp & Jarvenpaa, 2000; Jarvenpaa & Leidner, 1998). Perhaps a reason for this omission is that, although cost and efficiency imperatives are prompting the use of virtual teamwork in many organizations worldwide, academia is still largely regarded as an individual-centered and highly hierarchical setting where task-related communication flows vertically, not horizontally. That is, the predominant paradigm in higher education is that communication and information flow from the teacher to the student and back again. Peer-to-peer communication is not considered relevant, or at least not vital.

It is important, thus, to keep in mind some distinctions between academic and other organizational environments when looking at what existing research has to say with regard to the conditions under which trust among virtual team members evolves. Within corporate organizations, assumptions of common denominators regarding practices, authority, expertise, and/or consequentiality facilitates trust building even for geographically dispersed teams put together without mediating any previous acquaintance. In time, the initial mutual reliance generated by those denominators evolves into adjusted expectations, based on observed attributions among team members.

But in the increasingly heterogeneous context of online higher education, where those denominators cannot be taken for granted and where time constraints limit opportunities for members of virtual teams to know each other, trust does not seem to have a solid basis upon which to be built. Students come to the virtual classroom with uneven working styles, levels of self-discipline, technical skills, goals, knowledge of the subject, and, because of their relative independence from instructor's supervision, understanding of power and authority.

Dynamics of Trust

Does this mean that it is not possible to foster trust within online students' teams? Relevant studies on the issue are at best inconclusive, as scholars disagree on the factors conditioning the establishment of trust-based relationships. However, from the variety of existing explanations about the way trust evolves in different contexts, two main views can be identified: a developmental one, which sees trust growing incrementally as a result of long-term interactions; and a deterministic one, which sees trust as a condition preceding interaction, more likely to remain stable or decrease rather than increase over time (Crisp & Jarvenpaa, 2000; cfr. Tidwell & Walther, 2000).

The developmental view rests on the assumption that trust in teams only emerges gradually after members have been able to interact with each other and get acquainted (Lewicki & Bunker, 1995, as cited in Crisp & Jarvenpaa, 2000). Handy (1995) argues that trust requires *touch* (face-to-face interaction) to occur, as technology in and of itself cannot compensate for non-verbal clues that are important in human communication. Kimble, Li and Barlow (2000) support this position by contending that performance of effective global virtual teams is informed as much by exchanges in physical space, as it is by communication in the electronic space:

> *If a strong relationship is developed in the physical environment, members of the community are more likely to "go the extra half-mile" for each other. The feelings of identity and trust developed in this way provide a sound basis for subsequent electronic collaboration (p. 13).*

Case studies conducted by Jarvenpaa and Leidner (1998) on virtual teams of college students whose members never met before and lived in different countries suggest that those teams that manage to balance task-oriented communication and social-oriented communication are likely to perform better than teams with little or no social-oriented communication. As long as the social exchange complements rather than replacing the focus on the task it "can make computer-mediated groups 'thicker'" (Jarvenpaa & Leidner, 1998, p. 29).

In contrast, the deterministic view rests on the assumption that trust (or lack thereof) is brought into teams by members' personal traits and by the circumstances under which they get to work together. The model challenges the developmental view of trust, insisting that initial trust can be quite high even when there is no past interaction history or first hand knowledge of others' characteristics. Initial trust flows from characteristics of the trustor (e.g., an individual's disposition to trust and trusting stance in general) and shared institutional factors (e.g., common professional associations, structural assurances) (McKnight et al., 1998, cited by Crisp & Jarvenpaa, 2000).

Meyerson, Weick, and Kramer (1996) argue that temporary virtual teams created around specific tasks and with a short life span can manage to perform well despite their limited time for social bonding. Given the impossibility of generating trust over extended processes of mutual acquaintance, individual members will seek to reduce initial uncertainty about their teammates by importing category-driven information available to them, thus forming "stereotypical impressions of others" (Meyerson et al., 1996, as cited by Jarvenpaa & Leidner, 1998).

This kind of team will develop "swift trust" that evolves throughout two brief phases. Initially, trust is fed by perceived trustworthiness of the initiator or assembler of the team (who has previously had opportunity to know each member of the temporary group), and by a quick assessment of the risks and potential outcomes (Harrison, Dibben & Mason, 1997). Once the team members begin working together, trust is sustained by fast-paced, proactive, task-focused interaction in which each team member has a clearly defined role, based on his or her individual field of expertise.

> *Action strengthens trust in a self-fulfilling fashion: action will maintain members' confidence that the team is able to manage the uncertainty, risk, and points of vulnerability, yet the conveyance of action has as a requisite the communication of individual activities. In summary, whereas traditional conceptualizations of trust are based strongly on interpersonal relationships, swift trust de-emphasizes the interpersonal dimensions and is based initially on broad categorical social structures and later on action. Since members initially import trust, trust might attain its zenith at the project's inception* (Meyerson at al., 1996, as cited by Jarvenpaa & Leidner, 1998, p. 6).

The studies listed above represent only a sample of a growing scholarly production that is still struggling to both determine the conditions in which trust occurs and suggest practices to make it happen within formal and informal organizations. However, when considering teams whose members are separated by space (geographic location), place (organizational/institutional location), and situation (role, skills, knowledge, culture), most of this scholarly production finds itself siding with one of two extremes positions: trust among virtual team members is, by default, either ruled out or taken for granted.

Extrapolating "Real World" Experiences to the Classroom

We believe that the truth of the matter lies somewhere between these extremes. As we stated previously, conditions surrounding virtual teams in distance education settings are very different from those of virtual teams in other organizational contexts — a fact that might challenge extrapolation of the notion of swift trust to online classrooms. For example, in virtual classrooms instructors become the initiators of teams, even when they will not be part of them and may not be previously acquainted with their members. Moreover, role assignment within the team may not be determined by expertise, but rather by random selection.

Still, the study by Jarvenpaa and Leidner (1998) provides empirical evidence indicating that, in spite of higher levels of uncertainty about leadership, procedures, role assignment, etc., than those experienced by their counterparts in the "real world," some virtual teams in online classrooms manage to develop swift trust. They do so by engaging in a series of strategies that improve the efficiency and effectiveness of communication among members, consequently affecting overall team performance in a positive way.

But is swift trust enough in the context of online learning? We cannot forget that creation of virtual teams in an online classroom has to serve the overarching goal of effectively conveying curricular contents, beyond providing students with practical training on real workplace situations and use of information and communication technologies. Swift trust among members of virtual teams in online classrooms certainly contributes to the efficient accomplishment of short-term tasks, which is a valuable skill for students to acquire. However, according to Bitter-Rijpkema, Martens, and Jochems (2002) substantial collaborative learning and mutual knowledge elicitation seems to demand broader and longer-term interaction:

> *Construction of shared understanding and solutions requires more than simple exchange of explicit information. Elicitation of unarticulated ideas of participants lies at the basis of negotiated agreement upon common goals and collective solutions...Researchers emphasize the fact that knowledge elicitation doesn't arise spontaneously... Ideas for stimulation range from elicitation via external knowledge presentations, structured dialogues, argumentation elicitation and the use of artifacts to community formation... Empirical studies (Kraut et al., 1988) indicate that social interaction is so critical to successful knowledge creation that neglecting this aspect will limit collaborative knowledge construction (p. 2).*

Facilitators of distance learning environments should, therefore, introduce virtual teamwork to their online classrooms with two timelines in mind: one related to the efficient operation of teams under specific deadlines; another related to the development of long-run interactions conducive to participatory and collaborative knowledge creation, as well as coverage of the course content. While the idea of swift trust provides an adequate approach for the adoption of strategies concerning the former, some principles associated with the notion of "structured trust" and community of practice may also prove useful for the latter.

Bandow (2001) argues that "structured trust" facilitates team performance as it provides:

> *[a] framework around which teams and team members can function when they have little knowledge of others in the group. Standardized processes, contracts and other verbal and written agreements can all serve as forms of structured trust, and managers can facilitate teams to help establish trust structures. When individuals come together to work as a team, they bring many different opinions with them... Typically, verbal agreements are made within the team, but the problem with verbal agreements is that not everyone hears the same information, even if everyone receives it at the same time. Different assumptions are made based on individual perspectives...Left untouched, these misconceptions can grow into issues of monumental proportions that may never be overcome (p. 42).*

Communities of Practice and Virtual Teams in Distance Learning

In the preceding sections, we have discussed the importance of relationships and bonding for the successful implementation of virtual teams. As we have also mentioned, such bonding is more likely to occur the longer a group remains stable. However, it is a given that students are together for a short period of time represented by a semester, quarter, or trimester. Consequently, understanding the evolution of team formation and communities of practice in this particular setting is key to a successful online learning experience.

Lave and Wenger (1991) first coined the term "Community of Practice" (CoP) to describe a set of social arrangements maintained over time around an activity, defined by a specialized language, specific knowledge, unique procedures, and common resources, as well as by virtue of its relationship to other communities. Crucial to this idea is the notion of "Legitimate Peripheral Participation" (LPP), that is, the process by which the community is sustained over time through gradual incorporation of newcomers to the core membership. "Newcomers participate in the periphery, observing old-timers and taking part in legitimate practices. Increasingly, the newcomers are given more responsibility within the community and begin to engage in practices more central to the community" (Squire & Johnson, 2000, p. 24).

The notion of community of practice has appealed a number of education scholars in recent years, as it can be easily linked to other theories in the field, such as anchored instruction, cognitive apprenticeship, and social learning.[2] However, few studies have attempted empirical explorations of the establishment and maintenance of CoPs in distributed learning environments such as those typical of distance education (e.g., Barab, Squire, & Dueber, 2000; Squire & Johnson, 2000). Even scarcer are studies dealing with the role of information and communication technologies in promoting or hindering CoPs within virtual classrooms.

Still, the incipient literature on the subject seems to indicate that creating adequate structural conditions and processes for a community of practice within an online course should facilitate generation of trust necessary for virtual teams to operate. Findings from the case studies conducted by Jarvenpaa and Leidner (1998), and Kimble et al. (2000) corroborate that academic virtual teams that create procedures for communication and problem-solving (i.e., practices that build participants' identity as members of something larger than an aggregation of individuals) are able to overcome technical and cultural barriers inherent to virtual teamwork.

By the same token, researchers argue that time constraints of formal learning settings make it particularly difficult for teams to engage in the extended procedural and social exchanges that create a community of practice. This, in turn, has a negative impact on the process of building trust and discipline within teams. However, even if teams manage to create a community of practice, they rarely relate to other CoPs (Squire & Johnson, 2000). Moreover, community maintenance through legitimate peripheral participation does not stand much of a chance because a team's existence rarely transcends the term of the course in which it was created.

Engaging students in communities of practice demands giving them extended periods of time to participate in a community ...

[S]chool calendars and schedules imposed boundaries on students' participation, and seriously challenged educators' ability to engage learners in communities of practice within school settings...[A] student's participation in a community ended with the termination of the program. If students hoped to continuing participating within a community of practice, they would have to do so largely on their own. Thus providing students with opportunities to participate in communities of practice may require systemic change efforts to make lengthy relationships possible (Squire & Johnson, 2000, p. 42).

Balancing Trust and Control in the Virtual Classroom

Both developmental and deterministic views conceive trust as the result of reducing uncertainty with respect to other team members and the conditions under which teamwork takes place. Such uncertainty reduction is possible, according to the developmental model, through extended social interaction or, according to the deterministic model, by filling in voids of actual information with pre-formed ideas, stereotypes, attitudes, and assessments of risks and benefits.

Whereas some studies indicate that trust can not only be learned (and, therefore, taught) in scenarios of relatively short-term interaction (Birk, 2001), but also created in conditions that makes it self-reproductive (Falcone, Singh & Tan, 2001; Shaw, 1997); understanding trust building in terms of uncertainty reduction opens interesting possibilities for the design of strategies aimed at facilitating teamwork and collaborative learning.

Regarding facilitation of teamwork, a number of authors have underlined the advantages of clearly predefined rules of communication in generating and maintaining trust among team members. These rules range from the use of multiple technological platforms to requiring exchange of individual information among team members (e.g., biographical data, background, interests, photos, and goals) to establishing patterns of frequency and style of interaction. Such procedures for the internal operation of teams can contribute to the emergence of swift trust, as team members exchange some preliminary information about their motivations and capacities (for role assignment) and decrease their levels of uncertainty about issues of appropriateness and the organizational culture of the virtual classroom.

With respect to long-term strategies for ensuring collaborative learning, it is important to assess processes as well as results. Instructors or facilitators should not only keep track of communication among team members for timely intervention when conflicts are not adequately addressed, but also let students know that their work is being monitored throughout all phases. The presence of structured mechanisms of control helps reduce levels of uncertainty because it minimizes defection or opportunistic behavior while rewarding collaboration.

Responsibility and accountability are major problems with individual team members. Some do not see themselves as stakeholders, nor are they seriously troubled by the prospect of their behavior potentially lowering the team grade. These problems exist in face-to-face teams, but they can become more difficult to deal with in virtual teams. However, technology does allow the teacher to monitor all individuals and team contributions closely, as well as the evolving relationships of team members.

Control mechanisms have been associated with the notion of distrust, a condition that many times coexists with trust, even as the two terms are conceptual opposites. McKnight and Chervany (2001) explain that while we may trust a particular person in some situations, we may distrust him or her in other circumstances. Because organizations cannot anticipate members' responses in all situations, a balance between dependence and control is necessary (Shawn, 1997). When it comes to virtual teams, "looking at only the positive (trust) side of things can result in such detrimental thought patterns as 'group-think,' [whereas] looking at only the negative (distrust) side can paralyze action" (McKnight & Chervany, 2001, pp. 46-47).

Lewicki, McAllister, and Bies (1998, p. 439) highlight the complementary nature of the concepts of trust and distrust by defining them respectively in terms of positive or negative expectations regarding some individual's behavior. Thus, they argue that both concepts reflect "movement toward certainty," even if coming from different directions.

Conclusions

Preliminary empirical research is just beginning to assess the potential explanatory power and limitations of extrapolating the notions of trust and community of practice from organizational settings to distance education experiences. However, we believe that it is not too early to suggest some strategies to help overcome the problems described above. And although it has been indicated that a re-conceptualization of the way the academic sector approaches virtual teams is necessary, some measures within the current timeframe and structure of traditional distance education programs are possible.

The literature reviewed for this chapter and our own experiences as facilitators and participants in virtual teams, suggest that processes involving trust building (swift and structured), balancing trust and control, and developing communities of practice have as a common denominator a desire to reduce uncertainty. In this sense, we have several suggestions for educational practitioners who are considering the adoption of virtual teams for their classes:

- *Reliance on multiple communication platforms*. In the absence of face-to-face interaction among members of virtual teams, a variety of communication channels must be integrated into the online learning experience in order to provide students with levels of media richness that minimize the "noise" of missing cues in the exchange of messages. Students should be requested to alternate use of different communication platforms available in the virtual classroom for different tasks in the course, so that they not only demonstrate their ability to attain certain goals, but also gain a better understanding of processes and resources along the way. This strategy also takes into account the fact that students are likely to have varying skills across various communication platforms.

- *Rethinking expectations, processes, and outcomes*. In connection with the previous point, it is crucial for instructors to candidly reflect on the functions that virtual teams serve for the overall purposes of their online courses. Not all subjects and instructional goals benefit equally from incorporating teamwork as part of the course's dynamics. Nevertheless, if requesting teamwork is deemed crucial, instructors should allocate enough time within the course's term, and even before it begins, for social bonding. Faculty must be willing to reward efficient communication, problem solving, decision-making, and crisis management within teams, at least as much as effective outcomes are rewarded.

- *Defining basic rules of the game.* In lieu of the well-defined organizational cultures that members of virtual teams find in business settings, the instructor should provide online students with a basic set of principles to guide interaction inside the virtual classroom. Such a set of rules should go beyond offering orientation on typical "housekeeping" matters (e.g., submission of assignments, participation in class discussions, grading policies) to also suggest best practices for team members' interaction, remind them of basic norms of "netiquette," and/or introduce students to some specialized terms related to the subject at hand.

- *Seamless, timely intervention.* Online instructors should assume the role of coach and facilitator of virtual teamwork, rather than one of patrol officer or controller. In this sense, instructors would assume a position equivalent to that of experts within a community of practice, as they gradually surrender control of the learning process to students. However, instructors must be ready for timely interventions to help groups overcome crises in the early stages of team formation. In virtual classes, the roles of students and instructors are transformed to fit the environment. While many traditional classes have become more student-centered, the removal of some sensory cues further affects student-teacher and student-student interactions. The same technologies that break down the barriers of space and time erect new barriers between students and between students and instructors. Instructors become coaches, facilitators, or — in a certain sense — team managers as they guide the collaborative work and learning of students. As Meyerson et al. (1996, p. 192) suggest in reference to the establishment of swift trust in distributed teams, "unless one trusts quickly, one may never trust at all." Therefore, instructors should be prepared to promptly pinpoint dysfunctions and facilitate problem-solving for teams facing special communication challenges, in order to prevent these challenges from becoming major disruptions in the life of the team.

- *Facilitating connection between communities of practices inside and outside the virtual classroom.* Instructors and providers of student services within educational institutions could work together in gathering and facilitating information about trade organizations and other communities of practices with which virtual teams could cultivate relationships. Teams should be encouraged to establish formal or informal ties with other CoPs that are relevant for their *raison d'être* as a group, as this would not only give them an opportunity to look at a course's contents in connection with "real life" scenarios, but also allow students to expand their social and professional networks by participating in other CoPs.

- *Creating spaces for maintenance of course-originated CoPs over time.* Coordinating offices of online and distance education programs in universities and colleges could offer an innovative service to instructors and students by establishing portals or interactive spaces where communities of practices generated by teamwork in different courses continue to exist after their initial academic term is over. The purpose of such a space would be many-fold. First, it would create conditions for successful CoP experiences to survive beyond the limits of a virtual classroom. Second, it would allow the spontaneous creation of a meta-community of practice comprising the universe of online students who are participating or have participated in course-specific CoPs — a community where newcomers could learn best practices from peers who have become experts by virtue of their accumulated experience in virtual teams and online courses. Finally, the space should prove a valuable source of information for the sponsoring college or university, as it would reflect opinions, concerns, and feedback from students who actively participate in the institutions' distance education initiatives.

In light of the germinal status of the existing literature on the subject, our suggestions to create favorable conditions for the development of trust and communities of practice in virtual classrooms are, for the time being, modest ideas in progress. However, we consider them as a starting point for future research aimed at realizing in the electronic space Lave and Wenger's (1991) comprehensive view of authentic generative social practice.

Endnotes

[1]   Classes were composed of students in an Organizational Communication course taught in a small private college. This discussion preceded their reading assignments on the functioning of teams in organizations.

[2]   The notion of anchored instruction refers to the establishment of relevant connections between instructional contents and "real life" issues (Cogni-

tion and Technology Group at Vanderbilt, 1993). Cognitive apprenticeship occurs when learners become familiar with experts' thought processes and end up adopting their analytical strategies (Collins, Brown &
Newman, 1989). Social learning defines, in the context of our discussion,
the process in which community members learn from their peers, by
observing their behavior and progress within the group as a whole (Lave
& Wenger, 1991).

References

Bandow, D. (2001). Time to create sound teamwork. *The Journal for
Quality and Participation*, 24(2), Start page 41. Retrieved Oct. 16,
2001, from ProQuest database.

Barab, S.A., Squire, K.D., & Dueber, W. (2000). A co-evolutionary model
for supporting the emergence of authenticity. *Educational Technology,
Research, and Development*, 48(2), 37-62.

Birk, A. (2001). Learning to trust. In Falcone, R., Singh, M., & Tan, Y.H.
(Eds.), *Trust in Cyber-Societies*, (pp. 1-7). Berlin: Springer-Verlag.

Bitter-Rijpkema, M., Martens, R., & Jochems, W. (2002). Supporting knowledge elicitation for learning in virtual teams. *Educational Technology &
Society*, 5(2). Retrieved from http://ifets.ieee.org/periodical/vol_2_2002/
rijpkema.hmtl.

Cantu, C. (1997). Virtual teams. *CSWT Papers*. Retrieved from http://
www.workteams.unt.edu/reports/Cantu.html.

Cognition and Technology Group at Vanderbilt. (1993). Anchored instruction
and situated cognition revisited. *Educational Technology*, 33, 52-70.

Collins, A., Brown, J.S., & Newman, S.E. (1989). Cognitive apprenticeship:
Teaching the crafts of reading, writing, and mathematics. In Resnik, L.B.
(Ed.), *Knowing, Learning, and Instruction: Essays in Honor of
Robert Glaser*, (pp. 665-692). Hillsdale, NJ: Erlbaum.

Cramton, C. D. (2001). *The virtual knowledge problem and its consequences for dispersed Collaboration*. Retrieved from http://
www.webuse.umd.edu/abstracts2001/abstract_2001_cramton.htm.

Crisp, C.B. & Jarvenpaa, S.L. (2000). *Trust over time in global virtual teams*. Unpublished manuscript.

Falcone, R., Singh, M., & Tan, Y.H. (2001). Bringing together human and artificial agents in cyber-societies: A new field of trust research. In Falcone, R., Singh, M. & Tan, Y.H. (Eds.), *Trust in Cyber-Societies,* (pp. 1-7). Berlin: Springer-Verlag.

Gould, D. (1999). Virtual organization. Retrieved on June 28, 2002, from the World Wide Web: http://www.seanet.com/~daveg/vrteams.htm.

Handy, C. (1995). Trust and the virtual organization. *Harvard Business Review,* 73(3), 40-50.

Harrison, R.T., Dibben, M.R., & Mason, C.M. (1997). The role of trust in the informal investor's investment decision: An exploratory analysis. *Entrepreneurship Theory and Practice,* 21(4), 63-81.

Henry, J. E. & Hartzler, M. (1997). *Tool for Virtual Teams: A Team Fitness Companion.* New York: McGraw-Hill.

International WHERE+HOW (2002). *The International Distance Learning Course Finder.* Retrieved from: http://www.dlcoursefinder.com.

The Internet Research and Development Centre. *Virtual University Journal.* Retrieved October 2, 2002 from http://www.irdc.com/virtual-university-press/vuj/welcome.htm.

Jarvenpaa, S. L. & Leidner, D. E. (1998). Communication and trust in global virtual teams. *Journal of Compute-Mediated Communication,* 3(4). Retrieved from http://www.ascusc.org/jcmc/vol3/issue4/jarvenpaa.htm.

Jarvenpaa, S. L., Knoll, K., & Leidner, D. E. (1998). Is anybody out there? Antecedents of trust in global virtual teams. *Journal of Management Information Systems*, 14(4), 29-64.

Katzenbach, J. R. & Smith, D. K. (2001). The discipline of virtual teams. *Leader to Leader,* 22. Retrieved from http://www.pfdf.org/leaderbooks/l2l/fall2001/katzenbach.html.

Kezbom, D. (2000). Creating teamwork in virtual teams. *American Association of Cost Engineers*, 42 (10), 33-36. Retrieved October 16, 2001, from ProQuest database.

Kimble, C., Li, F., & Barlow, A. (2000). *Effective virtual teams through communities of practice.* Retrieved from http://www.mansci.strath.ac.uk/papers.html.

Lave, J. & Wenger, E. (1991). *Situated learning: Legitimate peripheral participation.* New York: Cambridge University Press.

Lewicki, R.J., McAllister, D.J., & Bies, R.J. (1998). Trust and distrust: New relationships and realities. *Academy of Management Review,* 23, 438-458.

Lipnack, J. & Stamps, J. (1997). *Virtual Teams.* Retrieved from http://www.netage.com/Learning/mini_book/Chapter_1_Summary.html. http://www.netage.com/Learning/mini_book/Chapter_2_Summary.html. http://www.netage.com/Learning/mini_book/Chapter_9_Summary.html.

Lurey, J. S. & Raisinghani, M. S. (2001). An empirical study of best practices in virtual teams. *Information and Management*, 38(8), 523-544. Retrieved October 16, 2001, from ProQuest database.

Mayer, R.C., Davis, J.H., & Schoorman, F.D. (1995). An integrative model of organizational trust. *Academy of Management Review,* 20(3), 709-734.

McKnight, D.H. & Chervany, N.L. (2001). Trust and distrust definitions: One bite at a time. In Falcone, R., Singh, M. & Tan, Y.H. (Eds.), *Trust in Cyber-Societies,* (pp. 27-54). Berlin: Springer-Verlag.

Mehrabian, A. (1971). *Silent messages.* Belmont, CA: Wadsworth.

Meyerson, D., Weick, K.E., & Kramer, R.M. (1996). Swift trust and temporary groups. In Kramer, R.M. & Tyler, T.R. (Eds.), *Trust in Organizations: Frontiers of Theory and Research,* (pp. 166-195). Thousand Oaks, CA: Sage Publications.

Moore, J. & Barab, S. (in press). The inquiry learning form: A community of practice approach to online professional development. To appear in *Technology Trends,* 46.

National Center for Education Statistics. (2002). *Contexts of Postsecondary Education.* Retrieved from http://nces.ed.gov/programs/coe/2002/section5/indicator38.asp.

Online-Educa. (2002). *Online-Educa Berlin: 8th International Conference on Technology Supported Learning & Training.* Retrieved from http://www.online-educa.com.

Shaw, R. B. (1997). *Trust in the Balance.* San Francisco: Jossey-Bass Publishers.

Squire, K.D. & Johnson, C.B. (2000). Supporting distributed communities of practice with interactive television. *Educational Technology, Research and Development,* 48(1), 23-43.

Tidwell, L. C. & Walther, J. B. (2000). Getting to know one another a bit at at time: Computer-mediated communication effects on disclosure, impressions, and interpersonal evaluations. Paper presented at the *7th International Conferences on Language and Social Psychology,* Cardiff, Wales.

United Nations Development Program. (2001). *Human Development Report 2001.* Retrieved from http://hdr.undp.org/reports/global/2001/en/pdf/front.pdf.

Chapter VI

Education Mirrors Industry: On the Not-So Surprising Rise of Internet Distance Education

Donald A. Hantula

Temple University, USA

Darleen M. Pawlowicz

Temple University, USA

Abstract

Internet distance education is analyzed as a natural consequence of fin de siècle industrial transformations. From this perspective, previous distance- and technologically-based educational innovations are discussed, not as having failed, but as not matching prevailing economic and social conditions. It is argued that in the evolution from a manufacturing economy, in which standard educational practices are based, to an information economy, in which greater autonomy, collaboration, flexibility, and a project orientation to work are the norm, educational practices will either follow the lead of industrial organizations or risk irrelevance. Implications for adapting educational practices to new economic realities and developing new research streams are presented, especially in terms of matching instructional technology to educational outcomes, virtual collaboration, and media naturalness effects.

Introduction

Computer-mediated education grew from near nonexistence to near ubiquity in the final decade of the twentieth century. Although appearing to come from nowhere (or maybe from outer space) along with the Internet, this "revolution" in distance education happened gradually, following changes in industrial and organizational practices. The Internet did not cause changes in education, but rather enabled educators to meet new demands for instructional practices and outcomes and adapt to a rapidly changing economic and social environment that was beginning to outpace academia. The most salient changes that occurred in the last decade were in computer hardware, networks, and software. These tools are components of a much larger technology, however, that of formal education. Kipnis (1997, p. 208) defined technology as "the use of systematic procedures to produce intended effects." As a technology, formal education has had several intended effects, and it is the changes in these intended effects that have spurred transformations in the use of instructional components such as computers, books, classrooms, school buildings, curricula, and audiovisual aids.

In this chapter, we discuss computer-mediated education as a natural consequence of fin de siècle industrial transformations. As the needs of industry evolved, intended effects of education also changed to reflect a new economic reality. Today, just as 100 years ago, educational institutions and practices are modeled on prevailing industrial examples of work and organization. This is especially the case in the United States where an overriding intended effect of formal education is to prepare students to fill roles within the prevailing economic system. Against this backdrop, it is only those components of education that reflect and reinforce the prevailing industrial system that are incorporated into the technology known as formal education. Components of education such as teaching machines and distance learning existed throughout the twentieth century but never became standard educational practice until fairly recently, because they were not acceptable in terms of preparing students to enter the prevailing industrial system. Working from this perspective, we then move to considering the educational and research needs brought to the forefront by recent economic and social changes, especially in terms of increasing acceptance of, and need for, educational practices that incorporate computer and other electronic technologies as a core component of the educational experience.

Education Mirrors Industry

Popular conceptions of education present educators and educational institutions as leaders of the vanguard. In many areas of research and scholarship this may well be the case, but in terms of educational practices, especially when it comes to incorporating technology into education, the educational system follows the lead of the industrial system. Educational institutions have been relatively stable and have not undergone any major transformations in the last two centuries, despite advancements in technology (Molebash, 1999). Indeed, the U.S. Congress (1988) found that educational institutions lag behind business by roughly a decade in adopting new technologies. One reason for this lag may be economic. Educational institutions, on the whole, do not have the same level of financial resources available for technology purchases as do business organizations. In this case, it may be prudent to wait for technologies to become less expensive, more reliable, and widely adapted before committing scarce resources to their purchase. Another reason may be a certain amount of intransigence on the part of educators and educational administrators, resistance to learning new technologies, and an allegiance to educational "traditions." However, in the case of Internet-based education, funds for computers and networking became available relatively quickly, and equipment was often provided free or at a substantial discount. Policies and incentives to increase faculty involvement of computer technology also proliferated rapidly (Noble, 1998).

Educational institutions customize many of their services according to what is dictated by industry. Jacques (1996) posited that educational institutions serve organizations by "manufacturing" employees who are suitable for the workplace. The classroom was designed as an industrial entity as it mirrored organizational practices. Specifically, educational institutions produce skilled employees congruent with organizational demands, thereby completing a system of supply and demand. However, Jacques asserted that educational organizations employ antiquated techniques and thought processes that subsequently lead to anachronistic management practices. If this holds true and educational institutions do indeed follow industry, it would not be surprising to find that educational institutions would lag behind organizations in the employment of new technologies.

Education emulated the factory. Straight lines of desks (often bolted to the floor), uniform curricula, standardized forms and procedures for evaluating students and faculty, strict scheduling, student achievement indexed according to hours worked and units completed all bear more than an accidental resemblance to the manufacturing process. As formal education grew in the U.S. in the early twentieth century, the Scientific Management movement informed and inspired educators to view schools in the same terms as manufacturing businesses (Spring, 2001), i.e., as "...essentially time- and labor-saving devices, created by us to serve democracy's needs" (Cubberly, 1919, p. 355). "Manufacturing" students who satisfied these industrial "needs" was the intended effect of education.

The type of output preferred was a standard "product" — a graduate who not only was trained in the basics of reading, writing, and arithmetic (skills of practical usefulness), but who was also socialized to industry (Robbins, 1997). Educators were trained to consider themselves as administrators or managers, seeking the most efficient ways to teach attendance, punctuality, attentiveness, conformity, rote learning and an acceptance of standardized work, piecemeal production, and adherence to a hierarchical order (Spring, 2001). These were the lessons to be learned so that the "industrial capabilities and character" could be shaped (Cubberly, 1909, p. 41). Principals were akin to factory managers, setting general policies and procedures under which teachers — shop managers of their own classrooms — made the process work. Thus it is not surprising that the physical design of school buildings and their interiors reflected the design of factories; the practices occurring within them attempted to replicate, as closely as possible, the prevailing industrial order.

A Short History of Educational Technologies

With the concurrent rise of both formal education and the factory system, it might be reasonable to assume that various technologies would have been quickly applied to produce more efficient education. However, this was not the case. Despite the prevailing machine age, schools, for the most part, did not adopt mechanized methods of education such as teaching machines. Instead, a more teacher-driven, craft model of education was the norm. Within the constraints of the classroom, teachers as skilled craftspeople assembled education from centrally approved and provided pieces in a custom shop. The craft of teaching was realized through regulating the flow and progress of students through mass-produced mandated material by explaining, illustrating, and answering questions. Teaching filled in the gaps between a standard curriculum and the individual needs of the students. Against this backdrop of a custom-production shop within an educational factory, such "educational technologies" were too expensive to be widely employed, as they would have had to be fitted to the uses of each teacher in each classroom.

In current parlance, "educational technology" refers to applications of one or more electronic or computer-based devices used in delivering education. "Distance education" refers to any educational arrangement in which the instructor and student are not in the same place at the same time. Educational technology may be used in connection with face-to-face classroom instruction or for instruction at spatial or temporal distances; distance education may or may not incorporate educational technology devices. Both educational technology and distance education have been used separately or in combination in the past. Currently, the combination of these two components of formal education is in the form of computer-mediated instruction.

Throughout the history of human communication, advances in technology have powered paradigmatic shifts in education (Frick, 1991). The book — a standard set of organized printed materials — is perhaps the most enduring technological change that has influenced education. Writing allows students to record lessons and instructors to produce educational material that could be used at other places and times. The book, however, disintermediated the instructor and student, allowing each to be at different places at different times. This did not mean the end of instruction; formal education became organized around the book as the fundamental element of instruction. Critical to distance education, books function as a central component of entirely aspatial and atemporal education. Mass production of books allowed a single author/ instructor to teach unseen multitudes of students. Indeed, through a skillfully written book, an instructor can continue to educate students long after the instructor has died.

The book alone, however, is often an insufficient means for providing effective education. Some type of additional guidance or instruction is often needed. The first distance education courses in the United States, dating back to the 1800s, were postal mail correspondence courses (Nasseh, 2002). Although many prestigious universities including Chicago, Cornell, Johns Hopkins, and Yale offered courses and degrees through correspondence at different times during the past two centuries, this method of distance education remained on the fringe in terms of adoption and acceptability.

Educational technologies such as recorded audio and films came into use during the early part of the twentieth century. Like the book, audio and video recordings may allow for disintermediated education, but were used more as adjuncts to classroom-based instruction than as replacements. The first educational technology that appeared to have the potential to replace classroom instruction was the teaching machine introduced by Pressey in the 1920s (Benjamin, 1988). Using Pressey's teaching machine, a student would refer to an item in a multiple-choice test then press the button corresponding to the "right" answer. If the chosen answer is correct, the next item is displayed; if the chosen answer is wrong, an error is registered and the student must continue to make choices until the right answer is chosen. Despite early promise, teaching machines were never widely adopted. A reluctance to adopt this new technology might have existed because the educational establishment was not ready for it (Skinner, 1968), or perhaps because its construction, "programming," and maintenance were beyond the skill and budget of most educators. Or, it was not widely adopted because teaching machines did not actually teach as much as test what had already been taught (and presumably learned).

Instructional radio was not well received (Wright, 1991), but the new technology of television appeared to have great promise, both as an adjunct to classroom instruction and as a means of distance education. In a particularly intriguing application of instructional television in the 1960s, the Midwest Program on Airborne Television Instruction took flight from an airfield near Purdue University, circling Indiana and five surrounding states to broadcast educational programming to nearly 2,000 public schools and universities, reaching almost 400,000 students in 6,500 classrooms in those six states.

However, by the 1970s, instructional television had faded due to teacher resistance, expense, and the inability of television alone to meet the various conditions for student learning, including testing (Reiser, 1987).

The 1950s and 1960s saw other attempts at using educational technologies, such as teaching machines, programmed instruction (Skinner, 1968), and the personalized system of instruction (Keller, 1968), all of which peaked in the late 1960s (Vargas & Vargas, 1992). Each of these technologies generated initial hope and excitement, but never became an accepted part of the educational establishment. As a result, one prominent teaching machine developer actively discouraged people from developing these technologies (Gilbert, 1982). When computers became common, computer-based educational applications were introduced (Crowell, Quintanar, & Grant, 1981) but were relegated to a small number of institutions (Hantula, Boyd & Crowell, 1989). Once again, educational technologies were used more often as adjuncts to classroom instruction or school-based instruction.

Establishment of the Open University in the UK in 1969 presaged the distance education evolution in the last decade of the twentieth century, including the advent of the University of Phoenix. But the major question to be answered is, why did it take so long? Educational technology and distance education have not been prominent in the past. Until more recently, technology has primarily been used as an "add-on" in educational settings (Papert, 1997). Part of the reason may be tradition; fully replacing lecture-based teaching would require a shift in the "accepted" and very traditional manner of teaching (Brothen, 1998). Technologies such as the overhead projector, which could be easily incorporated into the classroom under the teacher's control, were accepted because they did not threaten the status quo (Kipnis, 1994).

Education Mirrors Industry (Reprise): The Information Economy

The classroom/factory in which the compliant worker-consumer is the end product is no longer acceptable because factories are no longer the dominant models for most business organizations. The transformation from an industrial economy to an information economy has altered the way that organizations are run and the way education is configured (Sumner, 2000). Flat organizational structures, a project vs. job orientation to work, less centralized control, and flexible scheduling are current configurations that enable rapid response, new innovations, and the development of new global alliances (Alavi, Wheeler, & Valacich, 1995).

In this new economic model, outcomes depend not on goods but on information, and technology is the normative tool. We have seen a precipitous decline in the importance of spatio-temporal constancy; people commonly are not in the same place at the same time when "work" occurs. Because of globalization and the rapid pace of technological change, there is now an imperative to redraw the physical boundaries of the classroom, allowing learning to be continuous and education to occur in any place or at any time. With the rise of knowledge work and increased autonomy, the work model emerging is one of collaborative, rather than individual effort. Because knowledge work requires more flexibility and adaptability, individual employees have freer rein to determine how tasks will be performed. Part of this self-direction is the ongoing option to seek assistance and to reciprocate when the opportunity arises. Because computer technology is now ubiquitous in industry, computers are no longer the tools of the few. Combining the technological imperative with the nearly appliance-like nature of computers, the social and structural determinants are in place for computer-mediated distance education to become the norm. Educational institutions have changed the way education is accomplished in order to "manufacture" the needed graduates who have the requisite skills that the new workplace demands (Jacques, 1996).

Advantages and Disadvantages of Educational Technologies

Distance education technologies offer greater flexibility and increased autonomy for students. For example, students are better able to manage work and family issues due to greater flexibility in scheduling and the ability to "attend classes" during nontraditional work hours. This flexibility in time management also allows for self-paced learning, as well as fewer impediments to learning. Students do not have to attend class at a certain time and in a certain place, which results in decreased travel time and costs. Another important benefit is that institutions, instructors, classes, and other resources are increasingly accessible to students, regardless of their geographic location. Trends such as the greater need for life-long learning, the need for more part-time educational resources, and demographic changes such as an increase in older workers may further contribute to the demand for flexible educational opportunities. Finally, due to greater availability and access to educational resources, the student body becomes more diverse, which results in opportunities for interaction with students from around the globe. Due to increased globalization in organizations, it will be beneficial for these prospective workers to be exposed to a variety of diverse experiences.

While there are many advantages to the use of technology in educational settings, there are also some important drawbacks that should be noted. Mann, Varey, and Button (2000) reported that social isolation is a potential result of increased use of technology, particularly when technology replaces traditional social interaction. Employees in nontraditional work arrangements such as telecommuting and virtual organizations reported feelings of isolation and loneliness (Huws, 1984). While some individuals may experience more social isolation over time, others may be able to overcome these feelings as time passes. Thus, certain individuals may be better suited to distance learning and other nontraditional forms of technology-based education.

Also, the lack of feedback, the untimeliness of feedback, and information delays may be other disadvantages of educational technologies. A related issue is the occurrence of problems that cause delays and impede communication and learning processes. As a result, educational institutions need to be adequately prepared to prevent these problems, as well as to implement prompt solutions if these problems do arise. Finally, there may be a great deal of resistance to technological changes and other transformations that may come about. For example, researchers have reported managerial resistance to virtual teamwork and other types of nontraditional work within business organizations (Wiesenfeld, Raghuram, & Garud, 1999). Some of this resistance might stem from perceived threats to managers' identity and control. This type of resistance might also be anticipated in educational settings, especially from teachers who may be reluctant to adopt new instructional techniques and perceive change as a threat to their identity. Resistance from students, teachers, and other members of educational institutions may be a barrier to the implementation and success of distance learning and other programs based on educational technologies.

Future Trends in Education Technologies

By examining various trends and transformations that have taken place in organizational settings, it may be possible to predict some of the trends that might occur in educational institutions. The need for "technoliteracy," the rise of teamwork and inter-organizational collaboration, and the transformation of teaching and learning might be several of the most prevalent trends that will take place in educational settings in the future.

The Need for Technoliteracy

An important result of the increased use of technology in classrooms and organizations will be the growing need for "technoliteracy." Specifically, both teachers and students will need to become proficient with a variety of technological media (Banas & Emory, 1998), which will be somewhat challenging given the ongoing and rapid advancements in technology. Individuals will need to undergo periodic training to maintain technological literacy. Technoliteracy for teachers goes beyond knowing how to use various educational technologies, and includes knowledge of when to use them and how to select technological methods and media that are congruent with learning tasks (Hantula, 1998). For example, programmed instruction may be better suited to teaching fundamental or basic knowledge; technical skills may be best taught through methods that allow for practice and feedback on the skill. An important lesson to be gained from knowledge of organizational trends is that the most advanced technologies are not always suitable for certain types of tasks. Thus, emphasizing the congruency between the type of task and the technological media being used will grow in importance. This issue is not new. A prominent proponent of teaching machines, T. F. Gilbert (1960), summarized these concerns well:

> If you don't have a gadget called a teaching machine, don't get one. Don't buy one; don't borrow one; don't steal one. If you have such a gadget, get rid of it. Don't give it away, for someone else may use it. This is a most practical rule, based on empirical facts from considerable observation. If you begin with a device of any kind, you will try to develop the teaching program to fit that device (p. 478).

Indeed, the primary question to ask when implementing educational technology of any kind is not "what can I do with this thing?" but rather, "what will this thing allow me to do that I could not do before, or how will this thing allow me to better meet the educational needs of the students?"

The Rise of Teamwork and Inter-Organizational Collaboration

Networked and team-based learning will become more important in the future. There has been a proliferation of the use of collaboration and teamwork in most organizations, and organizations rely on numerous types of teams to accomplish various tasks and goals (Cohen & Bailey, 1997; Guzzo & Dickson, 1996). As a result, an emphasis on teamwork and collaboration in educational settings will better prepare employees for the business world. In addition, organizations are also relying more heavily on self-managed work teams (SMWTs), or teams that are autonomous and are responsible for managing and performing various tasks (Yeatts & Hyten, 1998). Due to the increase of these teams in organizational settings, it is plausible that SMWTs will become more prevalent in educational institutions of the future. For example, teams of students may have greater levels of independence and autonomy to complete projects and other assignments.

Traditional teams are co-located, meaning team members meet face-to-face in one place (Olson & Olson, 2000). The increased use of teamwork coupled with technological advancements and globalization has led to the use of "virtual" teams, in which teams of people work interdependently across space, time, and organizational boundaries through the use of technology. The rise in virtual teams is the result of the growth of teamwork in organizations and increased geographic dispersion of workers (Lipnack & Stamps, 2000). Unlike traditional teams, virtual teams utilize technology to facilitate communication and collaboration (Duarte & Snyder, 1999; Snow, Lipnack & Stamps, 2001). Increased access to technologies should also result in a dramatic increase in the use of collaboration and virtual teamwork in educational industries. For example, a student in France might collaborate with a student in the United States in order to complete a research project. The availability of distance learning will foster further collaboration between students and faculty members, and greater levels of inter-organizational collaboration should be expected. Indeed, virtual team collaboration in education raises the intriguing issue of inter-institutional communication and collaboration by students and instructors. Virtual project teams may be readily formed across institutional boundaries, and these may be invaluable in providing students with experience working with individuals who are located in other regions or even other countries.

Transformation of Teaching

Technological advancements in organizations have contributed, at least in part, to increased autonomy and independence for both employees and managers. Thus, it would not be unrealistic to anticipate the occurrence of similar changes in educational settings. For example, highly structured and traditional leadership functions have been transformed into roles where the leader serves primarily as a coach or facilitator (Cascio, 1999). This transformation of roles is analogous to a teacher shedding a more traditional role — disseminating information — to assume the role of facilitator in the learning processes in which students are allowed high levels of autonomy and independence and teachers guide discussions, make possible the sharing of information, and provide assistance when needed (Leidner & Jarvenpaa, 1995).

Autonomy for students would follow not only from the change in the teacher's role but also from an increase in collaboration. Individual students working on isolated tasks, seeking assistance only from the teacher when permitted, is an industrial model of education — one in which the teacher as foreman controls the pace of work and access to resources and information. When work was characterized by highly controlled, independent outputs, it made sense to socialize future employees to an individual system of working, grading, and ranking. However, in an organizational world that emphasizes collaboration and teamwork, such a model is no longer adaptive for higher education. Teacher-directed learning, drill and practice, and more "traditional" methods of teaching are certainly valuable when students are learning basic skills, but are less appropriate when students are learning higher level skills, or how to apply and implement advanced knowledge. Once a student possesses a modicum of knowledge, learning how to use it, share it with others, and build upon that knowledge base by consulting others rises in importance. Freeing students to seek knowledge and answers from one another, other instructors, books, and online sources should then become a part of teaching.

An increase of autonomy and sharing of knowledge demands skills of critical thinking, synthesis, and negotiation. Knowledge in a textbook or delivered in a lecture has already been reviewed and certified as accurate by authors, publishers, and the instructor; there is little reason for the student to question its veracity. However, when seeking knowledge from peers or other sources, a student must be able to critically analyze the information and its source. The degree to which all or some of the knowledge obtained is valuable has to be assessed, and then incorporated into the student's existing knowledge base. Balancing competing requests for help as well as soliciting information and guidance from peers over the course of an academic quarter, semester, or year requires subtle negotiating skills to insure that no student is exploited, misled, or ignored.

It would then be expected that the teacher's role should become less synonymous with information dissemination and more synonymous with arranging instructional events; changing from an actor or actress to a producer or director, in theater terms. Greater emphasis should be placed on the process of learning than on its outcomes. Perhaps grading could incorporate measures of value-added contribution to peer learning and projects. Close study of contemporary work process could also lead instructors to construct innovative process measures. Although these speculations await enactment and evaluation, it is clear that if teaching does not transform to a networked, technological, and collaborative endeavor, it risks irrelevancy.

Research Opportunities

Although educational institutions can learn much from organizations, there is a lack of empirical research that examines the role of various computer technologies in educational settings (Kosarzycki, Salas, Fiore, & Burke, 2002). Because there are many different types of technological media that may be used in a pedagogical environment, it is important to assess how these media impact learning. For example, are there certain types of media that are easier to use or are more engaging than others? What is the relationship between the communication media and the type of task to be learned? Moreover, are existing theoretical explanations of media usage substantiated in educational settings? Repeating the obvious but extraneous question of "traditional lecture class" vs. "online/technological/mediated class" will do little to advance knowledge or instructional practice (Hantula, 1998). This is not an either/or question. Technologically based education is a fact, and constructing straw programs for comparative purposes is a waste of research resources as well as a distraction from the more important questions of how features of these new technologies and media may be best adapted for instructional purposes.

Media Naturalness

Kock (2001) asserted that individuals might have an evolutionary bias for communication media that are most similar to face-to-face (FTF) interaction. Synchronous FTF communication, which uses auditory sounds and visual cues, has been the primary mode of communication in the evolutionary history of human beings. Subsequently, it is the most "natural" form of communication, and the more "natural" a communication medium is (in terms of its fit with the adapted behavior of the species), the more effective it should be (Kock, 2001).

Media Richness

Daft and Lengel (1986) proposed that technological media vary in terms of the amount of "richness" that they possess, with FTF communication at the high end and text documents at the low end. As a result of differences in media richness, individuals would be expected to favor certain media depending upon the nature of the task before them. However, Markus (1994) reports that there are also social reasons underlying use of certain communication media in an organization. For example, managers may rely heavily on e-mail because e-mail usage is encouraged as part of the norms or culture of the organization. These findings are important because they demonstrate that the most expensive and the most "rich" media are not always the most appropriate or the easiest to use for certain organizational tasks. For example, videoconferencing is a medium that is very similar to face-to-face interaction because of the presence of social and other important interpersonal cues. While it would appear that videoconferencing would be widely used and that users would report high levels of satisfaction with the interaction process (Patrick, 1999), the use of videoconferencing in learning has had very limited success (Kies et al., 1996; Rettinger, 1995). Although arguably "rich," videoconferencing is still a mediated form of communication that often has delays in transmission of sound or moving images, and due to the limitations of video screen technology, does not offer the amount of depth perception that is found in FTF communication. Whether these limitations in satisfaction with videoconferencing are due to technological constraints or are valid counter-evidence to media richness theory still remains to be determined.

Media Uniqueness

As previous attempts have illustrated, effective and accepted distance educational technology must do more than simply replicate the classroom or its typical tools in an electronic format; it must capture the strengths of the current arrangements and capitalize on the unique strengths of the new media. Instructional television and radio failed due to an absence of interactivity. Teaching machines were abandoned because they tested rather than taught and neither medium was as engaging as a live teacher (unless the teacher was truly dreadful). New electronic media present new issues, such as the preferred amount of interactivity (Haggas & Hantula, 2002), the effects of download delay in the transmission of information (Davis & Hantula, 2001), reading from a screen as opposed to a book, self-directed "attendance," and optimal use of components of multimedia technology.

If educational technologies are to be employed effectively, the biological, technological, and social aspects of media use require more explication. In addition, the rise of virtual collaboration and teamwork makes it essential to investigate the factors that contribute to the success of learning in these types of arrangements. For example, it is necessary to examine the factors that enhance satisfaction and productivity in virtual teams and to determine what barriers hinder communication and how they can be overcome. There is also the need for additional research about the benefits and drawbacks of educational technologies. It will be particularly important to assess problems related to resistance to these technologies at all levels, as well as to examine whether this resistance fades over time. Moreover, it will be necessary to investigate the role of organizational culture and support in the success of educational technologies. The eventual success of many of these technologies is dependent, at least in part, to the culture of the institution. Many educational institutions will adopt and implement these technologies, but offering a variety of resources and fostering a supportive atmosphere is perhaps more important, because these also are critical factors in organizational settings. Most importantly, researchers will need to explore effects such as information overload and psychological stress that may result from increased reliance on technology.

Implications

Technology will continue to alter the nature of learning in many educational settings, and it is difficult to fully anticipate the consequences of some of these changes. However, it is useful to further examine some of the most important changes in organizations in order to both anticipate what might occur in educational settings and better understand and learn from previous problems. For example, flexible and alternative work arrangements such as "hoteling" (where mobile employees can go to a hotel-like environment that contains equipment such as desks, computers, and phones to do their work) and telecommuting typify the types of organizational changes that have taken place. Will we see many of same arrangements in educational settings?

While it is evident that learning will become more automated, the idea of a fully automated educational experience in which a machine delivers all instruction, instructional events, and materials and all student interaction is mediated by preprogrammed machine-based technology, seems implausible in the near future. Privateer (1999) asserts that technology should be viewed as a tool to redesign educational curricula, rather than simply as a replacement for traditional instructional methods in higher education. Indeed, if a century of educational research and technological experiments have taught us anything, it is that it is the not the medium, it is the method that makes a difference (Clark & Zuckerman, 1999). Availability of technological media does not guarantee that these media will be properly integrated into instructional techniques. Instead, the greater challenge appears to be the human component of this process. Humans should endeavor to shape technology to fit both their physical and psychological needs (Kock, 2001) and not simply produce advanced technologies that they are not comfortable with. Ultimately, technology will continue to dramatically redefine learning and teaching and will have a profound impact on the educational institutions that enable these processes.

Brothen (1998) observed that there is an increasing gap between available technology and creative uses of it, and Molebash (1999) similarly states that, with respect to technology, education is moving along at a snail's pace while the world outside is speeding by at a supersonic rate. On the one hand, computer technology is more inexpensive, available, and powerful than ever before, but on the other hand, it appears that educators have not exploited its powers to transform teaching. Instead, it appears as if distance education technologies have been grudgingly implemented as a reaction to an increasing social and economic demand.

The Internet bubble has burst, much of the *fin de siècle* hype about "the new economy" has not been realized, and virtual schools have not replaced "brick and mortar" campuses. As education mirrors industry, the proliferation of educational technologies is perhaps preordained, but educators need not be simply along for the ride. In this new industrial order, will "formal education" as a technology evolve and thrive, or will it join the likes of teaching machines and Airborne Television Instruction in our closet of curiosities?

References

Alavi, M., Wheeler, B. C., & Valacich, J. S. (1995). Using IT to reengineer business education: An exploratory investigation of collaborative telelearning. *MIS Quarterly, 19(3),* 293- 313.

Banas, E. J. & Emory, W. F. (1998). History and issues of distance learning. *Public Administration Quarterly, 22(3),* 365-383.

Benjamin, L. T. (1988). A history of teaching machines. *American Psychologist 43*, 703-712.

Brothen, T. (1998). Transforming instruction with technology for developmental students. *Journal of Developmental Education, 21(3)*, (Spring).

Cascio, W. F. (1999). Virtual workplaces: Implications for organizational behavior. In C. L. Cooper & D. M. Rousseau (Eds.), *Trends in Organizational Behavior: The Virtual Organization,* (pp. 1-14). Chichester, UK: John Wiley & Sons.

Clark, R. C. & Zuckerman, P. (1999). Multimedia learning systems: Design principles. In H. D. Stolovich & E. J. Keeps (Eds.), *Handbook of Human Performance Technology (2nd ed.),* (pp. 546-588). San Francisco, CA: Jossey-Bass Pfeiffer.

Cohen, S. G. & Bailey, D. E. (1997). What makes teams work: Group effectiveness research from the shop floor to the executive suite. *Journal of Management, 23(3)*, 239-290.

Crowell, C. R., Quintanar, L. R., & Grant, K. L. (1981). PROCTOR: An online student evaluation and monitoring system for use with PSI format courses. *Behavior Research Methods & Instrumentation, 13*, 121-127.

Cubberly, E. P. (1909). *Changing conceptions of education.* Boston, MA: Houghton-Mifflin.

Cubberly, E. P. (1919). *Public education in the United States.* Boston, MA: Houghton-Mifflin.

Daft, R. L. & Lengel, R. H. (1986). Organizational information requirements, media richness, and structural design. *Management Science, 32(5)*, 554-571.

Davis, E. S. & Hantula, D. A. (2001). The effects of download delay on performance and end-user satisfaction in an Internet tutorial. *Computers in Human Behavior, 17*, 249-268.

Duarte, D. L. & Snyder, N. T. (1999). *Mastering virtual teams: Strategies, tools, and techniques that succeed.* San Francisco, CA: Jossey-Bass.

Frick, T. W. (1991). *Restructuring education through technology* (Faster back service No. 326). Bloomington, IN: Phi Delta Kappa Educational Foundation.

Gilbert, T. F. (1960). On the relevance of laboratory investigation of learning to self-instructional programming. In A. A. Lumsdaine & R. Glaser (Eds.), *Teaching Machines and Programmed Instruction.* Washington, DC: NEA.

Gilbert, T. F. (1982). Human incompetence: The autobiography of an educational revolutionist. *Journal of Organizational Behavior Management, 3*, 55-67.

Gordon, G. (1965). *Educational television.* New York: Center for Applied Research in Education.

Guzzo, R. A. & Dickson, M. W. (1996). Teams in organizations: Recent research on performance and effectiveness. *Annual Review of Psychology, 47*, 307-338.

Haggas, A. & Hantula, D. A. (2002). Think or click? Student preference for overt vs. covert responding in a web-based tutorial. *Computers in Human Behavior, 18*, 165-172.

Hantula, D.A. (1998). The virtual industrial/organizational psychology class:

Teaching and learning in cyberspace in three iterations. *Behavior Research, Methods, Instruments & Computers, 30,* 205-216.

Hantula, D. A., Boyd, J. H., & Crowell, C. R. (1989). Ten years of behavioral instruction with computers: Trials, tribulations, and reflections. In J. Hodges (Ed.), *Proceedings of the Academic Microcomputer Conference.* (pp. 81-92). Bloomington, IN: Indiana University Press.

Huws, U. (1984). The new homeworkers: New technology and the changing location of white-collar work. *Low Pay Pamphlet No. 28.* UK: Low Pay Unit.

Jacques, R. (1996). *Manufacturing the employee: Management knowledge from the 19th to the 21st centuries.* Thousand Oaks, CA: Sage Publications.

Keller, F. S. (1968). "Good-bye teacher..." *Journal of Applied Behavior Analysis, 1,* 79-89.

Kies, J.K., Williges, R.C. & Rosson, M.B. (1996). *Controlled laboratory experimentation and field study evaluation of video conference for distance learning applications.* Virginia Tech HCIL 96-02.

Kipnis, D. (1994). Accounting for the use of behavior technologies in social psychology. *American Psychologist,* 49(3), 165-172.

Kipnis, D. (1997). Ghosts, taxonomies, and social psychology. *American Psychologist,* 52(3), 205-211.

Kock, N. (2001). The ape that used e-mail: Understanding e-communication behavior through evolution theory. *Communications of AIS, 5,* Article 3.

Kosarzycki, M.P., Salas, E., Fiore, S.M., & Burke, C.S. (2002). *Emerging themes in distance learning research and practice: Some food for thought.* Poster session presented at the 17th Annual Meeting of the Society for Industrial and Organizational Psychology, (April 2002). Toronto, Canada.

Leidner, D. E. & Jarvenpaa, S. L. (1995). The use of technology to enhance management school education: A theoretical view. *MIS Quarterly, 19(3),* 265-292.

Lipnack, J. & Stamps, J. (2000). *Virtual teams: People working across boundaries with technology* (2nd ed.) New York: John Wiley & Sons.

Mann, S., Varey, R., & Button, W. (2000). An exploration of the emotional impact of tele-working via computer-mediated communication. *Journal of Managerial Psychology, 15(7)*, 668-690.

Markus, M. L. (1994). Electronic mail as the medium of managerial choice. *Organizational Science, 5(4),* 502-527.

Molebash, P. (1999). Technology and education: Current and future trends. *IT Journal.* Available online at: http://etext.lib.virginia.edu/journals/itjournal/1999/molebash.htlm.

Mungazi, D. A. (1999). *The evolution of educational theory in the United States.* Westport, CT: Praeger.

Nasseh, B. (2002). A brief history of distance education. *Adult Education in the News.* Available online at: http://www.seniornet.org/edu/art/history.html.

Noble, D. (1998). Digitial diploma mills. *First Monday.* Available online at: http://www.firstmonday.dk/issues/issue3_1/noble/index.html#d7.

Olson, G. M. & Olson, J. S. (2000). Distance matters. *Human-Computer Interaction, 15,* 139-178.

Papert, S. (1997). Educational computing: How are we doing? *Technological Horizons in Education, 24(11)*, 78-80.

Patrick, A.S. (1999). The human factors of videoconferences: Recommendations for improving sessions and software. *Journal of Computer-Mediated Communication, 4(3).*

Privateer, P. M. (1999). Academic technology and the future of higher education: Strategic paths taken and not taken. *The Journal of Higher Education, 70(1)*, 60-79.

Reiser, R. A. (1987). Instructional technology: A history. In R. Gagne (Ed.), *Instructional Technology: Foundations.* Hillsdale, NJ: Lawrence Erlbaum.

Rettinger, L.A. (1995). *Desktop Videoconferencing: Technology and Use for Remote Seminar Delivery.* Master of Science, North Carolina State University. Available at http://www.ncsu.edu/eos/service/ece/project/succeed_info/larettin/thesis/tit.html.

Robbins, S. A. (1997). Implications of distance education as an agent of sociocultural change. *Educational Telecommunications*, 1791-1798.

Skinner, B. F. (1968). *The Technology of Teaching.* New York: Prentice-Hall.

Snow, C. C., Lipnack, J., & Stamps, J. (2001). The virtual organization: Promises and payoffs, large and small. In C. L. Cooper & D. M. Rousseau (Eds.), *Trends in Organizational Behavior: The Virtual Organization,* (pp. 15-30). Chichester, UK: John Wiley & Sons.

Spring, J. (2001). *The American school 1642-2000.* New York: McGraw-Hill.

Sumner, J. (2000). Serving the system: A critical history of distance education. *Open Learning, 15,* 267-285.

U.S. Congress, Office of Technology Assessment. (1988). *Power on: Tools for teaching and learning, OTA-Set-379,* U.S. Government Printing Office, Washington D.C., (September).

Vargas, E. A. & Vargas, J. S. (1992). Programmed instruction and teaching machines. In R. P. West & L. A. Hamerlynck (Eds.), *Designs for Excellence in Education: The Legacy of B. F. Skinner,* (pp. 33-69). *Limited Edition.* Longmont, CO: Sopris West.

Watkins, B. L. & Wright, S. J. (eds.) (1991). *The foundations of American distance education: A century of collegiate correspondence study.* Dubuque, IA: Kendall/Hunt.

Wiesenfeld, B. M., Raghuram, S., & Garud, R. (1999). Managers in a virtual context: The experience of self-threat and its effects on virtual work organizations. In C. L. Cooper & D. M. Rousseau (Eds.), *Trends in Organizational Behavior, Vol. 6: The Virtual Organization,* (pp. 31-44). Chichester, UK: John Wiley & Sons.

Wright, S. J. (1991). Opportunity lost, opportunity regained: University independent study in the modern era. In B.L. Watkins & S.J. Wright (Eds.), *The Foundations of American Distance Education: A Century of Collegiate Correspondence Study.* Dubuque, IA: Kendall/Hunt.

Yeatts, D.E. & Hyten, C. (1998). *High-performing self-managed work teams: A comparison of theory to practice.* Thousand Oaks, CA: Sage Publications.

Chapter VII

Evaluating a Distance Education Program

Catherine Schifter
Temple University, USA

Dominique Monolescu
Temple University, USA

Abstract

In higher education, distance learning initiatives are very linked to the overall institution's educational mission. For such an initiative to succeed, a carefully designed distance education evaluation plan is necessary. This chapter describes key distance education program evaluation variables, using the Temple University's OnLine Learning Program as an example. In addition to describing the purpose of conducting a distance program evaluation and illustrating evaluation methods, the results from surveys and focus groups regarding students' satisfaction with their distance learning experiences are shared. We consider that a good distance education program evaluation plan should also impact the institution's general education policies and procedures.

Introduction

Evaluation of any program is a basic part of program development. As discussed in Chapter 1, if you look at distance education program development in terms of developing a business plan for a business, you need to know the program mission and scope and the audience to define the external and internal forces contributing to the program development; to identify exactly what services/courses/degrees/certificates will be offered and the performance (evaluation) measures to be used; to estimate the overall costs (income and outflow) of the program; and to consider future developments. Within the planning process the evaluation design and development are integral. At what point will you determine if the goals and objectives were met? How were they met? If they were not met, what happened to prevent them from being met? Each goal and objective should be assessed in terms of the mission and scope of the program. Evaluation of a distance education program requires attention to the same issues and questions, among others.

This chapter will first discuss basic issues of program evaluation, whether for traditional programs or distance education programs, and then will identify variables important to evaluation of university distance learning/education initiatives, using the Temple University OnLine Learning Program as an example. This chapter also presents the results from the research instruments used at Temple University (T.U.) to assess student satisfaction with two distance education modes (online and videoconferencing) of learning and teaching, and describes each instrument's advantages and disadvantages.

Basic Program Evaluation

What is the purpose of the evaluation? Who is it for? Once these two questions have been answered, the proper evaluation process, tools, and reporting structure can be selected or designed. There are many forms of program evaluation, including formative and summative, structured and informal, among others. A formative evaluation is intended to gather information specific to the goals and objectives of a program and to turn this information reflectively back to the program. This information provides guidance in refining and rethinking the program to ensure goals and objectives are met. Summative evaluation is used to assess whether the program has met its goals and objectives as defined by time (e.g., by 2002, the program will have at least one degree program available through distance delivery), to determine the impact of the program at that time, and to provide evidence for or against continuation of the program. Structured evaluation has a series of stages that comprise a cycle of activities that tend to be continuous. You identify a concern, study the issues involved, analyze and interpret the findings, make recommendations for change, implement the changes, and start over to see if the changes have the desired effect (Calder, 1994). Informal evaluation is ad hoc, crisis driven and immediate, less structured, and often not continued past the remedy of the crisis.

Overall, program evaluation must begin within the planning process and grow from the goals and objectives of the program as defined through the mission and scope (Bellanger & Jordan, 2000). Determining the purpose of the evaluation is key to knowing what data to gather and how and when to gather it. The purpose of the assessment determines which evaluation methods to use. Overall, evaluation should allow the organization or institution to learn from the past so to plan for the future. Should the program continue as is, expand offerings and opportunities, or be eliminated altogether? Questions include:

a.   Who is the audience for the evaluation?

b.   Is the program meeting its goals? And what are the signs of success?

c.   What evidence is there of student and/or faculty satisfaction?

Knowing who the audience is will influence the reporting format used. If the information is for the program staff, the information can be reported rather informally; however, if the information is for a vice president or the board of trustees, the report will be quite formal and include detailed information and instruments used, graphs of statistics, and the like. With each subsequent question, an example will be provided for how the audience will influence the reporting.

To determine whether the program is meeting its goals and being successful, the original mission, scope, goals, and objectives of the program must be reviewed. What goals and objectives were established with what time frame? If one goal was to have "one complete certification program available by 2002," but there is no complete certification program available by that time, there must be documentation as to what happened to demonstrate why the goal was not achieved. Was this a reasonable goal for the institution? Have there been changes in administration since the beginning of the program? The point is not to be defensive, but to document all intervening variables that impact upon the development of the program. Each goal should be assessed and documented in similar terms. Were goals met? If not, why not? To what extent were they met or not met, and what evidence is available to demonstrate success or failure? If the evaluation were for the program staff, the report would be short, describing the progress toward achieving the goal. If the evaluation were for the vice president of the university, the report would be formal with documentation of efforts to establish the certificate program.

One form of formative evaluation of a program focuses on customer satisfaction. The most common example is a survey completed at the end of courses. In terms of a distance education course, a satisfaction survey asks whether the customer (e.g., student or faculty) enjoyed the format of the course, whether the format impeded or promoted the learning/teaching process in any way, and whether the course was perceived as being similar to a traditional face-to-face course. An example of this latter question would be "I believe that having a course online is more challenging than having a course via a face-to-face mode."

Students and faculty would be asked to respond on a Likert-scale of "less, the same, or more." Other questions specific to the delivery media would be included as well. For example, questions in this area of the survey would ask about connectivity, download time, graphics, interactivity, and the specific delivery mechanism(s) used to determine satisfaction levels with the distance education infrastructure. This type of data is essential to knowing whether the program clientele were satisfied, no matter if the client was the student taking the course or faculty member teaching the course. If this information were intended for the program staff, it would be written up in a short report with raw data included; if this information were intended for the vice president, the report would include a detailed analysis of the survey data with graphs and charts comparing new data with old data to demonstrate trends.

Key Questions for Distance Education Program Evaluation

Distance education is already recognized as an effective teaching and learning tool (Simonson, Smaldino, Albright, & Zvacek, 2000). However, distance education program evaluation is intended to answer questions regarding the successfulness of a given distance education program, in light of the mission, scope, objectives, and goals of the program as mentioned previously in regard to basic program evaluation. Before undertaking any evaluation, you must be very clear about what questions are being asked and what data are collectable.

There are no clear or consistent guidelines for assessing the "quality" of a distance education program in comparison to a face-to-face program; however, certain features of a program can be investigated and provide some comparative data. Clearly, the teaching and learning environments for each are very different, but program features such as course content, level of interactivity, technology tools, and multimedia are important aspects of both face-to-face and distance education courses that can provide comparative guidelines for assessment.

Interactivity is an important component of any program, regardless the method of delivery. The general assumption is that a face-to-face course always provides a superior level of interactivity, but this is not necessarily the case. Distance education courses can make effective use of the Internet, e-mail, listservs, online discussion boards, synchronous chat rooms, and desktop videoconferencing to provide a level of interactivity that rivals that of a face-to-face course.

Key questions for distance education program evaluation include those for basic program evaluation, with the addition of two other important questions: (a) What are the incentives for faculty participation in the program? and (b) How does the university support the program?

Incentives for Faculty Participation in the Program

Why do faculty members participate in distance education initiatives? The literature indicates that faculty members participate to reach new students who might not otherwise take their course(s), to explore new ways to teach their discipline, for the diversity of experience (Dillon, 1989), and for intrinsic (e.g., prestige, self-esteem) rather than extrinsic (e.g., monetary rewards, course release time) incentives (Dillon & Walsh, 1992; Schifter, 2000a). A national study by Schifter (2000b) indicates that providing financial compensation to entice faculty to participate in distance education initiatives is a common practice among universities. There are several faculty compensation models for online course participation. These include a campus culture model in which participation in distance education is expected as part of one's employment, a "work for hire" model in which faculty are "hired" to work with a team of people to develop an online course package, and an individual support model in which the university provides support for individual faculty members who develop distance courses on their own. As discussed later in this chapter, the Temple University OnLine Learning Program (TU-OLL) applied the individual support model, which fit the initial program goal of determining if Temple faculty would want to teach online courses.

Initiatives that Require Support from the University

Evaluation of a distance education program should address not only its most immediate constituents (i.e., distance education students and faculty), but also the university community at large. Systems and initiatives implemented to support distance education, such as increased and improved computer help desk support, online registration and advising, online purchasing of textbooks, online payment of bills, and financial aid applications, also benefit all university students and faculty, not just those who take or teach online courses. In general, a university should allocate a budget for its distance education program that considers: (a) the hardware and software equipment (e.g., computers for faculty members, course management tools, new systems trial), (b) system backup and security measures for servers hosting the online courses, (c) distance education research, and (d) personnel. In addition, it is important to note that the support services that are currently available to on-campus students should also be made available to online students.

In summary, distance education program evaluation answers the same questions as basic program evaluation with the addition of questions about faculty participation and institutional support. As Schifter notes in Chapter II, understanding the culture of the institution will provide guidance in both asking the appropriate questions and interpreting the results.

The Online Learning Program Experience

This section will illustrate the guiding principles for launching the Temple University OLL Program, its infrastructure, activities, and evaluation methods.

Purpose of the Program

The Temple University OnLine Learning Program (TU-OLL) was created in 1995 with the initial goals of establishing a centralized university program for distance education to determine (a) whether Temple University students would take and be successful in taking courses offered via the Internet, and (b) whether Temple University faculty would offer courses through the Internet. Clearly, this program was not started as a for-profit university initiative, but as an "experiment" in distance education. This "experimental" program was initiated by the University's Teaching, Learning, Technology Roundtable[1] (TLT-R), backed by the Council of Deans and the Provost.

While some universities (e.g., Open University, University of Phoenix) initiated distance education course offerings that were meant to constitute comprehensive degree completion programs within a short period of time, Temple University adopted a less ambitious goal. Temple decided on a more measured approach that would allow exploration of the appropriateness of this mode of course delivery for its customer base. With this principle in mind, TLT-R members recommended that only credit-bearing courses be offered initially, but that eventually the scope of the distance education program should be broadened to include full degree-completion programs. This recommendation was due in part to the need to establish appropriate support systems for the distance education courses, faculty, and students.

The Infrastructure of the Program

The TU-OLL Program was launched with an office, a computer, and a part-time director. Its first year was devoted to enticing faculty members to experiment to adopt distance education initiatives, to understand the reasons why students would want to take online and videoconferencing courses, and to marketing initiatives. The Temple University Teaching, Learning, Technology Roundtable (TLT-R) recommended a number of faculty-support initiatives such as: (a) course release, (b) hardware and software, and (c) graduate assistants. This support was given to faculty members from various schools and departments, based on a yearly grant competition.[2] The TLT-R also recommended the creation of several student services (such as 24/7 help desk support and online registration) and stressed the importance of ensuring that all services available to on-campus students would be made available to online students.

Key to the TU-OLL Program's infrastructure was the fact that its members could count on several existing services already available at the University. Online faculty members could walk into one of the University's Instructional Support Centers (ISC) at any time to receive support for their online course materials. ISC also provided an onsite orientation about the available videoconferencing technology, with tips addressing issues for videoconferencing, such as: (a) ensuring eye contact by looking at the camera, (b) selecting the proper attire, and (c) carefully choosing the colors to be used on Microsoft Power Point slides. In addition, students could access their online courses via the computer labs, and they could also call the help desk office for technical problems.

Many of the infrastructure issues related to the program's distance education initiatives did not appear until two years after the program was launched and enrollment had increased. For instance, in its first year, the program could register 50 students in a semester from its office, and at the same time provide individualized services to its students such as tips on how to get started with their online course and obtain a T.U. e-mail address. Program staff also could act as liaisons between online students and their instructors. Nevertheless, as the program grew (in course offerings and student enrollment), adjustments to currently offered support services were sometimes necessary to make them more effective for online students.

For example, the University had initiated a telephone registration system for on-campus students the same year that the TU-OLL Program was launched. This registration system (Diamond Line system), however, did not differentiate between online, videoconference, and face-to-face courses. Students who thought they had registered for a traditional, face-to-face class were often surprised to discover that they had actually registered for an online or videoconference course, or vice versa. To address this issue, TU-OLL requested a unique course section number that identified a course as a distance education course. An online registration system for all university students became operational a few years after the telephone registration system was launched. Once again, adjustments to the system were needed to accommodate students taking online courses.

TU-OLL Program Activities

Even though the TU-OLL Program initial goals were discussed above, it is important to note that the TU-OLL Program's first generation of faculty members designed their online courses from scratch, using html code or html editor programs. These faculty members were expected to have expertise not only in course content, but also in computer technology and educational design. Two years after the first online courses were offered, the University adopted "course management tools" such as Top Class®[3], Blackboard Inc.,[4] and WebStudy Inc.[5] These course management tools facilitated creation and delivery of online courses.

Therefore, most of the primary activities of the program were isolated, administrative ones, focusing on distance education course development. With the University's adoption of course management tools and with the increase in the faculty's familiarity with distance education, the focus of the program shifted from faculty support to student services. The program director became a liaison between academic departments and computer services in order to assure that all services at the University were also available for distance education students (e.g., remote access to library resources, online registration, online textbook purchases, online tutorials, online advising, and even online writing sessions and career advising sessions). In addition to its focus on distance education course offerings, the TU-OLL Program, due to its experimental nature, also became a place where faculty would go to test new technologies (e.g., desktop videoconferencing, online chat sessions with file sharing applications, online focus groups, and online conferencing).

TU-OLL Program Evaluation

The program grew exponentially since its inception (from less than 50 students in its first year to 1,000 students a semester in 2002). And since its first year, it has had in place several, mostly formative, evaluation measures.

Evaluation of student and faculty satisfaction is critical for the success of any distance education program. Throughout the existence of the program, several methodologies, including surveys and focus groups, have been adopted in order to measure student and faculty satisfaction with the teaching and learning initiatives promoted by the program and with the technological support provided by the University. In addition, all evaluation tools adopted also focused on gaining information (from faculty members and from students) that could be used to improve the services offered by the program.

Even before the TU-OLL program was created, three colleges within Temple University had been experimenting with videoconference (VDC) course delivery. With the advent of the OLL program and expansion of VDC course offerings, assessing student and faculty satisfaction with this course delivery mode became important. With permission, TU-OLL adopted a survey instrument for videoconference (VDC) course satisfaction that had been used by the University of Southern Mississippi for the previous two years (see Internet Resources) to evaluate all of Temple's VDC courses.

In 1997, face-to-face focus groups were conducted to learn how students "felt" about taking online classes and being part of a virtual learning environment. The focus group data and information gleaned from the literature on student attitudes toward distance education helped us create an online customer satisfaction survey (see Internet Resources) that has been used every semester thereafter to determine whether the initial goals of the program were being met. In 1998, with the realization that online students could benefit from alternative evaluation solutions, an online focus group was pilot tested.

The focus group pilot test was created with Microsoft Front Page™, and it incorporated online discussion boards in order to provide a more flexible communication environment. A study by Monolescu and Schifter (1999) has demonstrated that asynchronous communication (such as a discussion board), when incorporated into a focus group, can be a powerful tool to evaluate students' online course experiences. This study also revealed that because online courses require a different array of preparation, infrastructure, and course methodology, the evaluation of students' online course experience required a different evaluation paradigm.

However, it was not until the Fall 2002 semester that TU-OLL launched two new versions of its online focus group pilot test: (a) one via Blackboard Inc that is primarily text based, and (b) one via Snitz Inc., with image-enhanced capabilities (see Internet Resources). Both online focus group versions were adopted for students and faculty members. The main difference between the student and faculty online focus groups was that the student version was created to allow students to remain anonymous throughout their participation, but the faculty version required that faculty members identified themselves while posting their comments.

For both online and VDC courses, the aforementioned student satisfaction evaluation tools provided data that supported the assertion that students were and continue to be interested in taking distance education courses. Results of the student satisfaction evaluation instruments will be discussed in detail in the following section.

Student Feedback

Online Surveys

The Temple University OnLine Learning Program has administered a student satisfaction survey (see Internet Resources) at the end of each semester since the first semester it offered distance education courses in 1995. In the spring of 1999, 600 students were in enrolled in 24 different online courses in anthropology, architecture, business, communication, computer sciences, education, music, and physical therapy. In the 2001-2002 academic year, approximately 2,000 students were enrolled in 88 different online courses. The following responses have been shared repeatedly by the online students who took at least one online course within the last five years:

a.   Regarding administrative issues, the students responded that:

•   at some point they received technical support from their peers, professors, or the University Help Desk;

•   they had no problems sending assignments or communicating with their instructors or peers via e-mail or listserv; and

•   they have started their online course(s) already informed about the course pre-requisite, technological requirements, and other relevant information needed for it.

b.   Regarding demographic issues, the student survey responses demonstrated that:

•   the majority of the students have been between 20 and 25 years old. Also, in agreement with the distance education literature (Furst-Bowe, 2001; Berge, 1998; Gibson, 1998), more female (56.4%) than male students (43.6%) are enrolling in distance education courses. This number is also consistent with the overall female enrollment at the University's non-distance education courses (57.7%).

c.   Regarding the instructional method and student performance issues:

•   The majority of the students who responded to this survey in 1999 stated that they were spending an average of 15 hours a week following their professors' course instructions. However, in 2000, this number dropped to an average of six hours a week per course. We believe that this drastic time change may be related to (1) the novelty of this course delivery mode in the year 1999, (2) the familiarity of the online students with the technology being used for the courses by the year 2000, and (3) the fact that within the past years the program website has provided tips on how to get started in an online course and tutorials on several of the technologies adopted by these courses.

•   The number of students that agreed with the statement "the same courses offered face-to-face would offer more content" has been decreasing with time. Almost 50% of the students who responded to this survey in the

Table 1: Students' Most Valued Online Course Features

Semester	Content	Web format	Classmates interaction	Professor interaction	Listserv	Chat	Survey responses
Fall 97	34 (85%)	21 (52.5%)	15 (37.5%)	23 (57.5%)	17 (42.5%)	11 (27.5%)	40
Spring 98	27 (90%)	26 (86.7%)	12 (40%)	22 (73.3%)	10 (33.3%)	7 (42.5%)	30
Fall 98	59 (79%)	46 (62.2%)	29 (39.2%)	47 (63.5%)	23 (31.1%)	12 (16%)	74
Spring 99	27 (27.5%)	62 (63.3%)	50 (51%)	58 (59.1%)	43 (43.9%)	20 (20.4%)	98
Fall 99	48 (88.9%)	41 (75.9%)	23 (42.6%)	43 (79.6%)	35 (64.8%)	18 (33.3%)	54
Spring 00	101 77.7%)	95 (73%)	56 (43.1%)	94 (72.3%)	50 (38.5%)	31 (23.8%)	130
Fall 00	43 (79.6%)	38 (70.4%)	21 (39%)	30 (55.5%)	18 (33.3%)	10 (18.5%)	54
Spring 01	16 (88.9%)	17 (94.4%)	12 (66.7%)	13 72.2%)	13 (72.2%)	6 (33.3%)	18
Fall 01	81 (87%)	73 (78.5%)	36 (38.7%)	53 (57%)	24 (25.8%)	20 (21.5%)	93

Note: 1. Data is displayed by raw numbers followed by the percentage of total responders. 2. Students were allowed to select more than one response, therefore, the percentages across rows do not total 100%. 3. For completeness of the data, all data in the table has been included since the start of the TU-OLL Program. Student participation in the survey was voluntary.

spring of 1999 agreed with this statement, while only 24.7% of the students who responded to this survey in the fall of 2001 agreed with it.

- As seen in Table 1, the most valued online course features by students are (1) the course content, (2) the online course web format, and (3) student interaction with the professor of the course.

- As seen in Table 2, the fact that students were "faceless" or anonymous during their online class interactions (via e-mail, listservs, or chat discussions) did not seem to impact on their amount of course participation. The two main reasons indicated were: (1) having time to think about how to express an idea, and (2) personality.

Table 2: Reasons Impacting on Online Students' Amount of Course Participation

Semester	Having time to think about how to express an idea	Personality	Feeling more freedom to express an idea	Feeling more comfortable writing than talking	Feeling anonymous	Feeling more comfortable with this medium due to the fact that they were faceless	Number of responses received
Fall 97	20 (50%)	23 (57.5%)	17 (42.5%)	15 (37.5%)	13 (32.5%)	8 (20%)	40
Spring 98	21 (70%)	21 (70%)	13 (43.3%)	14 (46.7%)	11 (36.7%)	7 (42.5%)	30
Fall 98	53 (71.6%)	44 (59.5%)	35 (47.3%)	33 (44.6%)	19 (25.7%)	14 (19%)	74
Spring 99	62 (63.3%)	59 (60.2%)	33 (33.7%)	30 (30.6%)	25 (25.5%)	15 (15.3%)	98
Fall 99	34 (63%)	32 (59.3%)	21 (39%)	23 (42.6%)	14 (26%)	16 (29.6%)	54
Spring 00	89 (68.5%)	71 (54.6%)	48 (37%)	50 (38.5%)	38 (29.2%)	30 (23%)	130
Fall 00	33 (61%)	32 (59.3%)	17 (31.5%)	19 (35.2%)	15 (27.8%)	12 (22%)	54
Spring 01	12 (66.7%)	13 (72.2%)	6 (33.3%)	9 (50%)	6 (33.3%)	2 (11%)	18
Fall 01	56 (60%)	59 (63.4%)	40 (43%)	36 (38.7%)	28 (30%)	28 (30%)	93

Note: 1. Data is displayed by raw numbers followed by the percentage of total responders. 2. Students were allowed to select more than one response, therefore, the percentages across rows do not total 100%. 3. For completeness of the data, all data in the table has been included since the start of the TU-OLL Program. Student participation in the survey was voluntary.

- In terms of student satisfaction with the online course taken, 90% or more of the students stated that: (a) they enjoy the online learning experience, (b) their course expectations were met, and (c) they were satisfied with their online course experience.

Through the surveys, the TU-OLL Program staff learned that, because online courses rely mostly on written information, it is very important that online professors and students begin communicating before the start of the semester. Communicating with faculty early in the semester prevents students from feeling overwhelmed or spending extra effort trying to catch up with their course work after the semester has started. The new feedback information that was gained each semester allowed the TU-OLL Program to constantly implement its activities and expand the information provided in its website, which helped make prospective online students more aware of what it takes to succeed in an online course.

Another important lesson learned through the TU-OLL Program surveys was that T.U. students who enroll in online distance education courses come to these courses with various levels of computer literacy and need to start their online distance education courses knowing in advance what technologies will be used in the online courses for which they register. Also, after six years of experience, the TU-OLL Program has gained enough knowledge about the general infrastructure and services needed to support (1) online distance education degree-completion programs and (2) the continuing education, non-credit, online distance education courses that are now being launched at the University.

Online Focus Group Results

Interesting data was gathered from both the face-to-face and online focus groups conducted by the TU-OLL Program. The following student comments illustrate the contribution of qualitative forms of feedback in an evaluation plan:

- Who should enroll in the University's online courses?

  "An excellent point was made that the courses should not be offered to freshmen. I agree that the traditional learning/ education experience should be well ingrained in the student before they could truly appreciate the benefits of an online course. A student must be self-motivated and organized in order

to maximize the opportunity offered through online learning" (Student 1).

• What are students' thoughts regarding course interactivity?

"I felt there was a high level of interactivity among the students and other classmates. Again, the anonymous environment, I am certain, added a great deal to this open interactivity. It was difficult for me, however, to get any kind of personal feeling for any of the students" (Student 1).

• Why did students choose to take an online course?

"My primary reason for taking an OLL course was to take advantage of the flexibility in my schedule. Of course, it was also a course that appeared very interesting and thought provoking. I would not have taken any course just because it was online. The course work and information that was shared on the listserv far outweighed my expectations for the course. The level of discussion that took place was challenging and informative. I took this course during a summer session, which added to the challenge. I believe it was an advantage in that the postings required seemed almost to be on top of each other, but it kept the flow going. There was no time to sit back and get lazy" (Student 1).

• What features/technologies/characteristics are relevant for future online course's success?

"I think that the most successful online courses are those whose content fosters discussion, varying points of view, and sharing relevant personal experience. A good online course really enhances your communication skills because you don't have the other person's body language to help in interpreting the responses, and you become aware of how others can react to something you say (or type) very differently than you intended it" (Student 2).

178 Schifter & Monolescu

"I think that very technical courses are more difficult online, unless you have a group with an equal level of skill who will participate in the problem-solving process" (Student 3).

• What are the disadvantages of taking an online course?

"The obvious disadvantage of not being able to receive immediate feedback from the professor and students did present itself. Our class experienced some technological problems at the onset of the course, which were frustrating. However, once these details were worked out on the listserv, and the professor made herself available either through phone or e-mail, the problem resolved itself" (Student 1).

Videoconferencing Courses

The videoconferencing survey instrument (see Internet Resources) was adapted from Southern Mississippi University. Most of the questions address the quality of audio and video transmissions and student satisfaction with the amount and quality of their course content. Based on the results of these surveys, Temple University made the following changes and additions to its videoconferencing rooms: (a) adjusted the location of ceiling microphones to reduce air duct noises, (b) included a television monitor at the back of the room so professors could see students in both classrooms[6] at the same time, and (c) added Internet drops in the VDC rooms.

The videoconferencing surveys consistently showed that students in the remote classrooms had to devote more effort to their courses than the students who were in the same location as their instructor. Students indicated this disparity was due to being distracted by: (a) audio delays (sometimes two seconds or more when not using a dedicated closed system or a T1 telephone line), (b) looking at a slide or only the head of the professor, (c) faculty clothing (certain busy fabric patterns create a fuzzy screen), (d) instructor or student arms, hands, and/or body motion (which in videoconferencing transmission cause visual distortions on the monitor or screen), and (e) the equipment itself (size and location can be distracting). Nevertheless, the remote students are the ones who seem to value the use of this technology the most because, according

Copyright © 2004, Idea Group Inc. Copying or distributing in print or electronic forms without written permission of Idea Group Inc. is prohibited.

to their survey responses, without this equipment they would not have access to the particular course/program for which they enrolled.

Retention and Grades for the 1999-2001 Academic Years

There are no national statistics about distance education retention and completion rates. However, "anecdotal evidence and studies by individual institutions suggest that course-completion and program retention rates are generally lower in distance education courses than in their face-to-face counterparts" (Carr, 2000, p. 39). As seen in Table 3, even though the drop-out rates for Temple University distance education courses are slightly higher than other

Table 3: OLL Program Student Drop-Out Rate and Grades

Course Level	Section Level	Students	MG	NR	W	WF	CR	NC	P	R	AU	GPA
0 - 199	Not 700	334507	4010	4398	16924	162	1857	235	2230	843	66	2.86
			1.2%	1.3%	5.1%	0.0%	0.6%	0.1%	0.7%	0.3%	0.0%	
	700	1281	37	27	94	3	1	0	0	1	0	3.14
			2.9%	2.1%	7.3%	0.2%	0.1%	0.0%	0.0%	0.1%	0.0%	
200-399	Not 700	119013	1327	1001	3688	52	1930	698	2697	55	52	3.22
			1.1%	0.8%	3.1%	0.0%	1.6%	0.6%	2.3%	0.0%	0.0%	
	700	1208	24	39	66	0	0	0	0	1	1	3.34
			2.0%	3.2%	5.5%	0.0%	0.0%	0.0%	0.0%	0.1%	0.1%	
400 and >	Not 700	50158	1047	190	498	8	122	0	1707	4428	24	3.68
			2.1%	0.4%	1.0%	0.0%	0.2%	0.0%	3.4%	8.8%	0.0%	
	700	1528	56	12	32	0	0	0	46	0	0	3.68
			3.7%	0.8%	2.1%	0.0%	0.0%	0.0%	3.0%	0.0%	0.0%	

Notes: 1. A 700 level section means that the course is offered online or via videoconferencing); 2. Course levels 0- 399 represent undergraduate courses; 3. Course levels above 400 represent graduate-level courses; 4. MG = missing grade; 5. NR = grade not reported; 6.W = withdrawal; 7.WF = withdrawal failing; 8.CR = credit; 9. NC = non-credit; 10. P = Pass; 11. R=Registered; 12. AU=Audit; and 13. G.P.A.= Grade Point Average.

Temple courses, the distance education student grade-point average (GPA) is not significantly different from the GPAs of students taking traditional face-to-face courses (especially graduate-level courses).

Conclusion

As this chapter has attempted to illustrate, a formative evaluation plan can help guide a new distance education program or redefine the program's aims and provide good feedback for future initiatives in the administrative, academic, faculty/student services, or marketing areas. We reiterate Lau's (2000) call for the need for institutional commitment to distance education initiatives and the need for adequate infrastructure as *key* factors contributing to the success of the initiatives; however, there is also a need to be aware of the impact of institutional culture on distance education initiatives.

Therefore, we suggest that a carefully designed distance education evaluation plan is also necessary to a program's success. The information gained from such a plan helps program leaders gather feedback needed for the institution's decision-makers to allocate the appropriate fiscal and infrastructure resources required to support it. In addition, we suggest that a distance education program must be responsible for providing an environment that fosters the enhancement of distance education students' course completion rates. By increasing completion rates, a distance education program can help an institution guarantee a more predictable subsequent fiscal budget (Parker, 1995).

As technology evolves, the needs of distance education students change. A distance education program must have a communication link with all of its constituencies to keep them apprised of the various implementations that will obtain from these changes. A good distance education program evaluation plan should reflect not only the performance of its courses, students, and faculty members, but also should be able to impact the institution's distance education policy and procedures. Most importantly, it should impact on the program's efficiency in achieving its institution's educational goals.

Acknowledgments

The authors would like to thank Dr. Karen Paulson (NCHEMS-National Center for Higher Education Management Systems) for her contribution to this chapter.

Endnotes

1   The University's Teaching Learning Roundtable (TLT-R) was established in 1994 to serve as an advisory committee to improve teaching and learning through the appropriate use of technology (see Internet Resources).

2   The TU-OLL Program had an initial goal of determining whether Temple faculty would teach in a distance education environment. To that end, a Request for Proposals for courses to be developed or converted for distance delivery via online or videoconferencing was sent initially to all faculty across the university. To provide guidance to the TU-OLL staff for supporting proposals, a committee of faculty who were already involved in distance education was constituted to provide a peer review process. Each proposal was reviewed for the design of the distance course, appropriateness for distance delivery, and overall reality of the proposal (i.e., was the proposal realistic in concept?). Proposals were ranked by these criteria, and only those that were deemed of highest quality were forwarded for support. Support consisted of faculty release time and funding for technology and specialized software, as needed. Not all proposals were supported. After the first two years of this process, the process was limited to those proposals that demonstrated a department moving toward offering a sequence of courses — not random offerings.

3   According to WBT system's website (http://www.wbtsystems.com/company), TopClass™ has an open architecture that allows you to integrate it with other applications.

4   Blackboard Inc. is a course management tool that provides online faculty and students with an easy way of adding their course materials and assignments, in addition to providing online tools for synchronous (e.g.,

virtual classroom) and asynchronous (e.g., e-mail and discussion board) communication.

5   WebStudy Inc. is also a course management tool that provides similar features to Blackboard. WebStudy Inc. also provides online professors with the ability to record voice messages either to explain the course materials posted or to provide students with personalized voice feedback on their assignments.

6   All Temple University videoconferencing rooms have PictureTel equipment (two video monitors in front of the room, two video cameras, ceiling or table microphones, a Socrates podium with a VCR and document camera, and a monitor at the back of the room.

References

Belanger, F. & Jordan, D. (2000). *Evaluation and implementation of distance learning: Technologies, tools and techniques*. Hershey, PA: Idea Group Publishing.

Berge, Z.L. (1998). Changing roles of teachers and learners are transforming the online classroom. Online_Ed, (August 30), Doc. N. 74. Retrieved from http://www.edfac.unimelb.edu.au/online-ed.

Berge, Z.L. & Collins, M.P. (1995). *Computer-mediated communication and the online classroom*. Volumes I, II, and III. Cresskill, NJ: Hampton Press.

Calder, J. (1994). *Programme evaluation and quality: A comprehensive guide to setting up an evaluation system*. London: Kogan Page.

Carr, S. (2000). As distance education comes of age, the challenge is keeping the students. *Chronicle of Higher Education*, 46(23), A39-A41.

Dillon, C. (1989). Faculty rewards and instructional telecommunications: A view from the telecourse faculty. *The American Journal of Distance Education*, 3(2), 35-43.

Dillon, C.L. & Walsh, S.M. (1992). Faculty: The neglected resource in distance education. *The American Journal of Distance Education*, 6(3), 5-21.

Furst-Bowe, J. (2001). *Identifying the needs of adult women in distance learning programs*. Retrieved from http://www.uwstout.edu/provost/jfb/proposal.htm.

Gibson, C. (1998). *Distance education in higher education: Institutional responses for quality outcomes*. Madison, WI: Atwood Publishing.

Lau, L. (2000). *Distance learning technologies: Issues, trends and opportunities*. Hershey, PA: Idea Group Publishing.

Monolescu, D. & Schifter, C. (1999). Online focus group: A tool to evaluate online students' course experience. *The Internet and Higher Education*, 2, 171-176.

Parker, A. (1995). Predicting dropout from distance education. In D. Seward (Ed.), *One World Many Voices: Quality in Open and Distance Learning,* (pp. 176-180). London: Eyre & Spottiswoode.

Schifter, C. (2000a). Factors influencing faculty participation in distance education: A factor analysis. *Education at a Distance*, 13(1). Retrieved from http://www.usdla.org/html/journal/JAN00_Issue/Factors.htm.

Schifter, C. (2000b). Compensation models in distance education. *The Online Journal of Distance Learning Administration,* 3(1). Retrieved from http://www.westga.edu/~distance/schifter31.html.

Simonson, M., Smaldino, S., Albright, M., & Zvacek, S. (2000). *Teaching and learning at a distance: Foundations of distance education.* Upper Saddle River, NJ: Prentice Hall.

Internet Resources

1. Internet Resources Temple University (T.U.) http://www.temple.edu.

2. T.U. OnLine Learning (OLL) Program http://oll.temple.edu.

3. T.U. Teaching Learning Technology Roundtable (TLT-R) http://www.temple.edu/tltr.

4. T.U. Blackboard's Portal http://blackboard.temple.edu.

5. WebStudy Inc. www.webstudy.com.

6.   T.U. OWLnet Interactive Web-Based Student Registration System http://owlnet.temple.edu.

7.   T.U. OLL Program Online Course Survey http://isc.temple.edu/oll/survey.

8.   T.U. OLL Program Videoconferencing Course Survey http://isc.temple.edu/oll/vdcsurveys.htm.

9.   T.U. OLL Program Online Focus Group http://oll.temple.edu/oll/OnlineFocusGroups/Studentollfocusgroup.htm.

Closing Remarks

Online Teaching, Copyrights, and the Need for Concerted Solutions

Gisela Gil-Egui

Temple University

Abstract

Most higher education institutions with online learning programs in the U.S. face similar challenges when it comes to establishing intellectual property (IP) policies that balance adequate stimulus for authors and appropriate investment return for the organization supporting their creative production. However, no university has yet been able to come up with a "golden standard" in this regard. While, by the time of writing this, Temple University was still in the process of discussing elements of a new IP policy for online contents, its preliminary experience on the matter reveals the benefits of proactive attempts at achieving consensus among all stakeholders, as opposed to adopting reactive or remedial stances.

Institutional change does not come about easily. The challenge of launching the OnLine Learning Program at Temple University was embraced by this university's community with both enthusiasm and caution. While many faculty members saw in this initiative an opportunity to explore emerging instructional technologies and settings, there were also questions in the air about the need for Temple to refine its policies regarding ownership of Intellectual Property (IP), in light of new possibilities for creation, reproduction, delivery, and retrieval of course contents.

The issue, which would later gain renewed attention with the project known as Virtual Temple (a for-profit distance education venture), made evident the importance of establishing a clear "default rule" regarding ownership of online instructional content produced within the setting of the University. Such a rule was to be designed in a way that it stimulate instructors to generate content, while providing Temple's administration with an adequate return for investment in equipment and resources necessary for faculty to create instructional online content.

Temple University already had an Invention and Patents Policy in force since 1985.[1] According to the University Counsel, George E. Moore, "the tradition had been that [Temple] did not assert its copyright (under the established work-for-hire legal doctrine) in textbooks, scholarly articles, and creative works that disseminated the results of academic research or scholarly study."[2] Still, some perceived the existing institutional approach as ill suited for the new copyright issues emerging from the application of online technologies to distance education. Thus, understanding the need for a formula that satisfies all the parties, Temple's former president Peter Liacouras appointed a Task Force on Intellectual Property in January of 1999 to develop a more precise copyright policy.

Nine representatives of the faculty and nine representatives of the administration composed the Task Force. The 18 members of this committee agreed, at its first meeting on March 1999, to name George Moore and Maurice Wright as co-chairs. As mentioned before, the former works as University Counsel and was designated convener of the Task Force. The latter, on the other hand, is a professor of music composition at Temple, with experience in both copyright protection and online teaching.

Thus, the Task Force was created in a way that it would, at least in theory, provide a setting where faculty and administration had equal representation in the formulation of a new IP policy. This effort emerged mainly from a shared concern that vagueness in the definition of ownership of courses materials could lead to legal contests whose resolutions would likely benefit one party to the other's detriment.

However, the initial intention of harmonizing different viewpoints into a coherent IP policy proved to be more difficult than expected. While waiting for Moore to convene the first meeting of the Task Force, the nine representatives of the professorate created the Faculty Senate Intellectual Property Discussion Group, with the idea of presenting a proposal reflecting the faculty's thoughts on the matter.

A series of drafts generated by this group were offered to the Task Force in 1999 and 2000. As discussion among the members of this committee progressed, consideration of different nuances surrounding content creation in academic settings seemed to complicate rather than clarify ideas. Therefore, in an attempt to provide a simple starting point, two members of Temple's Teaching and Learning Technology Roundtable[3] came up with a simple proposal: Ownership of intellectual property should be determined according to policies and traditions already in place, regardless of the specific technology used in its creation.

This parsimonious formula was considered by the faculty discussion group. In September 1999, a new proposal by Temple's professorate was offered. It reasserted the University's right to patent but removed references to specific technologies in the creation of intellectual property. The proposal also stated copyrights for the faculty who produced copyrightable material and incorporated a new scale for sharing patent income between the University and the inventors, according to the amount of net income generated by the creation at hand.

The Task Force discussed this proposal and accepted some of its definitions. However, a provision to recognize authors' copyrights within Temple's patent policy was not supported by the committee as a whole. As George Moore explains, "There has never been a tradition that *all* copyrightable material generated by a faculty member as a University employee is ceded to the faculty member"[4] (italics added). The disagreement persisted until the dissolution of the Task Force in 2001, due to organizational changes related to the retirement of President Liacouras.

Intellectual property then became a bargaining point for the faculty's union, Temple Association of University Professionals (TAUP), during its contract negotiation in 2001. As a result, that year's contract for faculty included a resolution by the professorate to work together with Temple's administration in developing a formal policy on copyrights. Such was the status of the matter at the moment of writing this epilogue.

In Maurice Wright's opinion, discussions about intellectual property at Temple University have moved from a setting where every member had similar power and a mandate to reach a consensual ground, to another setting in which two parties are confronting rival agendas and might try to maximize gains at the other's expense. Although initial meetings between parties in this new context have been cordial, Wright regrets that the university missed an opportunity to define an IP policy in 2000.

Still, Wright thinks that the unfinished labor of the Task Force on Intellectual Property was not a waste of time. Some of the concepts suggested, as well as the legwork done in terms of researching models and defining priorities should provide a head start for anyone who deals with the issue at Temple in the future.

An additional opportunity for analysis and assessment of the subject in a "power-free" setting was provided by Temple University's OnLine Learning Program during April 2001, when it organized the first Virtual Conference on Intellectual Property and Digital Information in Higher Education. For two weeks, experts and people concerned with copyrights and education at different levels (instructors, administrators, librarians, publishers, and students), from different parts of the country and different organizations, "met" via the Internet to discuss the status of the matter nationwide.

The event made evident some of the points that are becoming the focus for new discussions about copyrights and academia:

- *The dilemma of timing:* While ambiguities in the legal framework make it imperative for higher education institutions to define explicit policies as soon as possible, the reality is that most of these institutions still wait to see which one of the existing policies proves to be an effective model before designing an IP policy on their own. This may appear as a prudent attitude, but it comes at the cost of discouraging creation.

- *The scope and significance of policies:* As stated by David Post, a law professor at Temple and a participant in the conference, "What the initial position [of a policy] *is* becomes less important than just having *some* clear initial position from which to engage in negotiations."[5] When facing scenarios where radically opposed opinions impede the formulation of consensual solutions, both faculty members and administration are better off with a clear (even if biased) policy than with no formal reference at all in place. This initial rule, however, does not have to be a contractual straitjacket –rather, it is supposed to be a default point from where nuances and particular circumstances surrounding ownership can be jointly redefined by the interested parties.

- *Is content the only thing that matters?* Although debates on ownership over course materials and intellectual creation seem to rely heavily on the idea that content is the most valuable asset in academia, recent cases inside and outside Temple University are challenging such a perception. Within Temple, there have been several instances in which faculty members who originally designed and taught online courses, and later moved to another institution, have willingly relinquished all materials and contents to new instructors taking charge of those same courses. Similarly, there have been a few occasions in which instructors have taken with them course contents they developed, when transferring to other institutions. Elsewhere, the best known case is that of the Massachusetts Institute of Technology (MIT), which decided in 2001 to publish on the Internet the syllabi and contents of nearly all its courses, so that anyone can read them online for free.[6] In all these examples, the underlying assumption is that content is not the element that brings the most value to the teaching experience, but only one aspect of a comprehensive process that involves adequate delivery, institutional support, formal structures, assessment, customization according to the needs and capabilities of the students, constant updating, and adaptation to available resources.

In general, Temple University's experience illustrates the difficulties of defining copyrights over academic materials in light of emerging technologies for online teaching. More importantly, it highlights the need to establish mechanisms to guarantee an open dialog among all stakeholders in the matter. Although no formula has yet proven to satisfactorily cover all the issues raised by new technologies in the creation of intellectual property, examples of innovative copyright policies that are getting national attention — such as those of Carnegie Mellon University, University of Delaware, or the University of North Texas — are characterized by plural approaches that protect both individual creation and institutional investment.

Moreover, the burst of the "dot.com" bubble and the ambiguous results of many commercial ventures into distance education seem to indicate that assuming an absolute for-profit approach in the definition of IP policies at the institutional level may not be a good strategy. Different parties in the debate need each other to succeed and, therefore, must work in good faith to establish agreements that are mutually beneficial.

Acknowledgments

I thank Maurice Wright and George E. Moore for their valuable comments and suggestions in putting together these notes.

Endnotes

[1]   Details about this policy can be found at http://www.patents.temple.edu/ip_intro.htm.

[2]   Moore, G.E. (2002). Quote from an e-mail message to the author of this text, dated on September 17, 2002.

[3]   An advisory committee created in 1996 by Temple's Provost and Council of Deans to improve teaching and learning through the appropriate use of technologies. Details about it can be found at http://www.temple.edu/TLTR/.

[4]   Moore, G.E. Ibid.

[5]   Post, D. (2001). Excerpt from an interactive session held on April 18, during the Virtual Conference on Intellectual Property and Digital Information. Philadelphia, PA, April 17-30.

[6]   Massachusetts Institute of Technology (2001). MIT to make nearly all course materials available free on the World Wide Web. *MIT News*. Retrieved on July 2, 2002, from the World Wide Web at http://web.mit.edu/newsoffice/nr/2001/ocw.html.

Section II

Case Studies in Distance Education

Chapter VIII

Creating and Using Multiple Media in an Online Course

Maurice W. Wright

Temple University, USA

Abstract

The adaptation of a traditional, face-to-face course to an online format presents both challenges and opportunities. A face-to-face fundamentals course treating the science of musical sound and the methods used to code and transform musical sound using digital computers was adapted for online delivery. The history of the course and the composition of its audience are discussed, as are the decisions to create movies, web pages, electronic mail, and a paper textbook for the course. Practical choices for technology, which reflect the conflicting benefits of choosing simple versus more sophisticated technology, are outlined and the reactions of the students to these choices are discussed. An anecdotal comparison between an online and a face-to-face course section is offered, along with ideas for future development.

Background

Computers in Musical Applications is a course that has been offered in the Esther Boyer College of Music for 16 years and serves as a prerequisite for three music technology courses. The course was designed to provide students who expressed an interest in electronic and computer music with a detailed knowledge of the principles of acoustics and computer engineering that define the processes of digital recording, editing and synthesis of sound, and, to a more limited extent, digital video. When the university faculty adopted a core curriculum in 1986 that required a two-course sequence in science and technology, *Computers in Musical Applications* was proposed to serve as a second-semester core science course. The course would follow an acoustics class that was offered by the Physics Department and required of all music students. Since 1986, it has been offered each year with section enrollments ranging from 10 to 60 students.

Initially the course was taught in a traditional, face-to-face format that included a weekly, two-hour lecture class and a one-hour laboratory section comprised of small groups of students taught by a graduate student. The textbook for the course (Dodge & Jerse, 1985) was the same one used in a subsequent software synthesis class. The transition in 1986 from a small, self-selected class of technology enthusiasts to a large group of students with varied interests was challenging and was made more so by external factors such as the absence of a large lecture room with desks, difficulty in recruiting lab instructors with the necessary background and teaching skills, students' lapses in retained knowledge from the acoustics class, and complaints about the purchase of an expensive textbook of which only a few chapters were used. Another challenge was offered by the academic schedule of music students. Music ensembles such as orchestra carry only a one semester-hour credit but meet at least three hours per week with additional rehearsals and performances according to the college performance schedule. Faculty are expected to routinely excuse students from academic classes several times in a semester to participate in rehearsals and performances, and graduating seniors miss additional classes during the week of their senior recitals. As a result, class attendance is less than consistent. Also, the instructor is asked to provide considerable time outside of class teaching missed material. Finally, many music students are foreign students for whom English is a second language, and who struggle with comprehension in lecture classes. An opportunity arose to revise the course to address these challenges when *Computers in Musical Applications* was offered as an online course.

Course Design

Students in the online course used a textbook, a CD-ROM, course web pages, and e-mail. The online course was designed for asynchronous delivery and could accommodate any student's schedule; however, examinations had to be taken on campus unless special arrangements were made in advance of the examination date. Face-to-face group orientation sessions were added to the online class in later years to help students start the course, although all orientation materials were available online. The textbook's 10 chapters correspond to 10 major lecture topics for the course and contain all the basic material from which examination questions are composed (see Appendix A).

There is a midterm and a final examination with 50 to 60 multiple choice questions, most requiring calculation. Easy questions test one fact or formula in a form that is familiar to students from their class materials, but more difficult questions combine several facts and formulas in problems that also contain unfamiliar data.

The CD-ROM contained 10 condensed lectures in the form of QuickTime movies, each about 10 minutes long. Also included was a freeware application and 33 sound examples used for lab experiments, which gave students ample opportunity to experiment with digital manipulation of sound. The creation of the CD-ROM and course website will be discussed later in this chapter.

The face-to-face laboratory sections were replaced by 10 laboratory experiments designed to use Dale Veeneman's SoundHandle software.[1] Students can use SoundHandle to view waveforms and edit short sounds, create sounds using various waveforms and noise, and compute and view the frequency spectrum of sounds using the Fast Fourier Transform[2] (Veeneman, 1995). The lab experiments involve the measurement and perception of sound, the confirmation of Nyquist's limit,[3] and the source of and quality of digital noise. Students e-mail their lab reports to the instructor for grading and comment. There are opportunities within these experiments for qualitative discussion via return e-mail, which also allow the instructor to develop some rapport with the students (see Appendix B).

The course website serves as the portal to the class, presenting the syllabus, the orientation material, the lab assignments, and the weekly schedule of requirements. The current URL is www.oll.temple.edu/MUS-ST-C315/cma. Each student must use the CD-ROM, the textbook, the website, and e-mail to complete each week's assignment.

The course took a more intensive approach to mathematics than the prerequisite acoustics course because that course emphasized a qualitative approach to the subject. According to the published description (Temple University Undergraduate Bulletin, 2002), the prerequisite acoustics course includes:

> *Elementary principles of wave motion and discussion and analysis of musical sounds from a large variety of sources including live voices, instruments, oscillators, synthesizers, and recording media of all sorts. Factors, which permit the performer and listener to understand and more fully control musical sounds. Demonstrations and video to relate the signals received by the ears to visual and technical analysis. For music students, but useful to anyone interested in communications. Open to all students (p. 20).*

Minimal Mathematics

Many students who have completed the prerequisite acoustics course are not familiar with the simple mathematics that explain the frequencies of partials in a harmonic series — one of the most basic properties of musical sound (Pierce, 1992). All periodic sounds, which comprise the sounds of pitched musical instrument, contain harmonic overtones of varying intensity that occur above the fundamental pitch. Unique combinations of overtones contribute to the timbre, or tone quality, of a musical sound. The pattern of overtones is easily described with simple algebra. The most complicated mathematical concept in *Computers in Musical Applications* is the logarithm, used to calculate decibels. This subject is treated in the text, the web pages, and the labs. The binary number system is also discussed at length.

The Value of Multiple Media

Before this course became part of the University's core science curriculum, it served as a pre-requisite for music technology courses, and thus was elected by students who were, for the most part, interested in the science underlying the technological application. Those students were satisfied with fairly succinct "chalk-talk" lectures with recorded audio examples and the opportunity to ask many questions. However, students required to take the course as a science requirement were less interested and demonstrated varying degrees of motivation. Based on a review of course evaluations, I tried to create online course materials that would approach the subject matter from several perspectives at once.

Richard P. Feynman (1999), Nobel Laureate and Physics Professor at the California Institute Of Technology, was asked about his teaching philosophy in a interview broadcast by the BBC in 1981:

> *All those students are in the class: Now you ask me how should I best teach them? Should I teach them from the point of view of the history of science, from the applications? My theory is that the best way to teach is to have no philosophy, [it] is to be chaotic and [to] confuse it in the sense that you use every possible way of doing it. That's the only way I can see to answer it, so as to catch this guy or that guy on different hooks as you go along, [so] that during the time when the fellow who's interested in history's being bored by the abstract mathematics, on the other hand the fellow who likes the abstractions is being bored another time by the history — if you can do it so you don't bore them all, all the time, perhaps you're better off. I really don't know how to do it (p. 20).*

Feynman's refreshingly honest suggestion to try many ways to present ideas and information is a reasonable goal for an online course. Movies and web pages are only some of the presentation methods that can be used. Within each method lies the possibility for multiple modes of presentation as well. A video can include animation, a talking-head lecture, physical examples, and metaphor. There is also room for humor if it helps to deliver the message. John Allen Paulos (1988), in a popular book about mathematics, writes:

> *Both mathematics and humor are combinatorial, taking apart and putting together ideas for the fun of it–juxtaposing, generalizing, iterating, reversing (AIXELSYD ["Dyslexia" spelled backwards]). What if I relax this condition and strengthen that one? What does this idea — say, the knotting of braids — have in common with that one in some other seemingly disparate area — say, the symmetries of some geometric figure? Of course, this aspect of mathematics isn't very well know even to the numerate, since it's necessary to have some mathematical*

ideas first before you can play around with them. As well, ingenuity, a feeling incongruity, and a sense of economical expression are crucial to both mathematics and humor... (p. 76). If mathematics education communicated this playful aspect of the subject, either formally at the elementary, secondary, or college level or informally via popular books, I don't think innumeracy would be as widespread as it is. (p. 77).

Paulos' encouragement of humor again suggests the value of multiple meanings and surprise shifts in point of view — elements easily incorporated in movies or web pages. Most students who sought help at office hours admitted to "math anxiety," and seemed almost afraid of simple equations. Whenever possible, mathematical concepts were presented in a playful, cartoon-like style. For example, the second lecture-movie treats the use of binary numbers to express the quantity of variety, progressing from two-value decisions (e.g., yes/no, male/female, dead/alive) to four value decisions (e.g., North/East/South/ West), and so on. To show how three binary digits completely capture an eight-valued decision, a "waiter" offers the viewer the following breakfast choices:

111 Eggs, Potatoes and Onions

110 Eggs and Potatoes

101 Eggs and Onions

100 Just Eggs

011 Potatoes and Onions

010 Just Potatoes

001 Just Onions

000 Nothing at All

The waiter character is played by a 10-year-old boy wearing a white wig and glasses, intended to project a harmless, non-threatening persona. If the student's memory is jogged the next time he or she orders breakfast, the metaphor will help the student recall the lecture topic and, possibly, better remember that numbers can represent codes as well as quantities.

I created the 10 QuickTime movies for the CD-ROM using a VHS camcorder, a PowerMac 8500 computer, and Adobe's Premiere and Photoshop software. Each of the 10 subject units for the course was described on the course website, and included reading from the text, a lecture-movie, a series of web pages, and a lab assignment. The introduction to the lecture-movie provides an excellent opportunity to employ metaphor, because the viewer will form an opinion that will color the visual experience that follows. The framing image for the movie portion of the lecture is a handsome, red-brick mansion with a long walkway, adapted from a photograph of the Governor's Palace in Williamsburg, Virginia. This Virtual Lecture Hall image denotes stability, tradition, and the 18th century (an era familiar to music students). The soundtrack combines a recording of feet crunching on gravel, perhaps the student trudging to the front door, and soft, gentle music.[4] The effect is intended to be soothing and elevating. This visual is used to introduce the first four lectures. The topic for the fifth lecture is the synthesis of musical sound, a technology that has changed the lives and livelihoods of musicians. Digital sampling technology continues to reduce the need for "commodity" musicians begun by the introduction of recording and radio broadcasting, while creating new opportunities for technologists and "star" performers. During the introduction to the fifth lecture, the Virtual Lecture Hall bursts into flames, accompanied by a synthesized recording of an excerpt from the beginning of the last movement of Beethoven's Ninth Symphony. The sixth lecture examines different kinds of synthesis strategies (e.g., "additive" synthesis, in which overtones are combined to make a complex waveform, and "subtractive" synthesis, in which a complex source is filtered to remove overtones). The introduction to this lecture shows the burned shell of the mansion, with workers changing the shape of the exterior, and a dumpster in front to collect parts of the reduced structure. The transformation is a metaphor for subtractive synthesis, in which the mansion is "filtered" down to a different scale. The seventh lecture is an overview of filter theory, which is the general principal governing the creation and use of filters for subtractive synthesis and digital signal processing techniques like reverberation. A picture of the remodeled mansion, now a bank with a drive-through window, accompanied by the Destiny *leitmotif* from Wagner's Ring, introduces the lecture. The somber tones are rendered by the sounds of air blown over the top of glass bottles, an example of filtering heard in the lecture. A brief trip by virtual auto brings the viewer to a squat, cinder block building with a flat roof where the Lecturer discusses digital filters against the geometric pattern of 1960s era wallpaper. Thus the comfort and security of the Virtual Lecture Hall is replaced by something decidedly artificial and possibly unstable, a visual metaphor that introduces the discussion of artifacts and instabilities in digital filters. The introductions to the subsequent lectures are intended to be equally provocative, presenting the student with metaphors that color the discussion of the subjects at hand.

Students learn to use different media by the course requiring them to confront a densely constructed movie, use a simple CD-ROM, connect to the Web, run a simple software application, and send reports by e-mail. Through these activities, students become aware of the interfaces to different applications and learn to devise strategies for shifting among applications to accomplish a task. Using multiple media in this way has a teaching value in and of itself, especially if the physical features of the various media are discussed as part of the course.

Creating Video Sequences

The author of media materials must decide whether to purchase production services or to personally assume that responsibility. In an academic environment, the institution may provide production services, or a publisher might contract with an instructor for specific components of a media project. But the questions of control and decision-making authority over the production process must be grappled with as it would in any collaborative endeavor where budget issues are concerned. To maintain control of the process, the author can do most of the work, purchasing services only if necessary. Cameras and editing software are readily available. Apple Computer (2002) now offers a desktop computer with software for word processing, drawing, painting, spreadsheets, databases, video editing (with tutorial materials), and video input/output capacity, all for about $1,000. A digital video camera is also available for about $600. According to the most recent report from the Bureau of Labor Statistics (2002), $1,600 today is equivalent to $310 in 1968, which is approximately what a good electric typewriter would have cost. Clearly, video production equipment is affordable for most college professors and does not require a great amount of expertise.

An instructor who can stand and lecture to a class can learn to lecture to a camera. You mount the camera on a tripod, focus on a stand-in, and then record some test shots. When lecturing from notes, you can use a medium close-up shot so that your note pad is visible. You need not mimic television announcers to create interesting and effective video. Indeed, there is something to be gained by not mimicking the rituals of broadcast television.

Unless the image of the lecturer is especially compelling, other images should also be introduced during the editing process. These images can be scanned using a flatbed scanner and image processing software; however, the high resolution of such scans is often wasted when converted to a video image. If images are intended for use in video, they can be scanned easily and quickly using a video camera by aiming a light source at a stand on which the image is placed. You can then capture the video as a still image. Effective graphics can also be created with simple drawing or painting software and even animated images can be rendered in a sequence of still frames.

Despite the "Fair Use" provisions in the Copyright Law, educators should consider creating their own graphic and sound materials and obtaining permission from copyright owners for other material. Many institutions offer digital images online. Temple University's Digital Diamond Collection (2002) contains hundreds of photographs from the *Philadelphia Bulletin* newspaper and other sources, and the process for obtaining permission for their use is included with each image in the searchable collection.

Editing images and sounds can be the most time-consuming part of the process because large amounts of information must be manipulated and organized. The following strategies help to make editing move more quickly:

- Become familiar with the editing software by completing the tutorials.
- Use a reduced frame size, e.g., 320 by 240 pixels, for the first project.
- Avoid complicated video effects by learning how to make effective cuts.
- Do not try to compete with the presentation style of commercial television.
- Make a series of short movies and combine them later.

A simple recording of a seated lecturer, enhanced with effects to illustrate the lecture topic, and combined with text and images, provides an opportunity for visual illustration not available in a face-to-face lecture. A shot-by-shot analysis of a movie segment discussing digital noise is included in Appendix C.

Once the movie I created for the class was edited, it was compressed to fit the space available on the CD-ROM and to play back properly on moderately slow computers. One of the problems faced by the author of computer media is whether to assume that the user has a high-performance computer system of recent manufacture, or an older, more modest system. Unless the highest quality images are necessary, it seems more humane to consider the needs of the student with fewer resources. Although a rate of 30 frames per second will yield smooth motion on some systems, a slower computer might drop frames

Table 1: Data Rates for Uncompressed Video

Standard	Frames/Second	Bytes/Frame	Bytes/Second
NTSC Video	29.97	921,600	27,620,350
PAL Video	25	921,600	23,040,000
Motion Picture	24	921,600	22,118,400

or freeze intermittently. Ironically, smoother motion might be achieved with a slower frame rate (Adobe, 1994, p. 221). The movies used in *Computers in Musical Applications* were stored on CD-ROM with a frame rate of 10 frames per second.

Frame size and compression scheme also affect picture quality, data rate, and file size. The largest frame commonly used for multimedia measures 640 pixels wide by 480 pixels high, or 307,200 square pixels total (Apple Computer, 2001, p. 379). The standard Red-Green-Blue (RGB) color-coding uses one byte per color per pixel (Adobe, 2002, p. 78), so the total byte count for a single color frame is 307,200 times three, or 921,600 bytes. Multiplying this byte count by the frame rate yields the data rate. The video data rate for several standard frame rates (see Table 1) is about 24 megabytes per second (one megabyte = 1,048,576 bytes).

The audio portion of the program will add up to 176,000 bytes per second depending on the number of channels and the audio quality. A moment's reflection on the capacity of a typical CD-ROM reveals the scale of the data rate problem. A 650-megabyte CD will hold only about 27 seconds of video with a data rate of 24 megabytes per second. Furthermore, few computer systems can sustain a transfer rate from CD-ROM greater than one megabyte per second (WhatIs.com, 1999). CD-ROM transfer speeds are rated as 1x, 2x, etc., where the "x" means 150 kilobytes per second (one kilobyte equals 1024 bytes). It is my experience that a peak data rate of 400 kilobytes per second is a reasonable upper limit for CD-ROM movies, so there will need to be a significant reduction in data from the 24 megabyte per second transfer rate mentioned previously.

There are a number of ways to reduce and compress video data, but each method has a cost. The frame size can be reduced if a smaller image or lower-resolution image is acceptable. An image 320 wide by 240 high pixels would use 25% of the data of a 640 pixel by 480-pixel image. A motion sequence rendered at 10 frames per second would require 33% as much information as

Table 2: Effect of Image Quality on Data Rate

Frame Size	Pixels/Frame	Bytes/Pixel	Bytes/Frame	Frames/Second	Bytes/Frame
640 by 480	307,200	3 (color)	921,600	29.97	27,620,350
320 by 240	76,800	3 (color)	230,400	29.97	6,905,088
320 by 240	76,800	3 (color)	230,400	10	2,304,000
320 by 240	76,800	1 (grayscale)	76,800	10	768,000

the same sequence at 30 frames per second. A black and white movie requires only 33% of the data of a color movie. If the image size, the frame rate, and the color information were reduced, the savings would compound (see Table 2).

Even this 97% decrease does not bring the data rate below 400 kilobytes per second, so other methods of reducing or compressing the video data must be used. Video-editing software provides schemes for coding video data that the display software can decode during playback. The methods, called CODECs (for COder/DECoder), can achieve significant compression. The amount of compression depends on the nature of the scheme employed and how well it works with the particular data provided. Some CODECs preserve image resolution at the expense of smooth motion; others sacrifice resolution but preserve motion. An engineer who wishes to show the operation of a gear mechanism might want to preserve resolution and sacrifice color. An art historian may elect to preserve resolution and color but use a very low frame rate. A surgeon illustrating a technique for suturing may retain resolution and color and decide to play the images in slow motion. The choice of CODEC will vary depending on the program material; experimentation will suggest the best choice for a given set of constraints.

Creating Web Pages

Programs to design web pages (with tutorials) are available for free (Netscape Composer). A web page author will need to remember that the transfer of information over normal telephone lines is limited to 56,000 bits, not bytes, per second, and that most transfers occur at lower rates. To illustrate this phenomenon, I connected to five different Web servers using a 56 kBaud modem, a 733 mHz G4 processor, and an up-to-date Web browser (Microsoft

Table 3: Download and Reload Times for Five Web Pages

URL	First Load Time	Second Load Time
www.temple.edu/music	15 seconds	2 seconds
www.princeton.edu	30 seconds	5 seconds
www.kodak.com	30 seconds	7 seconds
www.microsoft.com	22 seconds	12 seconds
www.mapquest.com	40 seconds	30 seconds

Internet Explorer, Version 5.1), and downloaded a web page from each, then loaded each page a second time. The results are shown in Table 3.

Why did the initial loads take so long? Why were the reloads faster? Why were some faster than others? Each site has a number of small images interspersed among areas of text. During the initial load, the text is loaded first, then the background, and then the images. Each part of the download begins with the modem requesting a data transfer. Then there is a short delay, followed by the download of the file. Once the images are stored in the local computer, the page can be reloaded quickly from the local files. Some sites sell commercial space on their web pages and change the panels frequently, requiring a new set of downloads each time the page is requested. A popular site may have many users connected at once, all trying to get to the same data. When this happens, the delay after the image is requested will lengthen, and the rate at which the data is served will decrease. Transfer rates as low as 100 bytes per second are not uncommon, regardless of the speed of the Internet connection itself.

Web pages can be made to load quickly by avoiding graphic clutter and complex backgrounds. Text is quick to load, but a picture of text is not. A 200 x 290 pixel uncompressed color picture contains 174,000 bytes of data. By contrast, the text portion of this chapter thus far contains only about 25,000 bytes of data. Using the file transfer protocol, I was able to receive 174,080 bytes in 21.4 seconds, a transfer rate of 8,135 bytes per second. Even at this high rate (for telephone line transfers), students will grow impatient if the images take too long to load.

Because images are cached in the local computer, pages that reuse images will load faster than pages using unique images, so the designer is advised to create a library of reusable images. Although images can be used to guide the reader through a complicated topic, the value of each image is inversely proportional to the total number of images. Indeed a visually "busy" page might discourage deep thinking by encouraging a superficial race through the links, clicking with abandon to see what comes next. "White space" is soothing and conducive to thought. Less is more.

Pages that are image-dependent need to be tested thoroughly to be sure that the images will appear the same on different platforms and browsers. The simpler the page design and the less the page relies on specific browser features, the more portable the result will be. The World Wide Web Consortium (W3C) will check html code for compliance with its standards and will validate properly formed pages. To use this service, go to http://validator.w3.org.

Outcomes

The online version of *Computers in Musical Applications* was written in the Fall of 1996 and first used for classes during the Spring semester of 1997. It has been used each semester since then and sometimes offered in the same semester as the face-to-face course. Although a detailed, systematic comparison of grades for the traditional and online sections has not been undertaken, the grade distribution of the various sections seems stable and consistent. The course was given in both online (n = 17) and traditional (n = 21) formats in the Spring 2000 semester. The grade distributions (see Figure 1) were similar.

Figure 1: Comparison of Grade Distributions in an Online Section and a Traditional Section

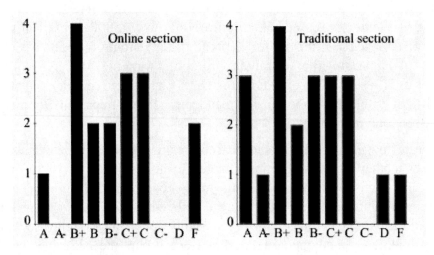

Table 4: Examination Scores in an Online and a Traditional Section

Test	Section	N	Mean	Standard Deviation
Midterm	Online	17	60	21.7
Midterm	Traditional	21	69	16.6
Final	Online	17	58	18.0
Final	Traditional	21	59	22.6

The scores on the midterm and final examinations are also comparable (see Table 4). Students who did not complete all of the laboratory assignments also performed poorly on the examinations. Two students in the online section turned in only two lab assignments, and one student in the traditional section turned in no lab assignment at all. These students' grades account for the "F" grades in each section.

When their scores are removed from the examination grades, the scores of the two sections remain similar (see Table 5).

The two sections were not completely separated because students who missed class in the face-to-face sections were encouraged to use the online materials. Conversely, students who were having difficulty with the online material were encouraged to attend the face-to-face lectures. A comprehensive, quantitative assessment of student evaluations of *Computers in Musical Applications* has yet to be completed, but a preliminary calculation shows that the instructor rating has improved from 4.0 (out of 5.0) in 1993 to 4.2 in 2000, suggesting that the effort spent in preparing the online materials may have had a positive effect on the teaching of the course in general.

Table 5: Examination Scores in an Online Section and a Traditional Section with Students Failing to Submit Lab Work Excluded

Test	Section	N	Mean	Standard Deviation
Midterm	Online	15	63	21.5
Midterm	Traditional	20	70	16.7
Final	Online	15	62	13.6
Final	Traditional	20	61	22.2

Thoughts for the Future

Preparation of multiple media for an online course was a labor-intensive process that was undertaken in the spirit of experimentation. The principal benefits of this process were the increased awareness of one's lecture style, the possibility of time-shifting class work for students, and a portfolio of movies, web pages, and lab experiments that could be recycled for future online and face-to-face classes. The biggest problem for the online students was the increase in opportunities for procrastination. The result was late submission of lab reports followed by poor examination results. To lessen students' propensity for procrastination, strict deadlines for submission of reports need to be given and enforced. Because I did not capture information related to students' access of website materials, there was no way to know whether a student had trouble understanding the concepts or was simply not accessing the course materials. Information that could prove useful could be gained by including short quiz questions throughout the course web pages to test students' knowledge of concepts and by tracking their use of and access to online course materials.

The online lab assignments are more time consuming to grade than face-to-face lab assignments because they are text-based and require the instructor to make corrections in spelling and grammar. Text-based feedback (via e-mail) is also required. Because of these requirements, students may not receive grades and comments on their lab reports for several days. In the interim, serious misunderstandings about important concepts might go unchallenged. An automatic lab-grading program used in conjunction with the instructor's comments would be helpful for students. The most often heard complaint about the course is that the material "will not be useful in real life" or that the student "expected it to be more hands on." Perhaps a proficiency requirement for one or two software applications could be included in the course syllabus, but the rigor of a course where the instructor would function as a human manual reader for commercial software is doubtful.

Whether the concepts introduced in *Computers in Musical Applications* are introduced with the assistance of innovative multimedia technology or whether they are presented in a more traditional format, the value of the more abstract and quantitative science and engineering concepts that underlie commercial software programs is great. Long after the current generation of computer equipment is obsolete, concepts such as Nyquist's limit will remain valid, and the decibel will continue to be the logarithm of the ratio of two quantities. Students who have acquired a basic, but not oversimplified, understanding of the technology used in musical pursuits will be better able to understand how it affects them and their careers.

Endnotes

[1] SoundHandle is a shareware program whose author generously granted permission to duplicate for the class. SoundHandle will work with older or newer Macintosh computers and supports several file formats.

[2] Fourier's transform can be used to analyze the frequency content of periodic waveforms. The calculation converts a signal representation in time space to an equivalent expression in frequency space, and viceversa. By altering the parameters of the transformation, a sound can be shortened or lengthened in time without altering its pitch, or its pitch can be altered independent of duration. The Fast Fourier Transform, an efficient algorithm for computing the discrete Fourier Transform, is a ubiquitous digital signal-processing tool.

[3] Nyquist's limit is a physical law that determines the range of frequencies that can be represented in a digital signal, and is one of the two most important (the other is quantization noise) determinants of fidelity for digital recording and synthesis of sound.

[4] Filtering a recording of applause created the soothing music heard during the opening sequence. The process is explained in the class unit on filtering.

References

Adobe Software. (1994). Premiere: User guide (Version 4.0).

Adobe Software. (2002). Photoshop: User guide (Version 7.0).

Apple Computer. (2001). Final cut pro: Users manual (Version 3).

Apple Computer. (2002). The E-Mac. Retrieved July 6, 2002 from http://www.apple.com/emac.

Bureau of Labor Statistics. (2002). Consumer Price Index, May 2002. Retrieved July 6, 2002 from ftp://ftp.bls.gov/pub/special.requests/cpi/cpiai.txt.

Dodge, C. & Jerse, T. A. (1985). *Computer music: Synthesis, composition, and performance*. New York: Schirmer Books.

Feynman, R.P. (1999). *The pleasure of finding things out*. Cambridge, MA: Perseus Books.

Paulos, J. A. (1988). *Innumeracy: Mathematical illiteracy and is consequences*. New York: Hill and Wang.

Pierce, J. R. (1992). *The science of musical sound*. New York: Freeman Books.

Temple University. (2002). Digital diamond collection. Retrieved July 6, 2002 from http://diamond.temple.edu:81/search.

Temple University. (2002). Undergraduate bulletin. Retrieved July 6, 2002 from http://www.temple.edu/bulletin/ugradbulletin/ucd/ucd_physics.html.

Veeneman, D. (1995). SoundHandle (Version 1.0.3). Retrieved July 8, 2002 from http://wuarchive.wustl.edu/systems/mac/amug/files/music.

WhatIs.com. (1999). Optical media: CD, CD-ROM, DVD and their variations. Retrieved July 6, 2002 from http://www.nightflightstudios.com/Tech_Write/Opti_Media.htm.

Wright, M. W. (1995). *Computers in musical applications.* Unpublished manuscript.

Appendix A

In the 1995 version of the text (Wright, 1995) one reads:

> *He [Harry Nyquist] tells us that a sampling rate of S is needed to capture frequencies as high as S/2. Stated another way, if samples are taken every T seconds, then events with periods of 2T seconds or greater will be correctly represented. The notion of the Nyquist limit is easier to understand when studying digital representation of audio signals. If we know that the frequencies in an audio signal fall between 20 Hz and 10,000 Hz then Nyquist's limit says that we must sample at a rate of at least 20,000 samples per second to capture the highest frequencies. Conversely, a system sampling at 20,000 Hz can correctly represent frequencies up to 10,000 Hz. (p. 21)*

One easy question on the 1995 midterm examination, drawn from that section of the text, reads:

If the sampling rate is 50000 Hz, what is the Nyquist frequency?

A. 100 kHz   B. 50 kHz   C. 25 kHz   D. about 20 kHz

At least 15 other examination questions depend on an understanding of Nyquist's limit, and are drawn from examples in the textbook.

Appendix B

Here is a typical lab assignment (images omitted). Underlined text links to help pages and text in italics are questions that must be answered in the lab report:

Laboratory Assignment #5
Quantizing Noise

Discussion

As the number of amplitude levels used to describe a function decreases, the quantizing error increases. Quantization noise is more noticeable than analog hiss because it is not steady state: it tracks the amplitude of the signal and contains frequency components that vary according to the frequency components of the signal.

Open SoundHandle (*remember how to use it?*) and open Lab05Sound01. Listen to the sound and examine a small part of the waveform. Then **Edit-Select All**, followed by **Modify-Scale...**as before, the "Left Scale" refers to the scaling value at the beginning of the window, the "Right Scale" to the value at the end. Rescale the whole window by 10%. This reduces the level by 20 decibels. Listen to the file. *Did the noise level increase?* Now scale the reduced signal by 1000% (+20 db). *Did the noise level increase?* Examine the waveform. *How does it differ from the original?*

Perform the same experiment on the file Lab05Sound02, but scale it by 5% and 2000%, respectively. *Describe the noise that results from the rescaling. Why does it have this quality (hint: examine the "before" and "after" waveforms carefully).*

Mail in your notes (*remember how?*).

The student has responded by transcribing the questions from the lab. They are preceded by a hyphen, and the student's answers follow immediately after:

- Are there increases in noise?

  Yes, I heard the noise increase and volume decrease at the same time.

- When reduced signal by 1000%, did noise increase?

  Not necessarily. The whole thing got louder but the ratio of noise and sound is the same.

- How does the waveform differ from original?

  The waveform is less precise and it is rougher.

- Describe the sound of lab05sound02 after reduced.

  They no longer have a smooth tone but have a tone with lots of noise.

- Why do they have this quality?

  Because as they got re-scaled (especially by 5%), they lost preciseness in amplitude. Instead of having many different levels of amplitudes, they only have three levels.

The student received full credit for this lab report.

Appendix C

Here is an example from a movie used in *Computers in Musical Applications*, a transcription of a segment about sampling theory. This is a relatively complicated section, but the zoom effects and superimposition of text is done efficiently by the computer editing software:

5:14   Medium shot of seated lecturer, reading from notes: "One can think of the sample rate as the time resolution of the sample process, and the error in measurement as the amplitude resolution."

5:22   Medium shot, continued. Begin posterize effect, reducing the image to only a few brightness levels. Reading continues: "As an image is represented by fewer levels of resolution, artificial boundaries appear."

5:30   Freeze frame on posterized image. Voice over: "Something similar happens with sound."

5:33   Dissolve to graphic of high-resolution sine wave. Voice over: "Consider a sine wave captured at two different resolutions."

5:36   Graphic of high-resolution sine wave. Voice over: "In the first case the wave is represented with many levels."

5:39   Dissolve to graphic of low-resolution sine wave. Voice over: "But in the second, only 16 levels. The shaded areas in the second diagram represent the errors of measurement."

5:45   Zoom out and pan right. Voice over: "The ratio of the maximum signal that can be represented..."

5:50   Zoom continues. Superimpose text: "Maximum Signal/Error Noise." Voice over: "...to the error noise in a digital representation is called..."

5:55   Zoom continues. Additional superimposed text: "Signal-to-Noise Ratio." Voice over: "...the signal-to-noise ratio and is directly related to the size of the sample word in bits."

6:00   Extreme close-up of lecturer, looking directly at camera. Voice: "Each additional bit of resolution in the sample word doubles the signal-to-noise ratio..."

6:06   Extreme close-up, continued. Superimpose text: about six DB per bit. Voice: "...increasing it by about six decibels."

6:08   Medium shot of lecturer in chair. Reading: "This error signal could be annoying because it is not a steady hiss that could be easily ignored but instead a signal of varying intensity and possessing frequency components that change according to the frequencies present in the input signal. To maximize fidelity in a sampled system, high sample rates and accurate measures can be used. But if high sample rates and very accurate measurements are used, the amount of data that has to be stored and transmitted becomes significant.

6:40   Extreme close-up of lecturer, looking directly at camera. Voice: "Beyond some point we cannot appreciate improvements in frequency and amplitude range and the digital signal..."

6:47   Jump cut to same close-up to remove pause. Voice: "...although discrete in time and amplitude."

6:51   Iris wipe to outdoor scene with trees waving gently in the breeze. Voice over "...seems perfectly natural."

6:53   Outdoor scene. Sound of air, birds, etc.

6:58   Dissolve to graphic of a house. Text: "Copyright © 1997 by Maurice Wright."

7:02   Same graphic. Text dissolves to: "Produzione Propria."

7:03   End of movie. Freeze on graphic and house.

This one-minute and 49-second segment uses a single long take of the lecturer reading from notes and looking up to the camera from time to time. The two close-ups were added later to stress important facts. The two sine wave graphics were created in SoundHandle, the same software the students use for lab assignments, and were pasted into a painting program so they could be colored and perfectly aligned. The dissolve from the high-resolution image (see Figure 1) to the low-resolution image (see Figure 2) is intended to help the viewer recognize the appearance of an under-digitized waveform, whose distorted shape will later be the subject of a lab experiment.

The outdoor scene was a wide-angle view of the author's backyard, the choice of grass and trees emphasizing the phrase "perfectly natural" with a visual pun. The text superimposed over the final image, "Produzione Propria," means "homemade."

Figure 1: Sine Wave Quantized to 256 Levels

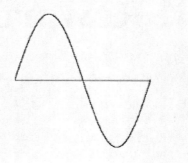

Figure 2: Sine Wave Quantized to 16 Levels

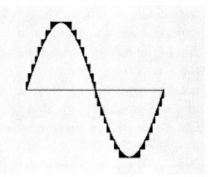

Chapter IX

Teaching a Studies-in-Race Course Online: The Challenges and the Rewards

Karen M. Turner

Temple University, USA

Abstract

Colleges and universities are increasingly using the latest communication technologies to offer courses to students on campus and beyond. This chapter is designed to answer whether a course dealing with the potentially volatile issue of race can be effectively taught as an online class. The course, Race and Racism in the News (JPRA 320), was designed in 1997 by examining the literature pertaining to teaching online/distance courses and studies-in-race courses, as well as incorporating studies concerned with preserving the anonymity of control groups and those that looked at differences between face-to-face and computer-mediated discussions. This course was developed to effectively incorporate online instruction with race studies aimed at teaching racial sensitivity to journalism students. The course has been offered seven times between 1997 and 2002. Student feedback over the five-year period indicates that such a course can advance the national dialogue on race. Many White students, in particular, said in the required end-of-course survey that the course anonymity provided them with a freedom from political correctness and they could participate more honestly than they would have in the traditional face-to-face classroom setting. Also, students have said they are now aware of the subtle ways race impacts the coverage of news. The effectiveness of this course could have implications beyond the classroom. It is believed that students sensitive to the subtleties of racism in news coverage will make better media professionals in our increasingly multicultural world. In 1997, former President Clinton challenged the country to engage in a race dialogue. This kind of course can be added to the mix of ways in which such a dialogue can be started and maintained.[1]

Background

For years, students have learned through the use of various media: printed materials from correspondence courses, audio and videotapes, and radio and television broadcasts. Now, with the explosion of Internet use, college students are finding many more courses are available online. Online course instruction, however, brings both opportunities and challenges.

The online learner typically uses communication tools such as the World Wide Web, e-mail, discussion boards and/or listservs. But the mastery of these tools used in a course context has posed pedagogical challenges as well as opportunities for both the educator and the student.

The Temple Challenge

In March 1996, Temple University promoted the creation of online classes by funding a select number of faculty members to convert or develop courses for the Spring and Fall 1997 semesters. This decision was made after launching two online courses in the Spring 1996 semester with exciting results. The University saw the development of online courses as a way to enable it to expand the student population, to retain existing students, and to improve the readiness skills of some of the students (J. W. England, personal communication, March 18, 1996).

I answered the request for proposals to develop an online course. It was viewed as a wonderful teaching opportunity to marry research interests in news coverage with the use of ever-evolving communication technologies.

The proposed online course, *Race and Racism in the News*, was selected and placed on the Fall 1997 and 1998 schedules. Meanwhile, the non-profit Poynter Institute for Media Studies in St. Petersburg, Florida, was beginning its Research Fellows program. The Research Fellows program was designed to support the completion of practical research in areas that address one of Poynter's missions, that of promoting journalism excellence and integrity by university faculty. Being selected as a participant in Poynter's first Research Fellows class provided me with additional resources, the most important of which was an advisory team of media experts. There was concern that teaching a course about race would be challenging because of the potential for a high level of emotional conflict. Teaching such a course online, where there is no traditional classroom interaction and mediation, would present even more of a challenge and call into play creative teaching skills — perhaps some yet to be developed.

Setting the Stage

With support from Temple University and Poynter Institute, I embarked on a journey to develop a model of an effective undergraduate studies-in-race course that used electronic teaching tools as the primary delivery vehicle. The major question that had to be addressed as part of course development was whether online technology is an effective method for teaching a studies-in-race course. In reading the literature, I sought answers to three critical issues:

a)   How to develop an effective online course;

b)   How to develop an effective studies-in-race course; and

c)   How to develop an effective online studies-in-race course.

Effective Distance Education

The term distance education or distance learning applies to situations where the teacher and students are in different locations. I turned to distance education research to help develop an effective online course. The research indicated that distance teaching can be as effective as the traditional face-to-face classroom instruction setting (Gottschalk, 1996a, 1996b; Logging on, 1998; Moore & Thompson, 1990). However, what is necessary is careful planning and organization, focused and clearly expressed course requirements, and understanding what students need to be effective learners (Berge & Collins, 1995). Gottschalk (1996c) sets forth several instructional content and design strategies for an effective distance course:

- Establish course goals that are broad statements of instructional intent;

- Establish specific objectives that explain how the goals will be achieved;

- Create a course content outline based on the identified goals and objectives, anticipated instructional problems and student needs;

- Review existing instructional materials being cognizant that what may have been effective in a conventional classroom setting may need to be supplemented or reconsidered;

- Organize and develop the course incorporating student-relevant examples that relate the content to a context understood by the students;

- Develop and select instructional materials and the appropriate integration of delivery methods, considering student needs, content requirements and technical constraints;

- Review goals and objectives to determine whether the instructional methods and materials are meeting the established outcomes through pretest instruction or the first actual use, which can serve as a field test;

- Develop an evaluation strategy to test the effectiveness of instruction; and

- Revise the course based on the evaluation findings and feedback.

Teaching Online

Effective use of the Internet is a must when creating a distance education course, particularly one offered primarily online. Early on in the course, students should be encouraged to regularly use e-mail, participate in class chat room sessions, post to the course listserv, and become familiar with surfing the World Wide Web.

Gottschalk (1996e) presents several instructional possibilities for skillfully integrating Internet use into such a course:

- Develop a classroom home page where information about the class can be posted such as the syllabus, exercises, literature references, relevant World Wide Web links, and the instructor's biography (see also Gottschalk, 1996f);

- Use e-mail for informal and quick one-on-one correspondence between instructor and students (these messages can be read at the convenience of the recipient and stored for later reference);

- Establish a course listserv, which encourages student-to-student interaction and provides the instructor with an additional communication delivery system to post updates such as assignments and tests; and

- Engage students in dialogue with other students, faculty, and researchers by encouraging them to join an electronic list(s) on topic(s) related to the class.

When developing a course, educators have a myriad of instructional media options. Using such an integrated approach is highly desirable (Berge & Collins, 1995; Gottschalk, 1996a). For example, an online course could use a course text, reserve readings, rental or reserve videos, a course website with links to relevant material published on the Internet, a listserv, an electronic discussion board, a virtual classroom for real-time lectures, e-books, and e-mail. The instructor must be aware of the availability of such resources and plan accordingly. As I discuss later, I held two face-to-face sessions in 2002, primarily because there were videos I wanted to share with the class that were difficult to secure off-campus.

When deciding how to mix media, the instructor and students must be comfortable using the delivery systems selected (Gottschalk, 1996b). Even though the technology plays a key role in delivering course content and advancing the learning process, the instructor must not prioritize the use of technology over the desired instructional outcomes (Gottschalk, 1996a). As discussed in Chapter 1, when planning a course, the educational goal cannot take a back seat to the technological choices.

Certain instructional tasks, such as student-to-student interaction and timely teacher-to-student feedback (Moore & Thompson 1990) are necessary elements of the course organization. This feedback must be institutionalized as an on-going process, so the instructor can make improvements as the course progresses (Gottschalk, 1996d). Also, the instructor must be sensitive to differing communication styles, the cultural backgrounds of the students, and his/her own cultural assumptions and biases about these students (Herring, 1993; Gottschalk, 1996b; Wolfe, 2000).

Teaching a Studies-in-Race Course

"If we acknowledge our own fears yet still move ahead and risk having the conflict we fear, we empower students to find their own courage" (Frederick, 1995, p. 90). One of the most difficult challenges facing those teaching a studies-in-race course is determining how to best engage students in learning about issues of race. A desired goal is to create an open and honest intellectual exchange that brings about an understanding of the complexities of differing views; however, there are many forces at work preventing students from talking and learning about race and racism. Tatum (1992) identifies three major sources of student resistance:

- Racism is considered to be a taboo topic for discussion, especially in racially mixed settings.

- Many students, regardless of racial-group membership, have been socialized to think of the United States as a just society.

- Many students, particularly White students, initially deny any personal prejudice, recognizing the impact of racism on other people's lives, but failing to acknowledge its impact on their own. (p. 5)

A college course may be the first opportunity some students have to discuss issues of race, multiculturalism, and diversity in a public forum with others from a variety of backgrounds. The instructor must often navigate the many strong emotions ranging from guilt and shame to anger and despair that students bring to the class (Tatum 1992).

Meacham (1995) states that there seem to be two significant and contradictory concerns held by faculty when teaching these courses. The first is that the students will be too polite, too correct, and too nice and thus will not engage intellectually with the issues raised in the assigned readings. The second concern is that students will say things that will lead other students and faculty members to feel uncomfortable, defensive, and angry so that the antagonism of ideas and interests will lead to open hostility among the students.

So how does one raise these often emotionally charged subjects for meaningful study and discussion? This has been the subject of much analysis (Frederick, 1995; Higginbotham, 1996; Meacham, 1995; Tatum, 1992). The research indicates there are several elements that the instructor should incorporate into a race course:

- It is essential that the classroom be a safe place for discussion (Tatum, 1992, p. 18).

- A sound intellectual framework for discussion should be established in the beginning of the course to help students better evaluate evidence and consider alternative perspectives (Meacham, 1995, p. 29).

- Discussions should be used for expressing ideas and issues, not personalities (Frederick, 1995, p. 90).

- All assumptions should be outlined, including definitions of terms such as race, racism, and prejudice (Tatum, 1992, p. 3).

- Students must become empowered as change agents — heightening their awareness of racism without also exploring strategies for change is a prescription for despair (Tatum, 1992, pp. 20-21).

- The instructor must clearly know and clearly articulate the goals for the course. It has been suggested that students complete a questionnaire in the first week of class explaining why they are taking the class and what they perceive are the goals of the course. Such an evaluation may help identify possible areas of conflict early on (Meacham, 1995, p. 26).

In addition to having students complete a questionnaire, Meacham (1995) suggests conflict is less likely to occur if instructors are in touch, not only with what students are saying out loud, but also with what they are thinking and not expressing. One way to do this is to end classes early and ask students to write anonymously their thoughts about the class discussion. Another way to manage conflict is to raise only issues that can be resolved over the term or the class period. Dealing with the more difficult and challenging issues requires more day-to-day planning and structure. It is a good idea to deal with potential conflict in a straightforward manner by establishing informal procedures. Some of the strategies an instructor can implement are shifting the class away from awkward or conflict-laden situations, stepping back from the issue itself to review what happened procedurally in the discussion, and modeling harmonious behavior that encourages listening so students can learn how to characterize both sides of an issue. Classics Professor Dan Tompkins and English Professor Roland Williams, two Temple University professors who have taught several studies-in-race courses, agree that the role of the instructor is an extremely important one (D. Tompkins & R. Williams, personal communications, May 3, 1998). Additionally, Tompkins says a real challenge for him is to raise at least some questions that force the students to confront their inherited or unanalyzed notions about race and ethnicity. He cautions that it is important not to slide off into the "easy" and less contentious area of "ethnicity" — to do so would betray the hard-edged nature of his course. He emphasizes his desire for his students to recognize that class is a major influence on student behavior and attitudes. Williams sees his role as providing students with basic skills that will enable them to adapt easily to a constantly changing world. Williams identifies these skills as the ability to write well, to engage in critical analysis, and to negotiate differences — to question their own preconceived notions of race and human character and discover common ground. He states the goal has been met if his students leave the course with a willingness to judge people individually.

Case Description

Temple University has a diverse student population. In 1997, 41% of the roughly 28,000 students belonged to a minority group. Fifty-eight percent were White, 22% were African American, 11% were Asian American, 3% were Hispanic, 0.3% were Native American, and the remaining 6% were Other. This Other category includes foreign students and anyone who chose not to identify an ethnicity. Over the five years I have taught the course, the student demographics have remained almost unchanged. In Fall 2001, 42% of the 30,500 students self-identified as belonging to a racial minority group. Fifty-eight percent were White, 20% were African American, 10% were Asian American, 3.5% were Hispanic, 0.3% were Native American, and the remaining 8% were Other (H. Goodheart, personal communication, April 13, 1998; T. Walsh, personal communication, October 7, 2002). These stats are for the entire Temple student community. The racial minority percentages would be higher if we were looking at only the undergraduate programs, as professional and graduate programs tend to have higher numbers of white students.

Since 1992, Temple University has required that students take a three-credit studies-in-race course. Its purpose is to give race issues broader attention as a subject of academic study. It is believed that by contributing to students' intellectual understanding of the phenomenon of racism, the University will better prepare its students to live in the increasingly multiracial, multi-cultural world. The *Race and Racism in the News* course was created to offer a studies-in-race course in an online environment. I was particularly challenged because I did not adapt an existing course to the new technology but rather chose to create a new course. Many of the issues faced in the Fall 1997 semester were associated with new course development and becoming acclimated to electronic teaching technologies. After reading the available research on developing distance/online courses and race studies courses, I was ready to combine the concepts to develop an online race course.

Process

One of the first major tasks was to identify a consultant who could create the course website, maintain it during the Fall 1997 semester, and later train me on web creation and maintenance. Once the consultant was hired, the next step was to determine the appearance of the site in keeping with university policy and decide what information would be posted. I was very concerned with anticipated problem areas such as attendance and listserv participation. Existing Temple University course sites and those at institutions such as the University of Texas, the University of Kansas, and Washington State University were viewed for ideas. I also requested that the University Computer Services staff create anonymous user identification e-mail accounts for the students to use for course listserv discussions. With complete anonymity assured, I believed students' online conversations should be more honest and uninhibited. I also talked with the university computer staff about holding "real-time" class discussions. Although I did not use synchronous class discussion for the Fall 1997 class, I hoped to add that component in the future. To preserve the pure online nature of the course, a face-to-face class meeting was purposely not scheduled until the midpoint of the semester.

Content

While dealing with the various technical issues, I also had to engage in course development. Solid planning and organizational skills are necessary for teaching any course, but when offering a course online, these elements become even more important. Also, the instructor must develop and clearly articulate the course goals and objectives.

The course goals and objectives for *Race and Racism in the News* were:

- To engage students in a critical examination of how issues of race and racism are covered by local and national media and how racism is manifested in that coverage, with an emphasis on broadcast media;

- To create an environment to discuss race issues freely and with civility; and

- To prepare students to live and work in a multiracial and multi-cultural world through observation and analysis of the subtle racism that exists in news coverage.

After receiving suggestions from colleagues who had taught similar courses in the traditional classroom environment, two required texts were selected: Wilson, C., II & Gutierrez, F. (1995). *Race, Multiculturalism and the Media* (2nd ed.) and Dennis, E. & Pease, E. (eds.) (1997). *The Media in Black and White.* These texts provided the contextual foundation for the course.

Because students would not attend face-to-face sessions, it was important to keep them engaged in the reading materials and monitor their progress. To help achieve these goals, students were given several writing assignments:

- *Introductory essay:* As a first assignment, students were asked to complete a questionnaire designed to assess their writing skills, computer experience, journalistic reading and viewing habits, and to gather demographic information.

- *Trade journal article review:* Students were asked to read and analyze a recent trade journal article of their choice, dealing with news coverage of race or race issues.

- *Weekly journal:* Students were asked to record their observations and opinions about the course content and methodology. This assignment was not meant to be a regurgitation of the class listserv discussion, but rather to supplement it. In the journal, they were asked to reflect on the issues discussed, write constructive criticism of the course materials, make suggestions for how to improve the course, talk about what is working and what is not, log questions, and record instances where the broadcast media (especially news) influences conversations they are involved in or overhear. These journals were e-mailed to me every two weeks.

- *Biweekly critique:* Students were asked to write an in-depth critique of a radio or TV news story or news magazine program segment that deals with race. In the one to two page papers, students were asked to clearly identify the race issue addressed, describe the content/subject of the story or program, talk about how well it was done, discuss what issues it raised and whether or not the program provided answers, talk about any stereotypes in the story, and describe if and how they would have handled the subject matter differently.

Using a Class Listserv or Electronic Discussion Board

The class listserv or electronic discussion board is a necessary part of an online class because this is where classroom discussion takes place. By sending e-mail messages to the listserv or by posting questions and comments to an electronic discussion board, students ask questions and express their views — similar to what they would do in a face-to-face classroom conversation. Instructors can use the listserv or electronic discussion board to post lectures, questions, and tests instead of, or in addition to, the course website. Postings are distributed to all those who subscribe to the listserv or have access to the electronic discussion board. Because there is no conventional face-to-face attendance, these electronic postings can serve as a means of monitoring student class participation. Requiring students to post a specified number of e-mail communications over the course of the semester clearly articulates the instructor's expectation and encourages participation (Guernsey, 1998). This finite posting requirement also addresses the research that indicates the participation levels of many women and some men are influenced by the communicative style of a message in computer-mediated communication settings (Carstarphen & Lambiase, 1998; Crowston & Kammerer, 1998; Herring, 1993).

In the Beginning: Fall 1997

How does one begin an online class? I raised this question to colleagues through the university online learning listserv. Some colleagues suggested meeting face-to-face for the first class, but several argued that a face-to-face session compromised the online learning approach. Primarily to preserve anonymity, I decided against a meeting and opted to e-mail students privately, providing them with the course URL. I decided it was easier to address start-up problems in a face-to-face setting; but that it was more challenging and more could be learned by solving these issues through the online technology. In July 1997, the course website was created containing preliminary information about the course, including class schedule information. It was clearly posted on the website that students would not meet face-to-face until perhaps midway through the semester; however, the Journalism, Public Relations, and Advertising Department assigned a course meeting time and room in the event I decided to hold a face-to-face class session sometime during the Fall semester. The meeting time and room number were published in the Fall 1997 semester course schedule booklet, which subsequently led to some confusion. On the first day of the semester, the students assembled in the designated classroom. I, however, did not. A student who was present that day told me that, while waiting in the classroom for me to arrive, one of the other students logged onto the course website and discovered that, in fact, no meeting had been scheduled for the beginning of the semester.

The Students

The semester began with 16 students and three on the waiting list. By the end of the semester, 13 students were still in the course. The final 13 described themselves as: Black female (2), Black male (1), White female (3), White male (4), Biracial female (1), Hispanic male (1), and Korean-American female (1). Nine were seniors and four were juniors. Three were 25-years of age or older, and one was self-identified as disabled. Ten of the 13 students had home computers and one had a personal website.[2,3]

Class Listserv

Initially, communication with students was done individually through e-mail. For those students for whom there was no known e-mail address, I had to engage in the time-consuming task of telephoning them. These students were advised to immediately secure an e-mail address. All students were referred to the course website. Students experienced a variety of technical problems from not understanding how to use e-mail to difficulty accessing the class website. A glitch using campus computers was discovered after several students could not send the introductory essay that was to be posted on the course website. The mail preferences had to be personalized, but this was learned only after many unsuccessful attempts. Eventually all the students found a way to send the assignments. Meanwhile, it took a few weeks to get the listserv up and running with the anonymous user-identification accounts. The University Computer Services Department had to create individual, anonymous e-mail accounts. Five weeks into the term, I sent the first message to the listserv asking students to check-in. Still some students had not picked-up their anonymous user- identification e-mail addresses from the department office. Two students accidentally changed their login identification so their real name appeared with their assigned student identification number. These students were immediately e-mailed and told to correct the problem. I sent a few messages to the listserv but received only private e-mail messages in response. I assumed the students were not logging onto the listserv. The web consultant was asked to post my messages on the course website as well. After almost four more weeks, it was discovered through a private e-mail message from Student #10 that the class had been posting messages on the listserv for three weeks. I had not been receiving any of these messages because I had not been informed that I had to subscribe myself to the listserv! The listserv was operational for 11 weeks out of the 16-week term.

As mentioned previously, the first assignment was to complete the Introductory Essay. This assignment was used as a writing assessment tool. Students had to answer questions designed to gather information on their computer literacy, course goals and expectations, and attitudes on race. They were asked to discuss their racial/ethnic identity, their family, their neighborhood, and any other relevant information or impacting circumstances. The essays dealing with identity were especially candid.

Below are some excerpts from student introductory essays:

Student #6 (23-Year-Old Hispanic Male)

My parents emigrated [*sic*] to this country in 1970, bringing with them a rich tradition and culture from their homeland, Nicaragua. Although I was born in this country, I was raised in the traditions and culture of Nicaragua. My parents always spoke to me in Spanish as a child, which helped me learn two languages. Families are extremely close in Latin American countries; my family is a very important part of my life. I have three brother, two sisters, a niece, a dog, and two of the most wonderful, generous parents in the world. My father is such a strong figure in my life; he is the perfect leader, the best provider, and someone that I respect more than anyone in the world. My mother is a saint for all that she does for me; she is like a sister and a friend, my blackjack partner. My father is a physician. As a result, he had the financial wherewithal to buy a house in the suburbs. I love where I live. It is beautiful, peaceful, and clean. As a child, though, it was difficult, at times, because we were the only Hispanic family in an all white neighborhood. I did establish many friendships, but I was always different. An older neighbor of ours would make racial slurs about us behind our backs; our neighbors would tell us. As far as I knew, he was the only one talking behind our backs. But, who knows?

Student #9 (19-Year-Old Biracial Female)
Growing up in a suburban Baltimore neighborhood I experienced racial issues at a young age. My parents are a bi-racial couple which in turn created an [*sic*] environment of different of cultures. My father is Greek and Italian while my mother is African-American. Although I am bi-racial, I have never been accepted by my fathers [sic] side of the family nor do I know a lot about his culture. Through the years I have been called every name from zebra to Oreo. When I sit and think about the behavior of these people I can only be amused...

Student #13 (21-Year-Old White Male)
I was born in Cologne, West Germany, in 1975, a multi-cultural oasis amidst a country and a people which are predominately White, German speaking, with limited experiences in other cultures. Cologne had large industries, such as steel and manufacturing jobs, and these jobs attracted thousands of foreign workers to move to our city in the late 1960s and early 1970s. In my kindergarten classes were children who spoke foreign tongues, ate different foods, and even smelled a little different. Despite these early experiences, I still had little experience with people of different colors. The foreign children where mostly Turkish, Italian and Polish, and thus in color, were essentially all White. The first person of African descent I ever saw was on a beach in Morocco, where in amazement, I touched his skin to see if any of the color would come off. Of course it didn't, but I realized that there were differences among humans...

I wanted the same candor and vulnerability expressed in the Introductory Essays to be shared with the class in the online discussions. By having the students communicate with one another anonymously through e-mail messages posted on the listserv, it was thought this could be achieved. An additional challenge for students was that their communication could not contain any gender or racial identifying language. This gender- and race-neutral restriction was added so students would examine their own assumptions in their conversations.

Computer-mediated communication has the potential to promote discourse based on ideas, not preconceived notions. It can break down many of the traditional communication barriers, including those that are racially and socio-economically based (Herring, 1993). In this instance, however, these barriers remained. The dialogue on the listserv rarely discussed the reading material and was often a place where students would vent feelings about discrimination at Temple, local newspaper coverage of Latinos, the Million Woman March, and bias in crime coverage. Also disappointing was the need several students felt to identify their race/ethnicity and gender in their postings. Arguably, these revelations gave those students a crutch for not articulating a position, but rather let the readers draw their own conclusions based on their own assumptions of what it means to belong to a particular group. I believe had I intervened in the conversations early on, I could have more successfully directed the tone and substance of the dialogue. But it was not until the students had been conversing for three weeks that I learned that listserv discussions were regularly taking place. By this time many students had already established their online personas and alliances.

To keep online discussions focused and productive, early and continued intervention and guidance regarding listserv discussions are necessary. When MSNBC conducted its 11-week race dialogue project in 1998, the 10 anonymous electronic bulletin board participants were coaxed with weekly questions from reporter John Hockenberry and editor/producer Ben Davis. Active involvement and prodding by the MSNBC staffers successfully focused the group discussion (B. Davis, personal communication, April 29, 1998).

Interestingly, the manner of the electronic course dialogue was consistent with research on gender differences in computer-mediated communication. I recognize that sweeping generalizations cannot be made with such a small student sample; however, an analysis of the listserv discussions showed that much of the communication was in keeping with gender-specific stylistic expression. Women's language tends to be supportive, apologetic, and personal, wherein men's language is more authoritative, challenging, and self-promoting (Crowston & Kammerer, 1998; Herring, 1993).

Reflections of Fall 1997

There were many problems the first time the course was offered, but everyone was patient. I e-mailed the students regularly to explain the various challenges encountered. Frequent communication was the key to keeping the students focused.

Following the fall semester, I recorded some recommendations as to what I found needed to be incorporated into the course the next time it was offered:

- Begin working early with computer services to ensure the availability of anonymous e-mail user-identification accounts, a listserv and an archived listserv, and a course website for the first day of the semester.

- Contact students by e-mail a week before the semester begins. Provide them with information on the e-mail user-identification accounts, the course website, the start date, and the introductory essay.

- Instruct students not to identify themselves by race/ethnicity and/or gender in their postings to the listserv. This approach was successfully used in the MSNBC project, which lends support to my finding that complete anonymity encourages more meaningful dialogue.

- Have more active involvement on the listserv by better directing the conversation. Perhaps as a first posting and a way to begin the course, the students will be asked to collectively develop a working definition of key terms such as race, racism, ethnicity, and prejudice.

- Better highlight the contextual foundation of the course by frequent postings of specific questions related to the text readings.

- Set up several hypertext links to additional materials.

- Hold at least one face-to-face meeting at the end of the semester.

- Get a separate e-mail account to better manage class correspondence and tell students to clearly indicate on the subject line what is being sent.

- Give specific dates by which assigned readings must be completed.

- Give a specific deadline by which written assignments must be received.

- Make sure texts are available on all university campuses.

- Send assignment receipt acknowledgments.

- Review weekly student participation on the listserv and periodically remind them what level of participation is expected.

- Give a midterm to better assess student progress.

- Consider password protecting the course website.

- Continue to keep and review an instructor course journal.

- Hold real-time chat room discussions during the semester with guest lecturers.

Recent Experiences: 1998-2002

In the years since *Race and Racism in the News* was first offered, there have been several support improvements — the most significant from my perspective being the widespread use and on-campus support of Blackboard, a course-management software package. During the Spring 2001 semester, I began using Blackboard as a teaching tool. Holding class discussions on the electronic bulletin board rather than through a class listserv has advantages. The students can, in a more organized way, respond to threaded forum questions I post. Also, computer services can more readily create the anonymous student identification accounts. I assign students identifications such as Race 1, Race 2, etc. This information is provided to our computer services office. When students post to the course Discussion Board through Blackboard, this is their automatic identity. When students respond to each other, they are told to refer to the anonymous identifications.

Race and Racism in the News has been modified several times since it was first offered. I continue to view the course as a work-in-progress and am committed to its original goals and objectives, which are:

- To engage students in a critical examination of how issues of race and racism are covered by local and national media and how racism is manifested in that coverage, with an emphasis on broadcast media;

- To create an environment to discuss race issues freely and with civility; and

- To prepare students to live and work in a multiracial and multi-cultural world through observation and analysis of the subtle racism that exists in news coverage.

To assess the impact the course has had, I administer a survey to the students at the end of the semester (see Appendix). One of the questions asked is, "Do you look at the media differently now that you have taken this course?" Based on the obtained responses, this course has had a significant impact for some students. Below is an excerpt from Spring 2002. This is one student's reflection of the impact of this course on her views of the media:

Student #4 (22-Year-Old Black Female)

I definitely look at the media differently as a result of this course. I am a critical consumer of everything I see or hear. I question the reasoning behind the placement of stories and the airing of particular stories. I am more open, sensitive, and understanding toward other races. It is easy to see the problems of my race, but I never knew the issues of others.

Two of the early changes made were modifications to the writing assignments. The Introductory Essay now asks students to write a short one-page essay describing when and what happened the first time s/he became aware of race. I participated in a Poynter Institute workshop where that question was asked. The responses at the seminar were so provocative and insightful that I thought such a question might provoke similar responses by college students. This expectation was confirmed. Below is one recent response:

(23-Year-Old Biracial Female)

The fourth grade was the first time I was made aware of race, and that some people in the world were not as open minded as the people I had been exposed to. I was on the school bus going home after school, and a little black girl said that I was a zebra because my mother's white and my father's black. I was not 100% sure what she meant, or why she said it, but I knew it had something to do with my race, and that it hurt. Over the years I have been referred to as everything from mulatto to the much more creative, Tiger Woods. The most difficult times for me were middle and high schools. That's the time when everyone is trying to define who they are, and aren't always as kind as they should be.

The responses continue to be candid when discussing their families. Following is one example:

(23-Year-Old White Female)
I am Italian/Irish Catholic and I have been brought up in a home where my father says... "A nig is a nig is a nig..." I am not proud of this and I do not think that I feel this way at all but it has been drained into my head for my entire life. My grandparents refer to African Americans as spiders. My family is very traditional in their opinions and I respect them. I would never bring home a man to my family that was not Italian or Irish. A Jewish man would not be accepted either. I grew up in Oaks, PA, which is a suburb near King of Prussia, and then moved to Tampa, FL. I experienced being a minority in Florida. Everyone there is of Latin descent and I was known as a "cracker."

The Introductory Essay has proven to be a useful method for assessing writing skills and it gives me a sense of the racial attitudes of the students — knowing the students, at least on paper, before the electronic class discussions begin has been beneficial.

The other major change to the writing assignments is that the trade journal article review has been replaced by a television news analysis assignment. Students do a content analysis of two newscasts of the same station but a week apart. They are asked to pay particular attention to who is seen and interviewed in the stories. I had been giving this assignment to my broadcast reporting class for a few years. I decided to give it to the *Race and Racism in the News* students after receiving feedback from several broadcasting students that, after completing the analysis assignment they cannot view the news the same way.

Other changes implemented include the following:

*   A "Getting Started" memo: I communicate with the students through the class listserv on the first day of class and post a Getting Started memo that directs the students to the course Blackboard site where the orientation materials and class rules are posted. A student cannot gain access to the class Blackboard site until s/he has subscribed using the assigned anonymous student identification number. I distribute these numbers electronically to each student.

*   Rules for attendance and discussion: The rules for attendance and bulletin board discussions are posted on the Blackboard site so students may refer to them at any time. Because there is no "attendance" in the traditional sense, attendance is measured through student participation on the electronic bulletin board. Students must post two substantive comments a week. When posting to the bulletin board, students are told they must never use their name or refer to their race, ethnicity, or gender. There have

been occasions when students would forget. When this happened, I would send the violator a private e-mail warning.

- The instructor as discussion starter and facilitator: I post discussion board questions at least once a week. Often I draw from the current headlines. I also keep the postings focused on course content. One posting that I have used a few times early in the semester as the first or second question is the following:

  Pretend you are visiting the U.S. from the planet Jupiter. This means you are devoid of experiences. You need to file a report with your colleagues on Jupiter about earthlings. Based on your exposure to radio, television, movies, newspapers, magazines and the Internet, how would you describe the following: (1) African Americans; (2) Asian Americans; (3) Hispanic (Latino) Americans; (4) Native Americans; (5) White (Caucasian) Americans; (6) Non-European immigrant groups, such as Haitians, Jamaicans, Southeast Asians, etc.; and (7) European immigrant groups. After you have filed your report, read the reports of your fellow Jupiterians. Any surprises?

Current Challenges

In Spring 2002, the class held two face-to-face meetings. The first meeting was in early March and the second in early April. The purpose of the first face-to-face meeting was to show and discuss video material that was not readily accessible to the students. The second meeting featured a guest speaker. Before the March meeting, I cautioned the students that the rules of anonymity were still in effect; they could not divulge their identification number. Student feedback indicates there were some concerns before the March meeting about finally meeting people whom they knew only through the electronic bulletin board. However, after the second meeting, students indicated in their journals that they enjoyed the face-to-face environment, and I did not observe any meaningful differences in candor or emotional level of the remaining online discussions, even though the students knew the general racial and gender demographics of the class. Much of the research looking at gender communication style and participation differences between classroom and computer-mediated communication environments has used White subjects. There is a need for more research in these areas of study also using students of color (Wolfe, 2000).

I plan to replicate the 2002 model when I teach the course again.

Conclusion

I set out in 1997 to develop an online studies-in-race course with an anonymity component that would facilitate civil discourse about the ways so-called minorities and minority issues are covered by the news media. This course has been taught seven times over the past five years. I have observed that the race conversations online are much more candid than in traditional face-to-face settings, whether they are on the electronic bulletin board or through electronic student journals that are shared only with the instructor. For some students, talking about race in any teaching environment is welcomed. But there are students for whom being anonymous gives them a newfound freedom to express their views on race. The following is an excerpt from a Spring 2001 student. It is a typical student comment:

Student # 9 (21-Year-Old White Female)
I do not believe that I would have enrolled in this course if it had been in a regular class setting. First, the anonymity originally offered remained one of its most attractive components, allowing me to voice my opinions without fear of direct, physical response. Second, the ability to discuss these issues from the comfort of my dorm room allowed me to both develop my ideas more completely and articulately, and allowed me to express my opinions with more honesty than if I were faced with an entire room of fellow classmates and a professor. I do feel that I tend to censor myself in classroom settings; this class afforded me the opportunity to leave self-censorship by the wayside.

Teaching a studies-in-race course online can be effective. However, the instructor must be organized, focused, constantly in contact with the students, and able to anticipate problems — both technical and pedagogical — before they occur. Creating a supportive environment is key. The students must feel that, whatever their views, they will be respected and addressed. Admittedly, this can be difficult when dealing with such a potentially explosive issue, but the instructor sets the tone for the class.

I received this unsolicited testimonial in 2002 from a student who had taken the course in Spring 2001.

Student #3 (35-Year-Old White Female)

I must say that your course awakened me to issues I had no idea I was blind to. As an undergrad, I had taken one required gender/race course, and it was great, but it did not enlighten me to my own feelings, beliefs, etc., on marginalized groups the same way your assigned journal writings, the coursework here, and the online discussions have. In fact, this course inspired me to pursue more courses at Temple involving similar issues, such as feminist views and ethics in journalism. What I'm most pleased with is that I feel I've become a richer human being through your course, realizing my position in the entire world rather than just my little corner of it and learning to value every human voice rather than just the ones I'm conditioned to respond to. It has certainly made me more objective as a journalist and given me the ability to listen carefully to all sides of an issue instead of just assuming I automatically know the "correct" one. For instance, the September 11th events easily could be seen from only a U.S., patriotic position, but now I'd like to understand where the Afghans and other middle eastern cultures are coming from as well.

What is exciting about marrying such a potentially explosive area of academic study with new electronic teaching techniques is that if done properly, the instructor, on a small scale, can advance the understanding and dialogue about race.

Acknowledgments

I wish to thank Poynter Institute Dean Karen F. Dunlap and her faculty for their guidance and support during the initial phases of this research.

Endnotes

¹   The term *race* is being used as socially constructed concept, not as a factual representation.

²   The racial identifiers such as Black and White are sometimes used rather than Caucasian and African American because these are the terms students used when self-identifying.

³   The census bureau created the term *Hispanic.* It is being used inter-changeably with the indigenous term Latino.

REFERENCES

Berge, Z. & Collins, M. (1995). Introduction: From marks in the sand to computer conferencing via fiber optics. *Computer-Mediated Communication Magazine, 2*(4), 6. Retrieved from http://www.december.com/cmc/mag/1995/apr/berge.html.

Carstarphen, M. G. & Lambiase, J. J. (1998). Domination and democracy in cyberspace: Reports from the majority media and ethnic/gender margins. In B. Ebo (Ed.), *Cyberghetto or Cybertopia? Race, Class, and Gender on the Internet*, (pp. 121-135). Westport, CT: Praeger.

Crowston, K. & Kammerer, E. (1998). Communicative style and gender differences in computer-mediated communications. In B. Ebo (Ed.), *Cyberghetto or Cybertopia? Race, Class, and Gender on the Internet*, (pp. 185-203). Westport, CT: Praeger.

Frederick, P. (1995). Walking on eggs: Mastering the dreaded diversity discussion. *College Teaching, 4*(3), 83-92.

Gottschalk, T. H. (ed.). (1996a) Distance Education: An overview. *Distance Education at a Glance* (University of Idaho Engineering Outreach Guide No.1). Retrieved Summer 1997, from http://www.uidaho.edu/evo/dist1.html.

Gottschalk, T. H. (ed.). (1996b) Strategies for teaching at a distance. *Distance Education at a Glance* (University of Idaho Engineering Outreach

Guide No.2). Retrieved Summer 1997, from http://www.uidaho.edu/evo/dist2.html.

Gottschalk, T. H. (ed.). (1996c). Instructional development for distance education. *Distance Education at a Glance* (University of Idaho Engineering Outreach Guide No.3). Retrieved Summer 1997, from http://www.uidaho.edu/evo/dist3.html.

Gottschalk, T. H. (ed.). (1996d). Evaluation for distance educators. *Distance Education at a Glance* (University of Idaho Engineering Outreach Guide No.4). Retrieved Summer 1997, from http://www.uidaho.edu/evo/dist4.html.

Gottschalk, T. H. (ed.). (1996e). Computers in distance education. *Distance Education at a Glance* (University of Idaho Engineering Outreach Guide No.6). Retrieved Summer 1997, from http://www.uidaho.edu/evo/dist6.html.

Gottschalk, T. H. (ed.). (1996f). Distance education and the WWW. *Distance Education at a Glance* (University of Idaho Engineering Outreach Guide No.11). Retrieved Summer 1997, from http://www.uidaho.edu/evo/dist11.html.

Guernsey, L. (1998). Educators ask whether interactively works in online courses. *The Chronicle of Higher Education*, A32.

Herring, S. C. (1993). Gender and democracy in computer-mediated communication. *Electronic Journal of Communication* [online], *3*(2). Available from http://www.cios.org/getfile\HERRING_V3N293.

Higginbotham, E. (1996). Getting all students to listen: Analyzing and coping with student resistance. *American Behavioral Scientist, 40*(2), 203-211.

Logging on: The diary of a distance learner. (1998). *Risk Management, 45*(3), 33-37.

Meacham, J. (1995). Conflict in multicultural classes: Too much heat or too little? *Liberal Education,* (Fall), 24-29.

Moore, M.G. & Thompson, M.M. (with Quigley, A.B., Clark, G.C., & Goff, G.G.). (1990). The effects of distance learning: A summary of the literature. (Research Monograph No. 2). University Park, PA: The Pennsylvania State University, American Center for the Study of Distance Education (ED 330321).

Tatum, B.D. (1992). Talking about race, learning about racism: The application of racial identity development theory in the classroom. *Harvard Educational Review, 62*(1), 1-24.

Wolfe, J. (2000). Gender, ethnicity, and classroom discourse: Communication patters of Hispanic and White students in networked classrooms. *Written Communication, 17*(4), 491-519.

Appendix

As part of the final exam, I require students to complete a questionnaire about the course. Here is an example of the 2002 survey:

Course Feedback

The purpose of this short questionnaire is to help me improve the course design. I am looking for honest, clear, constructive, and succinct responses. There are no "right" answers. You will automatically receive 20 points as a "thank you" for answering *all* of these questions. Since I am doing research in this area, I may contact you for further feedback.

1. *Do you look at the media differently now that you have taken this course? Explain your answer.*

2. *How will you apply what you have learned in this course to your daily work, personal interactions, future studies/employment, etc.? Explain your answer.*

3. *As you know, I conducted this course differently this semester by holding two class sessions but still used the Discussion Board for your anonymous postings.*

a) Since you had been discussing questions for a few weeks before we met as a class, what if any impact did the face-to-face meetings have on the class dynamics? Explain your answer.

b) Would this course have been more or less attractive to you had we met in a regular class setting? Explain your answer.

4.   *Would you have participated in the Discussions Board more or less often:*

a)   Had a certain number of postings not been required? Explain your answer.

b)   Had we met in a regular class setting, rather than the majority of the communication occurring only online? Explain your answer.

c)   What if the class was conducted online, but your identity was not anonymous? Explain your answer.

5.   *I have been told that sometimes there is a student expectation of "white bashing" in race studies courses.*

a)   Was there any concern or expectation of "white bashing" before the start of this class, either by the authors, your classmates, and/or the instructor? Explain your answer.

b)   What did you think of the texts? Explain.

c)   What did you think of the quality of the Discussion Board questions/responses? Explain.

d)   How can the "race" dialog be improved? Explain.

6.   *You know your classmates primarily through what they have said and how they have expressed themselves via the written word. Based on your best guess, identify the race (Black/White/Latino/Asian/Native American) or ethnicity AND gender of each and briefly explain how you reach your conclusion:*

Race 1:

Race 2:

Race 3:

Race 4: Etc.

7.   *Any additional comments…*

Chapter X

Media Entrepreneurship as an Online Course: A Case Study

Elizabeth J. Leebron

Temple University, USA

Abstract

This chapter describes the conversion of a traditional classroom course to one taught online. Creating a Media Business *has been part of the Business curriculum within a broad, traditional Mass Communications major, and its objective has been to introduce students to the theory and practice of starting an independent media enterprise. The attempt to transform any traditional academic course into a virtual one will invariably entail redefining pedagogical issues such as requirements, assignments, participation, and evaluation. Certain course content and objectives are more amenable to both the opportunities and constraints posed by the Internet. Our course was enhanced by the conversion because of its suitability for transfer from the tangible to the virtual environment. More specifically, for* Creating a Media Business, *the Internet is not merely a channel of information transmission, but very often an important, if not essential, part of the very business about which the students are learning.*

Background

In the early 1990s, Temple University's Broadcasting, Telecommunications, and Mass Media Department instituted a new course, *Creating a Media Business*, to introduce students to the knowledge and skills fundamental to building their own media enterprise. This undergraduate course, with a graduate-student component, was created to broaden students' professional vistas by exploring work possibilities outside the domain of established media agencies. Typically, students planning careers in the media often focus on securing positions in the extant TV networks, radio stations, telecommunications corporations, recording companies, advertising and public relations firms, and so forth. Of course, since the media have powerful and glamorous associations for many people, the job market with respect to these agencies is competitive, even in the best of economic circumstance, and even those newcomers fortunate enough to be hired must often begin their careers in positions somewhat different in kind (i.e., not just in level) from that to which they aspire. *Creating a Media Business*, then, was designed to allow students to explore opportunities outside the traditional business or corporate model, thereby enhancing not only the number, but also the range of professional possibilities on which they might plan. These possibilities might apply to career decisions before or immediately after graduation or to career changes following a more traditional stint in the media/corporate world. At any stage, the kind of entrepreneurial skills to which students would be introduced in this course are those which enable individual dreams to be realized.

Clearly, by the turn of the twenty-first century, many, if not most, teaching institutions began incorporating online/computer technology into the educational experience. William H. Graves (2000) defined virtual learning spaces as those not constricted by time or place. Institutions began to explore new teaching opportunities that required reorganization of content because the instructor was no longer the primary vehicle for dissemination of knowledge. The new e-learning environment in which students were able to learn through software applications as opposed to learning through a textbook became synonymous with some online teaching (Graves, 2000). Thus, the move to offer courses online and/or through distance-learning was initiated, if only in the name of routine progressiveness. However, from a rather robust roster of traditionally taught mass communication offerings, *Creating a Media Business* (after having been taught traditionally for three years) was one of only a handful of courses in the major designated for online conversion. This decision to move it into the virtual classroom was motivated by more than routine progressiveness.

Although one could iterate what many consider to be the almost universal pros and cons of virtual education (e.g., adaptable to individual schedules vs. lack of immediate, personal feedback, individualized learning vs. group learning, and physical presence at one time vs. virtual presence at asynchronous times), the most important aspect of this evolution of education is that the focus of convenience has shifted from the institution and its instructors (traditional instruction) to the students and instructional design (Graves, 2000).

Creating a Media Business was selected as an online offering because the very subject matter of the course, more often than not, involved the Internet. That is to say, although Creating *a Media Business* would likely benefit from the same cyber qualities that might serve any virtually offered course, it had the distinction, among many other courses, of being specifically related to the Internet. This special relation occurs in at least three ways. First, the independent business ventures, which students envision, are increasingly themselves online ventures. Second, even if the proposed entrepreneurial venture is not, itself, primarily located in the virtual world, it most likely will need to avail itself of that world's services, perhaps for advertising and publicity. Finally, inasmuch as the subject matter of the course is not narrowly academic, the kind of popular press and news accounts that might be used as instructional readings are more likely to be found on the Web than in conventional academic-library systems. The classroom of the future or the virtual classroom will incorporate more collaborative learning through sharing of content as well as group sharing of assignments.

The remainder of this chapter, then, discusses in some detail the now five year, online existence of *Creating a Media Business* in terms of prerequisites, student constituency, technology, instructional techniques, assignments, evaluation, and participation. For each of these issues, particular attention is paid to the differences between the traditional and virtual versions.

Threshold Requirements

In addition to certain basic academic requirements, including junior status for undergraduates and completion of the core requirements in the major, enrollment in this course required that students have certain minimal techno-skills and access. In particular, students needed to have ready access to a computer with full Internet capabilities. No specification was made with respect to carrier or operating system, although it was necessary that the student be able to interface with the University's software associated with both online and traditional teaching described in the next section. Basic proficiency in word-processing, e-mailing and Web surfing was also expected.

These minimal prerequisites no longer seem to pose any problem to urban students taking university courses. Moreover, in the event that a student did not have his or her own computer, the University computer laboratories provided sufficient access for participation. Of course, future research might consider how much the constraints of using on-campus technology might affect performance. While certainly visits to the university computer labs are not as restrictive as regularly scheduled, traditional classroom lectures, the student who can work almost entirely from home may be advantaged.

Student Populations

Although the general teaching objective remained unchanged in converting *Creating a Media Business* to an online course, the student constituency was somewhat altered by the transition. Diaz (2002) reported that students enrolled in online courses tend to be older with more college credits and higher GPAs than their traditional counterparts. From the time the online version of our course was launched, an increasingly larger percentage of the student population consisted of graduate students, culminating in 40% for the most recent semester it was offered.

Clearly, one of the universal benefits of the virtual classroom is the ability to attract a larger and/or different student population, particularly when compared to a traditional course offered during normal working hours. And, while an increase in older, more sophisticated students may be much welcomed by the instructor, consideration should be given to the possible difference this new constituency will make in terms of classroom participation. While, on the one hand, older students may set a loftier tone that, in turn, may be exemplary to their junior counterparts, on the other hand, that same social modeling may function as an intimidating hindrance. The addition of graduate and older, working-professional students in our course did, in fact, result in an elevation of student performance on a number of levels, including more postings on the listserv and better documented and reasoned arguments in these postings and assignments. Dille and Mezack's study in 1991, and Souder's study in 1994 (as cited in Diaz, 2002) reported age to be a significant contributor to students' performances in the online versus traditional classroom. Since, as will be described, there was a minimum participation requirement for each student, it was difficult to determine if additional undergraduate discourse was in any way thwarted as a result of the older students' participation. Interestingly, in terms of student reports on the subject, the older students were more likely to offer complaints about the contributions of some of the more outspoken younger students (in terms of their relative lack of worthiness) than vice versa.

As a final point on this issue, it should be noted that the possible problematic nature of the mixture of age/sophistication levels in a course might result both in the traditional as well as the virtual classroom. However, since the virtual classroom is, as already pointed out, more capable of attracting heterogeneity, then it might also be more likely encumbered by the problem. Moreover, in terms of the power of an intimidation factor, it could be hypothesized that the less sophisticated students might find the fleetingness of the oral contribution to be less daunting than its incontrovertible permanent written counterpart.

Technology

Blackboard, a comprehensive e-learning platform, was used to deliver and manage course materials on the Web. Both the students and the instructor used Blackboard to access assigned course material, track due dates, and communicate through e-mail, bulletin boards, or live chat. To the extent that an instructor misses the type of surveillance he or she can exert in the traditional classroom, it should be noted that Blackboard allows the instructor to track access and usage of the entire course site. Also, because it is specifically an educational platform, Blackboard provides an electronic grade book that enables students to view their progress in the course (http://blackboard.temple.edu –log on as guest).

Instructional Techniques

Much has been written on the difference between traditional in-class and online instruction (Herrington, Oliver, Herrington, & Sparrow, 2000; Relan & Gillani, 1997), and it is likely unnecessary to review those standard variations here. Moreover, the more conventional roles of the instructor in terms of assignments, facilitating participation, and evaluation are indicated in sections that follow. The course objectives and outcomes remained the same (see Appendixes A & B). However, one instructional aspect of *Creating a Media Business* was profoundly affected by the transition from physical to online classrooms, and this feature has implications for instruction in other applied or practice-oriented courses.

When traditionally taught, *Creating a Media Business* regularly featured guest lecturers — successful entrepreneurs who had negotiated the terrain of establishing their own media businesses. In professional-skills courses, practitioners are often able to share useful knowledge typically not easily replicated in textbooks. Moreover, in this case, many of the local entrepreneurs have the added advantage of being alumni of the school in which the course is offered. Clearly, it is encouraging for students to see instances where their chosen course of study has already been successful for others. Additionally, outside of New York City or Los Angeles, regional achievements often provide specialized insights useful to the largely local student population.

Although synchronous online sessions could be arranged, the course did not have a regular, online meeting time so as to effectuate an online lecture hall. Moreover, despite the omnipresence of online technology in both office and home, most businesspersons are not likely familiar with the conditions of online performances. Similarly, most students are still not used to attending such sessions. Add to these limitations that the scheduling of synchronous meetings tends to remove whatever advantage the temporal freedom of the online class provides. All this is not to say that guest speakers and synchronous online meetings should not play a larger role in the future, but rather that, thus far, an attempt was made to offer alternatives to the guest lectures.

Two other options for hearing from relevant professionals were established for the course. First, students were required to attend to case studies provided in several of the online business publications, namely, *Inc., Harvard Business Review, Entrepreneur,* and *Young Biz.*

Material published about the histories and strategies of media entrepreneurs, sometimes even in Q and A format, still allowed students to derive some of that personal/practical knowledge.

However, published accounts can fall short of live appearance because first, speakers may exert some level of editorial control or at least discretion over what they say in print (via paper or screen). Thus, the possible advantages of impromptu candor may be lost. Second, inasmuch as published articles are not crafted specifically for one's course, the questions posed to the subject may not be those that might best suit the interests and needs of the students. To this end, students were also required to establish personal contact and conduct interviews with members of the relevant business community.

Using online directory systems, students were able to locate the electronic addresses of relevant professionals in order to write and question them directly. In turn, each student could post and thereby share the results of these personal contacts with the other students. This, of course, increased the actual number of individuals from whom the class could hear. Still, the limitations of written versus oral discourse noted above are not necessarily ameliorated by this approach, and, probably most importantly, a new problem arose with this technique of one-on-one guest-contact. Although the results of private correspondence with a respected professional might prove to be exhilarating for the lucky student, a professional contacted by an individual student (even under the aegis of a university course) may not compare favorably with an invited lecturer.

After all, the guest lecturer comes to the classroom having already accepted the obligation of sharing, but busy entrepreneurs have no such obligation. As it turned out, it was not uncommon for students in *Creating a Media Business* to be frustrated by their inability to secure a decent interview, particularly in terms of crucial financial details such as number of employees or operating costs, etc.

While in-person speakers might, for all the reasons suggested above, be more forthcoming with a student audience, another option to consider is a pre-selected list of professionals (previously invited and screened by the instructor) from which the students could choose a candidate for individual correspondence. Inasmuch as the instructor was originally responsible for inviting and preparing guests in the traditional classroom, this pre-screened list, while limiting the student's opportunity to test his or her own initiative, would likely guarantee more consistent success without adding to the instructor's normal workload.

Assignments

In addition to the prerequisite skills noted earlier, all students in *Creating a Media Business* were required to subscribe to the class listserv. Also, as described earlier (see Technology), a single cyber platform was used to integrate the reception and dissemination of all classroom intelligence.

All members of this online class were minimally responsible for checking the website on a daily basis. This involved reviewing all posted announcements, assignments, references, letters, and discussions by checking the homepage and its links (as mastered by the instructor), the listserv (which might include material from the instructor as well as other students in the course), and e-mail (which could include material from the instructor, classmates, and business sources to whom the student had individually made inquiry.)

Participation beyond this daily consultation was also required. Generally, students were encouraged to contribute questions and comments about the posted/linked readings and assignments. In addition to written assignments, readings, and conducting whatever e-mail correspondence s/he found necessary, each student was required to post at least two comments per week to the listserv. Mandated commentary did not have to be lengthy, but it was required that it be substantive. That is to say, mere expressions of approval, disapproval, or value (e.g., "that was a very interesting article") were not sufficient.

The actual course assignments involved readings, written work, and oral presentation. When the course was set in a traditional classroom, a required textbook was the central source of written instruction (the text was actually a client service book produced by PricewaterhouseCoopers).

However, as mentioned previously, given that the subject matter was largely practical and immediate, newspaper, magazine, and journal articles are likely to be more appropriate sources of instruction than a standard text. Although the book was eliminated from the required reading for the online course, the reading assignments (required and recommended) increasingly involved material linked or uploaded to the course website.

It was estimated that, with the exception of the written assignments, the time it would take to make daily consultations with the webpage, to read all required materials, and to submit the necessary feedback would be equivalent to the number of hours per week normally consumed by traditional lecture attendance and required reading time, i.e., nine.

The first assignment was for students to introduce themselves to each other through words so that each of the other members of the class could develop a mental image of who their classmates were. The parameters for this exercise were wide. Student entries varied from one paragraph to a full page of text. Some wrote passionately about themselves, indicating what had led to their desire to look at building a business.

Others wrote about their personal lives and how their life experiences impacted their desire to be "their own boss." Still others wrote that they were not sure this was what they wanted to do but thought they could explore their potential to be an entrepreneur. The honesty was fortuitous as it opened lines of communication quickly. The students' personal profiles revealed details about their personal lives and feelings that they might not have shared if they were physically standing in front of twenty of their peers (see Appendix C).

Once profiles were posted, students began to consider where they wanted to live after graduation. Students were advised to think about where they would like to reside and then research that particular community using at least three websites. (See Appendix D). The guiding principle was that you cannot start a business if you are not happy with your environs. Following the selection of a locale, students identified business ideas they had been considering. The more narrowly focused the idea, the easier it would be to research the competition. Students wrote about at least one, but no more than three, business ideas and then discussed them via the listserv. Once they narrowed to one idea, they could undertake research toward producing the final assignment — the construction of a complete and professional business proposal for an entrepreneurial media enterprise, which was submitted in steps. The consecutive steps were as follows: (1) identify the type of business you intend to pursue, (2) articulate in 150 words or less the concept and your aspirations, (3) after selecting a community in which to introduce your business idea, review the competition in a 100-mile radius, and (4) from your list of competitors, select no more than 10 competitors that have been in business for five or fewer years and then profile them.

These competitor profiles were similar to case studies and provided a cursory review of real-life businesses that enabled students to see if their idea was practical, merited further consideration and would be competitive in the marketplace. They could also ascertain whether or not their product or service had something unique to offer that would help to make it competitive in the business world. Understanding the competition enabled students to draft a statement about their product or service's potential in the marketplace. Ultimately, they not only had to address the potential but how they would distribute or market to achieve sales.

Because the students shared the same major, the business ideas had a tendency to overlap. The final assignment, though accomplished in phases, was a team assignment for undergraduates. The rationale for assigning the business proposal as a group project was that it was a difficult task to accomplish in one month. The overlapping of ideas proved to be a factor in forming the teams. Creating a team concept online is challenging, and time again becomes an issue. Students were encouraged to set aside time (a minimum of one half hour, several times per week) to engage in a threaded discussion about their plans. All students had to consider matters regarding office space, financing of ideas, funding potential, phones, mail, benefits, payroll, sales, and other more mundane issues in writing their plan. A pivotal question that students had to answer was: Are you ready to be the one who is responsible for these issues as you bootstrap your way up through the entrepreneurial maze?

The final component of the course was a 15-minute oral presentation that was a summary of the business proposal. Prior to this point, students were not brought together in a traditional classroom setting but may have known each other through other courses.

All but the final step involved a written report that each student was required to post to the website. These steps encompass both the interviews described earlier and the written assignments that other students were required to read and to which they had to respond. These assignments allow for systematic exploration of the issues relevant to the course objective in a way that is compatible with the shape of cyberspace and conducive to exploiting what it uniquely has to offer. The final, oral business presentation was retained, even in the online version of the class, because such face-to-face interaction remains an integral element in entrepreneurial business endeavors — particularly in terms of soliciting capital and/or clients. Thus, despite the course's online status, it would seem remiss not to provide students with the benefit of crucial presentation experience they will likely need at some point in their careers.

Evaluation

Students were graded exclusively on the assignments described earlier — no examinations were given. Essentially, students were evaluated on two things:

1. *Quality of their Business Proposal* - Quality was determined by the worthiness as an overall project, and also in terms of the quality of the labor that went into producing each presented phase of the proposal. The student received a numerical grade for each posted assignment, as well as one overall grade after the final, oral presentation.

2. *Quality and Quantity of Labor Expended in Online Participation* - Although the instructor, given the participation requirements, ultimately determined all of these grades, our online course clearly provides each student with more qualitative assessment than s/he normally receives in the context of a traditional classroom. This befits the course because establishing a business is, by its very nature, a typically interactive enterprise involving multiple sites and levels of assessment. Student assessment can obviously occur in any type classroom, but for reasons that will be discussed in the next section, the online experience likely presents the better environment for such interaction.

Participation and the Success of Creating a Media Business

As already mentioned, the Internet resonates with *Creating a Media Business* because the very endeavor of media entrepreneurship, more often than not, involves the Internet — both as subject and object of its domain. Additionally, as discussed immediately above, the media entrepreneurial enterprise implicitly involves people and people interacting. The remaining question is whether or not an online format offers the best type of interaction for this sort of course.

If there were a practicum for the entrepreneurial experience itself — that is, if students were able to meet face-to-face on a daily basis as partners in a business venture while also conferring with and/or pitching to other professionals who would be necessary to implementing their media enterprise — one would probably have the optimal interactive situation for teaching students how to be media entrepreneurs. Such a practicum might very well be recommended as a follow-up seminar for those who successfully negotiate the course presently under consideration. However, absent this advanced seminar, the online version of this course may be the best way to introduce students to the media entrepreneurial experience.

Unlike the submission of a traditional paper or exam, work on assembling a business proposal is not so discrete or finite. It can be tried out, assessed, and put back on the table for more tweaking or massaging. The traditional classroom rarely can provide the time sequencing for such a "back-and-forth" process. However, daily Internet communication lends itself better to the objectives of a course such as *Creating a Media Business*. Sonwalkar (2001) discusses the five fundamental learning modes for online asynchronous learning. They include the apprenticeship, incidental, inductive, deductive, and discovery modes of learning. The discovery and apprenticeship phases are particularly important for the student interested in building a business because one learns by doing. In fact, writing the business proposal enables students to test their own knowledge in designing a plan for submission to funding agents or other prospective business associates. Whereas in traditional courses, students stick precisely to the resources provided, the online fluidity of time and space encourages students to go beyond what the instructor has provided or what they find after a routine survey. Certainly, the ease of being transported by a click of a button — the simplicity of so much of the universe being linked — allows students to initiate and incorporate more and more refinement, which is a necessary instinct in planning a successful business.

Finally, the feedback of peers, both typical of and critical to the development of a business enterprise, is probably more easily secured in an online course. Even though, as suggested earlier, a student may be more comfortable talking informally in a class than writing to a listserv, oddly enough the quality and quantity of feedback is likely to be better in the online context. According to Knowlton, Knowlton, and Davis (2000), online discussions enable students to "understand that there are real people that they are communicating with in cyberspace. As a result of discussion, students don't feel alone in the educational process, they become a part of an educational cyber-community of learners" (p. 54). Students engage freely in debate and discussion in the online environment; they challenge each other's ideas and assumptions and evaluate each other's work. Ultimately, they grow together as a community, which strengthens their ability to process course material.

Clearly, the quality of the discussion is improved, both because the student has time to formulate his or her comments and because, quite simply, it is a course requirement that student feedback be considered discourse. Ironically, the amount of contribution is also improved in the online setting because of this same principle — it is required. Students seem to contribute more than the minimum required and to engage in extended meaningful discourse online. This is in part due to the open-ended time element of the online discussion.

In the traditional classroom, if given the choice, students may indeed feel comfortable contributing oral, "armchair" comments, but fewer students participate in discourse and there is finite time in which to share one's opinions and knowledge. It would be extremely awkward in the traditional classroom to make specific demands about the frequency and nature of oral contributions, unless an instructor was literally to call upon each student to recite.

Future Considerations

Some issues to be decided for future terms include whether or not to set minimum standards for technology that would include age of the student's system and student access to certain software products. Another issue of concern is how often students should be required to check the listserv and post comments. Because I found that criticisms were not as guided as they could have been, posting a checklist with weekly assignments to structure discussion would be a good idea. Another consideration is to use a strategy for framing the discussion that would include not only a pointed question, but also a time limit (Brown, 2002). However, similar demands in the virtual context are seemingly more reasonable and less intrusive, thereby enhancing the work enterprise.

The one drawback of sharing business ideas online is that ideas cannot be copyrighted but are proprietary to the individual. To preserve the privacy of the ideas, students were required to e-mail non-disclosure statements. The statement simply indicated the student would comply with the text of the non-disclosure statement and would hold all information in the strictest confidence.

References

Brown, D. (2002) New learning tools: Exploring the hype. *Syllabus*, (February), 20.

Diaz, D. P. (2002). Online drop rates revisited: The technology source [Electronic version]. *Syllabus*. (May/June). Retrieved May 1, 2002 from http://ts.mivu.org/default.asp?show=article&id=981.

Dille, B. & Mezack, M. (1991). Identifying predictors of high risk among community college telecourse students. *The American Journal of Distance Education, 5*(1), 24-35.

Graves, W. H. (2000). The Dot. XXX challenge to higher education. *Syllabus*, (June), 30-36.

Herrington, J., Oliver, R., Herrington, T., & Sparrow, H. (2002). Towards a new tradition of online instruction: Using situated learning theory to design web-based units. *ASCILITE 2000 Conference*, (pp. 1-12).

Knowlton, D.S., Knowlton, H. M., & Davis, C. (2000). The whys and hows of online discussion. *Syllabus*, (June), 54-58.

Relan, A. & Gillani, B.B. (1997). Web-based instruction and the traditional classroom: Similarities and differences. In B.H. Kahn (Ed.), *Web-based instruction,* (pp. 41-46). Englewood Cliffs, NJ: Educational Technology Publications.

Sonwalkar, N. (2001). Changing the interface of education with revolutionary learning technologies. *Syllabus*, (November), 10-13.

Souder, W. E. (1994). The effectiveness of traditional vs. satellite delivery in three management of technology master's degree programs. *The American Journal of Distance Education, 7*(1), 37-53.

Appendix A

Course Objectives

* Explore media business opportunities
* Assess market
* Develop a mission statement
* Determine legal structure
* Understand capitalization requirements for new business

- Identify sources of financing
- Develop a business plan· Identify insurance requirements
- Understand budget and cost accounting
- Learn how to find sources of business information

Appendix B

Outcomes of the Course

1. Develop an understanding of entrepreneurship as it applies to the arts and entertainment
2. Develop an awareness for the trials and tribulations of media entrepreneurship
3. Understand of the need for pre-planning in building a successful start-up
4. Gain knowledge of branding
5. Develop an aptitude for entrepreneurship
6. Understand the concept of growth and the problems associated with it in an entrepreneurial venture
7. Develop an awareness of funding opportunities for start-up businesses

Appendix C

Sample Personal Profile

My name is XXX and I was born in Philadelphia on Friday, June 13, 197X. I was raised by both of my parents, as an only child. I am very spoiled at times and I think the world should revolve around me. However, I am a very giving person and I am probably the best friend anyone could have. I am not selfish to those that treat me with love and respect.

I am employed full-time and I work part-time Thursday, Friday, and Saturday nights as a cocktail waitress at Club XXXXX. Time is very important to me so I try to use it wisely.

I am told than I am very beautiful and loveable and have a great sense of humor. However, I am in no way conceited, and I take pride in my intelligence. I graduated from XXXX High School at number 10 in a graduating class of 450 students. At the end of my junior year I was number 1 in my class. I thought I was super smart so in my senior year slacked off. I went to XXX University for two years and decided to transfer because I was homesick. I then came to Temple as an accounting major but found that it was not my forte. Luckily, I doubled with marketing so I just continued. If I would have just come in as a marketing major, I would have gotten out last year, on time. However, I am graduating in May in the new Apollo so I guess it was worth the wait.

I want to use my marketing degree as an entry into the fashion world. I want to eventually design my own line of clothing. I applied to the Fashion Institute of Technology in New York to get into a one-year Fashion Buying and Merchandising Program. I have not received a response yet. Last year, my life took a turn for the worst. My father lost his job at XXX because they closed down. They transferred him to North Carolina. My mother moved with him a couple of months later, leaving me in Philly in our house. Our house was for sale but we eventually ended up renting it out... Now I am homeless but I found an apartment. It is very nice and I move in tomorrow. I have been living with one of my so-called friends for a month and I can't stand her. She makes me miserable so I just thank god with all my heart that my new landlord let me move in a couple of days early, opposed to Sunday, February 1.

I do not have a boyfriend but I am looking for one that has it going on like I do. I expect too much from a man — that is why I am constantly dating and getting rid of men that do not meet my criteria. However, most of my friends are male because they are very easy to talk to.

Finally, I am very down-to-earth, but I consider myself very trendy. I am a people person. I do not drink or use drugs. I pray everyday. I have good credit. I love clothes to death and I spend more than I can afford. I take pride in my appearance. I love children, but I don't want any until I am married. I send $12 a month to XXX through Children's International Program. I was up late one night and those sad faced children get to me. People tell me I am crazy and it is a scam but I tell them my heart is in the right place.

Appendix D

Sample Community Profile #1

I would choose to live in the Blue Bell area. This decision is based upon the location of the township. Blue Bell is centrally located to the Blue Route, PA Turnpike, Route 309, Route 73, and close to Philadelphia. Blue Bell is located in the Wissahickon School District. Houses retain their value and the school has a nationally high ranking. There are businesses located within the home in Blue Bell and have stability in businesses.

I had originally chosen Plymouth Meeting but upon research conducted on the Internet, I chose Blue Bell. Blue Bell has greater diversity in the community, value and more money generated. I obtained this information through the Mansfield University demographic census. This information is available at http://www.mnsfld.edu/~library/mu-demog.html.

I also obtained more information through the Montgomery County Chamber of Commerce located at http://www.wissahickon.org, Philanet http:www.philanet.com, and articles listed at Pennsylvania Women Working Together located at http://www.pa-wwt.com. I tried to obtain additional information from the US Census but the information was not currently available. I also used searches of Infoseek and Yahoo using Montgomery County PA as the search; here I was able to research prices of homes, school district website and view Blue Bell and Plymouth Meeting company sites on the Internet.

Upon researching the location, I have concluded I would prefer to live in and run a business from Blue Bell, although the price of housing is greater in Blue Bell than in Plymouth Meeting. Even though the business will be conducted from home over the Internet, Blue Bell is more centrally located, which is important in business meetings.

Sample Community Profile #2

The community that I will be profiling is the Bronx, which is a borough in New York City. The Bronx is the only mainland borough of New York City, which means that it is the only borough attached to another city other than Manhattan. It was named after Scandinavian farmer Jonas Bronck, the first European to settle the area in 1639. In the late 1800s, Irish and German immigrants were among the very first large communities of new Americans to settle in the Bronx. When elevated trains reached the borough in the 1900s, the borough became home to immigrants from Eastern and Southern Europe. After World War II, these groups were largely replaced by a Latino and African-American population. Today the 42 square mile borough is home to 1.2 million people.

The Bronx is home to post-secondary educational institutions, including the schools of the City University of New York, Manhattan College, and Fordham University. The Bronx also has public and private high schools, and public and private elementary schools.

The Bronx has a number of cultural museums and galleries, including The Bronx Museum of the Arts, which reflects the multi-ethnicity of The Bronx's communities, and the Edgar Allan Poe Cottage, which was this literary master's final residence. The Bronx also has museums for photography (En Foco), and a Jewish American Museum (Judaica Museum), The Bronx also has areas like The Bronx Zoo, which is open all year round and houses over 4,000 animals. The Bronx is also the place to watch the world famous Bronx Bombers, at Yankee Stadium, the home of the New York Yankees since April of 1923. And believe it or not, although the Bronx is a very urbanized area, there are still spots were sports lovers can go fishing, bike riding, play golf, and go horseback riding. The Bronx is also the spot for music and the performing arts, including the Bronx Arts Ensemble, The Bronx Symphony, and the Hehman Center for the Performing Arts.

Overall, The Bronx is a very diverse community with many things to see and do. It is part of the largest metropolitan area in the United States, so there is never a question of trying to find somewhere to go or something to do.

Chapter XI

The Uses and Impact of Academic Listservs in University Teaching: An Exploratory Study

Julie-Ann M. McFann

University of California, Los Angeles, USA

Abstract

The purpose of this study was to explore the impact academic listservs were making on teaching at Temple University when used in conjunction with face-to-face courses. Since the study was the first of its kind, an exploratory qualitative design was used to see if themes or patterns emerged. Results indicated that listservs were primarily used for housekeeping activities, although instructors voiced their desire to tap into the potential of listserv technology. The overriding discovery was that most instructors were using listservs without a predetermined teaching goal. A demographic profile of professors likely to use listservs is also included.

Introduction

Many instructors use online discussion groups (listservs) in conjunction with the face-to-face courses they teach. Although there has been some research on the impact of networked computers for aiding discussion, research regarding the pedagogical use of academic listservs in general is only now starting to emerge in a meaningful way. The purpose of this study was to explore the impact of academic listservs on teaching at a large, urban, Research I university. The ultimate goal of research regarding academic listservs is to see how they impact student learning. Before we can study how they impact learning, however, we need to find out why instructors were actually using listservs. It would be a moot point to study the effects of academic listservs on learning if most professors were not using them with that goal in mind. Because use of academic listservs at Temple University had not been studied, the focus of this study was purely exploratory to see what themes or patterns emerged. This research limited its focus to listservs rather than other types of asynchronous discussion groups, such as bulletin boards, because they are different in the way that information is delivered. Listservs are conducted via electronic mail making them more passive, whereas students must actively go to a bulletin board site to retrieve information and participate. Future research should be conducted comparing the educational impact of the two formats.

There is a dearth of empirical research regarding the effectiveness of listservs as a pedagogical tool (Edwards & Shaffer, 1999). Much of the literature on listserv usage in conjunction with face-to-face courses is anecdotal in nature or the research was conducted using the author's own courses. Generally, the research describes how the authors were using online communication in their courses. Findings were usually based either on their successes and failures with online assignments or on questionnaires distributed to students in the course that focused on student satisfaction regarding computer usage and/or the requirement to use computer networking. As Spotts and Bowman (1995) point out, "Most articles about technology use in higher education appear to be based on anecdotal evidence about outstanding professors who are using the latest innovations in dramatic and highly effective ways" (p. 56). Although the literature is mostly anecdotal and biased in favor of using listservs, the researchers independently drew similar conclusions about the benefits and disadvantages of online communication.

The major theme that runs through the literature is the idea of students learning from each other with the professor taking on the role of educational facilitator, an idea similar to that of cooperative learning situations. Bump (1990) notes that the radical feature of the online forum is "its tendency to make the controlling instructor obsolete" (p. 49). The literature indicates there are three areas where academic listservs seem to be making the greatest impact: student writing, content discussion, and class dynamics. Additionally, there are three impediments to participation: time, hardware access problems, and lack of technological skill.

Student Writing

Approximately 100 years ago, the educational philosopher John Dewey (1900) described the phenomenon regarding students' misunderstanding the act of writing for teachers as an act of arbitrary and artificial communication for the purpose of achieving a grade rather than an act of real communication. He noted that students feel like they have to "say" something related to their learning, whether or not they feel they actually have something to say. Based upon one of the themes that emerged from the literature, it appears that academic listservs are providing a venue for students to express their own thoughts and ideas to a "real" audience of peers rather than simply writing a paper for the professor to grade. In describing their experiences with having students write their papers online, Karayan and Crowe (1997), Batson and Bass (1996), Grassie (1995), Zack (1995), Miller (1991), and Bump (1990) all noted that an advantage of using a listserv in teaching writing is the students' desire to communicate with an audience of their peers. Students' writing becomes a public act instead of a private act between student and teacher. They *believe* their papers have a purpose other than a grade and understand writing as a means of communicating ideas. Because students have a clear sense of audience, they have an easier time writing for communication than writing an essay to be read by the professor alone (Miller, 1991).

Content

Grassie (1995) believes the biggest benefits of academic listservs "are the increased opportunities for enhancing the content discussion of the curriculum" (p. 5). Students are forced to ponder and deconstruct their notions and opinions about issues when they are confronted by a variety of perspectives on the same issues. In many cases, their thinking is changed because of dialogue with their classmates (Harrington, 1993). Pena-Shaff, Martin, and Gay (2001) believe that students are able to discuss topics in more detail online than they would have during the face-to-face lecture period, but they also point out that message threads are more like monologues than dialogues with others.

Class Dynamics

The literature suggests that listservs have a positive impact on classroom dynamics. Partee (1996) describes an academic listserv as a "virtual dormitory" because of the sense of community created amongst participants. Schwartz (1991) prefers the idea of a coffeehouse atmosphere with intellectual friendships being established. Karayan and Crowe (1997) report that many classes using electronic discussion reported that it fostered a greater sense of community and that students are reluctant for the interaction to end at the end of the semester. Class members expressed a "feeling" of closeness to each other that they did not experience in other classes. Grassie (1995) points out that the use of the forum "promoted a kind of camaraderie unusual in [major university] classes," with students learning each other's names quickly and regularly socializing outside of class (p. 6).

Impediments

Keeping in touch with students in the class and being able to be an active participant on the listserv can be difficult for many students (Breen, Lindsay, Jenkins, & Smith, 2001). There appear to be three impediments to participation: time, hardware access problems, and lack of technological skill. Students find participation very time consuming, and many, due to time constraints, are unable to participate (Davis & Ralph, 2001; Partee, 1996). While students are reading and responding to messages, new messages are being posted, thus creating a never-ending cycle of reading and posting.

Access to technology also presents a problem. Students without computers and/or Internet access from home are at a disadvantage, because they need to be at the university computer lab in order to participate (Davis & Ralph, 2001; Zack, 1995). McMahen and Dawson (1995) point out that, despite a teacher's best intentions, "the reality of insufficient hardware [on the part of the university] can prevent participation" (p. 324). During peak hours, computer labs may be over-crowded, thus preventing access for students to participate, or servers may slow down as they try to process the increase in online activity. Additionally, Breen, Lindsay, Jenkins, and Smith (2001) found that computer ownership did not reduce the demand placed on university computing facilities, because students who owned computers still used university labs for research and course-related work, thus contributing to usage during peak hours. Karayan and Crowe (1997) found that students without easy access to the technology feel more negative toward the online forum because of consequences the lack of participation may have on their grade, and believe that participation in an online forum should be optional rather than required.

For those students with lower levels of technological skills, the issue of time and access become even more acute because novice users expend more time and energy than their more skilled peers in accomplishing even the most basic tasks (Ross, 1996). In addition to completing their course assignments, these students are also trying to learn the technology. Ross points out that "students with low [computer-mediated communication] skills felt victimized by equipment that seemed to have a mind of its own" (p. 9). He continues by pointing out that experienced students report not only a lower frequency of technological problems, but also problems that are of a different quality than the novice users. While the novice users were challenged by how to send e-mail, the experienced users were challenged by issues such as how to send graphics. Bump (1990) believes that this leads to "technostress," especially when students are confronted with the huge amount of text that they must wade through that is generated by classmates' postings to the group. Because they are unsure of how to manage both the technology and the e-mail, they may feel overwhelmed and feel they have lost control. As their level of frustration increases, their level of commitment to participate in the group decreases, and they may drop out of the forum completely, missing many important instructional events (McMahen & Dawson, 1995; Velayo, 1994).

In spite of the negative aspects of the academic listservs, the general overall impression that runs through the literature is that it is a positive experience for both students and teachers that greatly enhances learning (Davis & Ralph, 2001; Gizzi, 1995; Grassie, 1995; Harrington, 1993; Karayan & Crowe, 1997; Morrison, 1993; Pena-Shaff, Martin, & Gay, 2001; Ross, 1996; Zack, 1995). Ross suggests that although novice users encounter difficulties, the problems are resolved and the novice users participate in the group as effectively as the experienced users.

To summarize, listservs appear to be making an impact in three areas: student writing, content discussion, and class dynamics. However, time, hardware access, and lack of technological skill are impediments to online discussion participation.

Research Design

Because information regarding faculty use of listservs including how they incorporated it into their teaching was unknown, a qualitative research design was used to look for themes and patterns to define faculty uses of listservs. The research questions for the study were: (1) Who utilizes academic listservs? Does a demographic pattern emerge? (2) Why do instructors utilize listservs? (3) What is the impact of the listserv use on the way the instructor teaches? (4) What listserv strategies have instructors employed that they felt were successful and/or unsuccessful? (5) How did the instructors use the listserv?

Data were gathered during a one and a half year time period (two Spring semesters, one Summer session, one Fall semester) from a variety of sources: face-to-face interviews, an experimental online focus group, participant observation of two graduate level listservs where I was a student member, three undergraduate listservs where I was the instructor (three different courses and semesters), and non-participant observation of three other listservs. Lastly, one professor provided archived class postings and another provided the archive of posted course material (e.g., study notes, summaries, etc.) for review. Although listserv messages were read, a formal content analysis was not conducted (see McFann, 2000, for a follow-up study analyzing listserv content). Rather, the messages were reviewed to see if what was occurring on the listservs was congruent with the interviews and to provide examples, where appropriate, in the results section.

Interviews and Online Focus Group

The primary source of data for this study was the interviews conducted individually or via an experimental online focus group. The e-mail postmaster for the university sent a memo via e-mail to all instructors using academic listservs asking if they would be willing to be interviewed for this study. Of the 63 instructors contacted, 23 responded, and 20 were subsequently interviewed—either in 30-minute face-to-face interviews (n = 17) or via the online focus group (n = 3). All interviewed were asked the same guiding questions (see Appendix) based on the research questions. Caution must always be taken when analyzing the results of a self-selected sample because of inherent biases. The sample size represents just under one-third of the instructors using listservs during the time frame of the study who, as will be shown in the demographics result section, are a cross-sampling of departments and gender in proportion to the University population. However, generalization of the results should be limited to academic cultures similar to Temple University.

Participant and Non-Participant Observations

A form of "participant observation" was used with two lists because I was a student in those classes. One of the instructors had decided to "give this list thing" a try. The other instructor had heard about academic listservs from colleagues and created the list the first week of class.

I was also a participant observer on the lists of three different foundational undergraduate education courses that I taught. Unlike the instructors of the lists observed as either a student-participant or non-participant, I corresponded quite extensively with all my students about their perceptions and impressions of their listservs.

Lastly, I was a non-participant observer of four classes. One was a graduate-level course, two were different sections of the same undergraduate course, and the fourth consisted of listserv archives provided by the undergraduate course professor of a different course he had taught the previous year.

Analysis Method

Open-ended interview responses were analyzed by listing the responses to each question and then grouping similar responses together as they emerged from the data. Because many of the respondents used similar words to mean different things, clarification of the terms was explored during the interviews to ensure researcher understanding of the terms used. Thus, meanings rather than specific terms were used when interpreting data. Determining the percentage of similar responses was the only statistical analysis conducted from the interviews.

Results

Interview Demographic Results

Although caution was necessary given the self-selection factor of the subjects, an analysis of the interview data found several trends in the demographics of instructors using listservs.

Subject Area Taught

The colleges and subject areas of instructors interviewed are shown on Table 1. As would be expected because of the size of the college in proportion to the rest of the university, the College of Arts and Sciences was the largest group of instructors represented (n = 10). All 10 instructors were from the Humanities, with English being the largest subgroup.

Two subsets of instructors emerged from the subject matter taught. Four of the instructors taught writing-intensive courses and four instructors taught the computer-related course within their field.

Table 1: College and Subject Area

College	Subject Area	Number Interviewed
Arts and Sciences	Classics	1
	English	3
	Intellectual Heritage	1
	Political Science	2
	Psychology	1
	Religion	1
	Sociology	1
Business	Economics	1
	Marketing	3
	Risk Management	1
Communications and Theater	Broadcasting	1
	Communications Sciences	1
Engineering	Architecture	1
Health Sciences	Dental Information	1
	Health Information Management	1

Table 2: Teaching Rank

Teaching Rank	Number	Percentage
Professor	7	.35
Associate Professor	3	.15
Assistant Professor	5	.25
Teaching Assistant	2	.10
Adjunct Instructor	3	.15

Teaching Rank

The teaching rank of interviewed instructors is shown Table 2. Slightly more than a third of the instructors at the university using listservs were full professors (35%). The results suggested a bi-modality of both full and assistant professors being the predominant users of academic listservs, with teaching assistants the least likely to use a listserv; however, the number of teaching assistants using listservs may have been impacted by the department in which the individual was teaching and whether the teaching assistant had full responsibility for teaching a course or was assisting a professor who was already utilizing a listserv.

As shown on Table 3, nearly half of the instructors had taught college for 10 years or less, causing a skewed distribution toward the 10 years or less range. The results suggest that faculty with less years teaching college are more likely to use academic listservs.

Instructor Age

As shown in Table 4, 75% of the interviewed instructors are over age 40. Only one instructor is under 30. Most of the instructors are between the ages of 41 and 60.

Table 3: Years Teaching College

Years Teaching College	Number	Percentage
0-10	9	.45
11-20	4	.20
21-30	5	.25
31-40	1	.05
40+	1	.05

Table 4: Instructor Age

Age	Number	Percent
21-30	1	.05
31-40	4	.21
41-50	6	.32
51-60	6	.32
61-70	2	.11

Instructor Gender

Seventy-five percent of the instructors interviewed for this study were male (see Table 5). This number is consistent with the United States Department of Education statistics that indicate 68% of professors, associate professors, and assistant professors are male.

Summary of Demographics

Based on the demographics from this study, the profile of an instructor who uses academic listservs may be a male professor or assistant professor teaching a humanities course, likely one involving intensive writing, over the age of 40, and with 10 years or less teaching experience in a college or university.

Interview, Focus Group, and Observation Results

Following are the results, by question, of the interviews and focus group. Data obtained through observations provide additional information for each question.

Table 5: Instructor Gender

Gender	Number
Female	5
Male	15

Academic Listserv Utilization

Because there was a great deal of overlap between Questions 1 and 3 ("What are the purposes of your listserv?" and "What do you believe are the benefits of using listservs?"), the results of the two questions have been combined.

1.   What are the purposes of your listserv?

3.   What do you believe are the benefits of using listservs?

Although numerous reasons for having an academic listserv were cited, several purposes were commonly reported. Not surprisingly, the instructors overwhelmingly used the listserv as a means of communication — both from instructor to students and from students to instructor, and as a means of disseminating information. In fact, the primary benefit of having a listserv was the ability to disseminate information and materials.

About a third of the instructors cited dissemination of assignments and materials, such as additional readings and study guides, as a purpose for using a listserv. They stated that it freed them of having to do everything, such as distributing materials or answering questions, during the class meeting time. A stated benefit was that in order to distribute a study guide, all they needed to do was access a stored file and include it in a posting to the list instead of having to photocopy it, which saved paper and money for the department. Also, a couple of instructors noted that, although it required heavy work during the first semester, once they had created the materials, it was already "canned" and ready-to-use in subsequent semesters with minor changes. A lot of the information that is disseminated could be considered "housekeeping" in nature, such as reminders that an assignment is due or telling students to bring certain materials to class.

Another frequently cited benefit is being able to communicate with students outside of the classroom in an asynchronous but continuous fashion. Students could ask questions and/or request clarification about assignments at their convenience, and the instructor or other students could respond at their convenience. For example, in one of the courses studied, there was some confusion regarding one of the major assignments that was due upon return from Spring Break. In a discussion that took place during the break, a student asked for clarification about the assignment, and several students agreed that they were also confused about the assignment. The instructor replied a week after the original question was posed. Because she was able to see that there was some confusion and that the students may not have done the assignment correctly, she was able to offer a solution online:

I intentionally "stayed out" of our listserv this past week, so you folks could provide each other input on your projects without my "interference." In reviewing the week's interactions today, I noticed they included comments from J., D., & M. regarding the nature of the first paper...Given that I may have just "dropped a bomb" on some of you, I offer the following suggestion: If what you have done doesn't come close to pages one and two, and you don't have time to address the list of elements on pages one and two by this Tuesday, then turn your paper in the following week. The relief some of you are experiencing at this moment is almost palpable over the computer! (Professor 1)

At times, students used the listserv to let the instructor and classmates know that they would not be in class or to find out what they had missed:

I accidentally missed class today...I was wondering if someone could summarize what I missed. I would be eternally grateful. Thanks! (Student 2)

A classmate responded approximately one and a half hours later:

Hi A.! Today in class we discussed the mudslinging tactics of [a politician], more about the checks and balances system between the president and Congress. On Wed., we're starting chapter 3. (Student 3)

Because the information was posted online, other students who were absent also obtained information about what they had missed. The professor saved time because he no longer needed to respond to the same request by several absent students. Additionally, since the information was available to them, they could not arrive at the next class session pleading ignorance of what had been covered in the previous session. One professor said that her students seem "more prepared for class" since she started using the listserv (Professor 4).

In addition to communication, the instructors used the listserv as a forum for discussion of issues, readings, and students' papers. Continuing discussions online that had started in the classroom also was cited as a benefit of having the listserv. Unfortunately, most of the instructors interviewed did not feel as successful with the level of discussion as they would like. They understand the potential of the medium for discussion but are at a loss as to how to create an environment where students spontaneously begin and carry on discussions related to course topics. This will be further explored in the Unsuccessful Strategies section.

Many instructors cited sub-benefits to online discussions, such as providing an opportunity for students who do not feel comfortable speaking in class, either due to language difficulties, intimidation, or shyness, to have a voice. Also, because there were no time constraints, students were able to think about and contemplate their responses before contributing to the discussion. At times, a student thought a question seemed silly or stupid. The online forum seemed like a "safe" venue to ask it. A student in one of the observed courses asked the following question:

> *Okay, in the spirit of your suggestion that this is the place to ask dumb questions, I will ask one. I am newly registered and have never voted before. What happens when I go into that little booth? (Student 1)*

The instructor was able to give the student reassurance that her question was not stupid and gave an in depth description of what the newly registered voters in his class would find when they went to vote.

Many instructors were able to gauge student understanding and correct misconceptions of the class topic based on the questions being asked and the direction of the discussion. This sub-benefit of the online discussion may be more important than most instructors realized, because it enabled them to see where their students' thinking and understanding had gone askew. Students sometimes seem confident that they understand the material being studied when in fact the discussion indicates they do not understand it. The instructor can quickly re-teach the material or correct the misunderstanding either on the listserv or during the next class session. This ability to observe student understanding and misunderstanding added another dimension to the teaching-learning process.

The professors also stated that having this extra venue improved in-class discussions and interactions. One of the reasons they indicated this was because the list "short circuits stereotypes," as one professor put it (Professor 6). During the interview, Professor 6 elaborated on his comment by describing a student who contributed a great deal to the class online discussion with insightful comments. The professor was shocked to discover that this student whom he had perceived as the top student in his class because of his listserv contributions was the same student who *looked* like the typical slouching student who does the minimum to get by in class. It caused him to rethink how he viewed students. Another factor mentioned by faculty involving in-class interactions was that class intimacy improved, both in-class and online.

About a fourth of the instructors used the listservs for joint assignments, turning in of homework, and/or extra credit. Two professors in writing-intensive courses noted that by making their students' writing a public act, the quality of writing improved. One of the professors said, "Peer writing gives [the students] a reason to communicate" (Professor 6). The other professor assigned two collaborative e-mail papers and "found it was the best writing they had done all semester" (Professor 13). The peer writing was a means of collaborative learning, and the students were able to learn from each other. This sentiment was voiced by one student during a discussion on what worked and on how to improve the class listserv:

> *Having the class post our assignments helped the listserv because it allowed us the opportunity to explore other's ideas and expand on their thoughts. It opened the door to allow one to argue for or against a certain opinion. It also allowed us to personally evaluate the quality of one's work. (Student 6)*

To summarize, instructors reported the primary purposes and benefits of using listservs are the ability to disseminate materials, communicate with students outside of the classroom about "housekeeping," and discuss course content. Additionally, they noted it gave shy, intimidated, and non-native English speakers a chance to contribute to discussions and increased class intimacy, which improved in-class discussions. For writing-intensive courses, they stated that peer writing and "writing as a public act" improved the quality of writing.

2. "Why did you originally begin to use a listserv? What were the motivations and/or what was the impetus?"

Six of the instructors began using academic listservs at the encouragement of a colleague or an assistant. As one instructor describes it, "I was convinced by [them] that it would be a good thing" (Professor 7). Another instructor stated,

"I went to a workshop [about listservs] and decided to try it" (Professor 17). Other instructors were already familiar with listservs and decided to try them with their teaching. "I had joined a listserv and saw how interesting that was, and then discovered I could do the same thing with my students," a professor said (Professor 18). For the computer-related courses, the professors reasoned that their students needed to know how to use the Internet so they incorporated it into the course. Another impetus was so that class members and the instructor could communicate and engage in dialogue outside of class. Thus, in addition to the desire to have students become familiar with technology and engage in discussions outside of class, colleagues and familiarity with listservs were influential in the decision to use academic listservs.

4.   "What do you believe are the disadvantages of using listservs?"

Although academic listservs appear to be the answer to everyone's teaching problems, there are disadvantages to them. A fourth of the instructors stated that the time demand of the listserv was its greatest disadvantage. They pointed out that, even though they liked the idea that having a listserv increased their availability, they were aware that they were always "on call" and were obligated to answer students' questions immediately. Answering a question could take anywhere from five minutes to almost a half of an hour, depending on the nature of the question and how in-depth the answer needed to be. If there were several questions, an instructor could use up quite a bit of time in one sitting. Also, especially in writing-intensive courses, the listserv generated a great deal of mail, and it was difficult at times to keep up with it.

Another disadvantage cited was the lack of student access to the needed technology. Several instructors used the phrase "real or imagined access problems" in describing reasons why students do not participate on the class listserv. The "real" problems prohibit students from accessing the list, whereas instructors commented that "imagined" problems were employed by the more techno-phobic or less motivated students. Two professors voiced their concern over the creation of technological "haves and have nots." Due to time constraints caused by family or jobs, many students who did not have access to computers at home were unable to find the time to get to a computer lab. Often, when they did find the time, the labs were overcrowded and they had to wait for a machine to become available. Computer and Internet illiteracy was also a problem. A task that would normally take about three minutes would turn into an hour's worth of frustration. Students sensed their valuable time was not being used to the best advantage.

However, this argument was countered by a professor who said there was a technological lack of self-discipline among students. He pointed out that the students did not seem to want to learn how to use the technology unless they were forced to do so by instructors. Students themselves acknowledged this phenomenon on one of the observed classes' listservs:

> *Overall, I think that the listserv was intimidating but it did give students a reason to get involved in computers (which many people avoid until they absolutely have to get involved).... Some students are not motivated to come to campus and use the computers unless they are already here attending a class. (Student 7)*

Another professor noted that students who either had the resources to buy a computer for their home or lived on campus and were able to go to the computer labs during "off hours" had the advantage over commuting students who had to make time to go to the labs.

Another disadvantage cited by professors was the inappropriate use of the medium by students. This inappropriate use took many forms. One form was the way students were too self-revealing due to the false sense of anonymity and "safety" of the list. Students may have revealed information about themselves that they would not have been comfortable revealing in a face-to-face situation. Students also were "suggestive," even lewd at times, in their postings. This issue has serious implications because it could be construed as sexual harassment, especially if a student's posting receives responses with unwelcome sexual overtones to them.

"Flaming," along with sexual innuendoes, was such a problem on one list that the professor refused to use academic listservs in the future in conjunction with her teaching. "Flaming" is an Internet term that could be defined as an irrationally nasty post, usually written in anger, regarding or in response to someone else. Flaming, professors believed, usually occurred when students resorted to using opinions rather than arguments in their postings. If the topic being discussed was a sensitive one, students were passionate about their opinions and wanted to be heard. However, because they were unable to read their classmates' body language, many misunderstandings erupted.

A final disadvantage reported by the instructors was that students did not seem to understand the purpose of the listserv. Instructors voiced their frustration regarding students not following instructions regarding posting to the list, often sending papers to the professor's e-mail address rather than the listserv, or being too informal in their writing (e.g., using all lower cases as is frequently found in chat rooms or not being diligent about grammar). Others said that instead of engaging in discussion, their students suffered from the "me-too" syndrome where a student would say, "I agree with what has already been said." An issue for some instructors was students posting social messages more often than academic messages. Finally, it was often difficult to follow the discussion of a particular topic because students would not stick to the subject heading and go off on many different tangents and digressions. It should be noted, however, that this problem occurs on all e-mail-generated lists, whether academic, professional, or recreational, but can be solved if a threaded discussion format is available.

In summary, the most frequently cited disadvantages of academic listservs are the time demands involved in creating materials for dissemination, training of students, and reading the volume of mail the list generates. Other disadvantages include the inappropriate use of the list by students who do not understand the intended purpose of the list.

5.   "Will you continue to use listservs in your teaching?"

In spite of all of the disadvantages of using a listserv, all but one of the 20 instructors indicated they would continue to use listservs. The one dissenting professor was very dissatisfied with her students' online behavior, which included flaming and suggestive comments in particular. Although she sees the potential of having a list, she indicated she would not use it again in conjunction with her teaching.

6.   "Is participation on the listserv required or optional for your students?"

6a.   "How much weight in your grading do you give to listserv participation?"

Surprisingly, these questions seemed to confuse most of the interviewed faculty, and some were unable to answer them. Even though more than half (n = 13) said the list was a requirement, only six specified a specific grading weight and included online participation as part of their class participation grade. Participation (in class and online, combined) accounted for anywhere from 10% to 30% of a final course grade. The symbiotic relationship between the two venues was noted by several of the instructors. They believed that students who did not feel comfortable talking in class could make up for it online — a particular benefit for shy or non-native English speaking students.

To summarize, most faculty make their lists a course requirement, however, they are not supporting this requirement with any grade weighting. Those who do designate a grade weight for online participation combine it with in-class participation for a total of 10% to 30% of the final grade.

Listserv Impact on Teaching

1.   "In what ways has using a listserv changed your teaching methods?"

Over a third of the professors did not believe that having the academic listserv had changed their teaching methods. Two professors remarked that it was too soon to tell if it had really changed their methods because they were so new to using the listserv.

For those that stated it had changed their methods, the primary response was that it had placed less of an emphasis on the physical classroom for them. They mentioned there was an added dimension to their teaching because the classroom walls no longer restrained them. One professor commented that her lecture time was more focused and that she could "move through things faster by not taking up as much class time" on the less important course topics (Professor 4). Because of the listserv, she could introduce material she wanted her students to learn, but she did not need to use in-class time to review it — thus saving in-class discussion for what she considered to be the more important course topics. For another professor, watching students develop their own understanding of the course content caused him to rethink the teaching-learning process and to have a "growing belief that classes create knowledge" (Professor 13). As a result, he put more of an emphasis on collaborative learning instead of a teacher-centered approach. Another said he was able to refer to the listserv discussion and resources during class as a means of facilitating student learning. Finally, several professors either sent prepared materials to their students via the listserv that they would have previously put on reserve in the library, or relied less on reserved readings because of the online dialogues.

Although more a change in perception on the part of the professor than a method change, many professors asserted that having the list changed their teaching because they were more available to their students. One professor noted that because he and the students had more contact hours with each other and were able to get to know each other on a personal level, the class dynamic became richer.   Another professor indicated that students seemed less restrained to speak in class. In essence, the online interaction impacted in-class interaction forcing professors to change how they interact with students.

In summary, over a third stated the listserv did not have an effect on their teaching methods. For the remaining faculty, the most frequently cited changes were the expansion of learning beyond the physical classroom, an increased availability to students, and a shift away from needing to cover all course topics during class sessions.

2.   "In what ways has using the listserv affected your quality of teaching?"

Although four professors did not believe the listserv had impacted the quality of their teaching, either positively or negatively, most professors stated that the quality of *learning* had been increased by the listserv. They surmised that students were more seriously engaged in the subject matter and came to class better prepared for the day's lesson. One writing instructor who used in-class group work extensively stated, "I like the feeling of knowing students have extra time to work on assignments [that previously they would have only been able to work on in class]" (Professor 3). Additionally, they thought the listserv improved learning because it enabled more collaborative learning to take place. As previously mentioned, several instructors believed that having the listserv improved learning because they were able to get a feel for student understanding and could make any needed clarifications right away. Likewise, if something was not working, the instructors were able to make midcourse corrections.

Two professors stated that the availability created by the listserv improved the quality of their teaching because they had far more individual student contact than they had ever had previously and that teacher-student communication was vastly improved. However, one professor who taught several sections of a writing-intensive course, noted feeling guilty and irresponsible for not reading every single posting to the listservs, even though he would always respond to mail sent directly to him. The term "richer" was used to describe how the teacher-student interaction had impacted the quality of their teaching.

In summary, four professors out of the 20 interviewed do not believe the listserv impacted their quality of teaching. The rest of the professors stated that the quality of learning, rather than their teaching, was impacted positively by the list because their students were more engaged in the material and better prepared for class. Also, because of the list, professors were able to gauge student understanding of the material and make any necessary corrections. Finally, two professors stated that student learning was improved because of the increase in teacher-student contact time.

Successful and Unsuccessful Listserv Strategies
Throughout the interviewing process, professors repeatedly asked for strategies to improve the quality of their listservs. They wanted to know what other professors were doing in order to make it work. Approximately a third of the professors did not have any list strategies they considered to be successful.

There appears to be a fine line between a strategy being successful or unsuccessful. What worked fabulously for one professor would fail miserably for another. Certain factors such as class size, group dynamics, course topic, and time available to students seemed to have had a profound impact on the lists. For example, a graduate course with less than ten students during a regular semester was very active in their discussions, while an undergraduate course with six students during a summer session basically used the list to turn in their assignments. No discussion regarding their practicums or class topics took place.

1.   "What listserv strategies have you employed that you felt were successful?"

Several instructors gave their students specific assignments regarding the list such as posting comments on the list about the class topic, providing a menu of questions to write about or respond to, posting their current event topic before class, or simply throwing out pointed questions and comments. Once the discussion began, the professors kept their personal contributions to a minimum while continuing to monitor the list. Other professors used incentives such as extra credit or participation points to encourage participation in the online discussion. A couple of professors had students grade themselves on their participation at the mid-semester point and again at the end of the semester. This enabled the students to see how important their contributions were, not only to their final grade in the course, but also, to their classmates' learning. The grades the students gave themselves tended to be in line with what the professor would have assigned to them. Finally, several instructors subscribed their students to the class listserv themselves, which enabled students to be online within the first or second week of classes. This strategy helped counteract some students' tendency to put off joining the list until later in the semester. In several lists that I observed, students sometimes did not subscribe until nearly the end of the semester (if they subscribed at all).

One professor identified an important listserv strategy, namely, that professors should give students enough lead-time to read any announcements or assignments posted on the list. A professor could not post an announcement the night before class and expect everyone to have read it by the next day. This strategy also has implications for those courses where students post summaries of their current event topics before class so that their classmates are better prepared for in class discussion. Unfortunately, the need for early posting was not always conveyed, or technological difficulties arose that prevented timely delivery:

> *Hi everyone! Please forgive me for not posting this listing yesterday. Our server here at work was down all day so I was unable to log on to the system... (Student 6).*

This student had posted the summary of her current events topic on the day she was to present it. Only two people in the class had been able to read the summary before the student's presentation. In another course observed, several students posted summaries of their presentations the night before class. Again, only a few students had been able to read their postings and, as a result, the students did not get a lot of feedback from their classmates.

Thus, the key to the success of an academic listserv seemed to be clarity, focus, purpose, and, as many professors described it, a "carrot on a stick." The instructors who had a successful listserv gave specific assignments related to the list, graded online participation, subscribed their students to the list, and gave their students enough lead time to read their listserv mail.

2. "What listserv strategies have you employed that you felt were unsuccessful?"

Even though three professors stated that all of their strategies had been successful, almost a third of the remaining faculty appeared to have similar problems with their listservs. The overriding theme among the unsuccessful strategies was the lack of expectation for participation being conveyed to the students. Six instructors declared their surprise that the students did not spontaneously begin to talk to each other on the list. They had expected students to talk without needing any guidance or directions from the instructor. Other professors did not *require* posting, so the students did not have any incentive to participate. Other professors required participation, but did not enforce the requirement in any way.

A strategy that seemed to have gone wrong was the idea of posting or having students post topics for debate. The strategy of posting topics for debate could be considered akin to the strategy of posing pointed or controversial questions to the list, which happened to work very well. In two classes, the posting of topics for debate, which the professors provided, nearly ground discussions to a halt. Students stopped dialoguing with each other, and only responded to the debate topics as if answering a question on a quiz or test. The expected debate between students never transpired. In another class where the students were to provide the topics, the discussion never materialized because students either did not post a topic to debate or classmates did not respond to the posting. When students were asked why this phenomenon might have taken place, one student stated:

> *I think the listserv has become less interpersonal as it was last semester. I think the debate topics are nice but they don't really debate anything. We either agree or disagree on one of the topics. There are little comments made on how other people respond. I don't think we have to change anyone's mind on their personal view but I think last semester you made the listserv like we as a class and individuals were trying to broaden each other's mind with our own personal views... (Student 7)*

Another class used case studies as a strategy with mixed results. Like the "topic of debate" strategy, the students were responding to the situation rather than to each other. It appears that the less elaborate method of simply posing a pointed or controversial question worked much better to elicit debate and dialogue than the more elaborate case study or topic for debate that involves providing background information to set up the context. Another advantage of a question rather than a debate topic was that it took less time to prepare a sentence or two than several paragraphs, and the questions were more spontaneous with what was happening in the discussion, the class, or the world.

However, even posing questions did not always create the desired effect of a give-and-take dialogue. On several of the observed lists, the students and the professors gave up trying to get a dialogue started. In fact, one of the lists basically stopped functioning about halfway through the semester due to lack of participation. There were several factors that may have contributed to this. The first factor was that the professor relied on the students to bring up the topics to debate discuss. Except to answer questions and disseminate information, the professor was not an overt presence on the list. Secondly, the professor stated that the students also did not participate during in-class discussions. The major factor may have been that the professor was teaching this particular course for the first time. Interestingly, in another course taught by this professor, the list was so active that the students requested that it remain open after the semester ended for them to continue their discussions, which they did for several months into the following semester before it also faded out. The difference in the level of success of the two listservs could be attributed to the subject matter and to current world events that related to that particular course.

In summary, the primary strategy cited as being an unsuccessful one was the failure to convey to students the expectation for their participation. Additionally, professors who relied on students to develop discussion topics, or who used topics for debate and/or case studies, were dissatisfied with the results.

Emerging Themes

There appears to be a love-frustration relationship between instructors and the academic listservs. Repeatedly during the interviews, faculty members voiced the sentiment that they believe the listserv could be a powerful and potent tool in their teaching (some have experienced the benefits already), but they don't know how to glean the full benefits from it. Two themes emerged that may be the root of the frustration.

The first theme that emerged was a general lack of predetermined teaching goals among professors who feel their listserv attempts are unsuccessful. Although they had the goal of using the listserv as a discussion tool, an overwhelming complaint was that the students "don't talk to each other." The frustrated professors had not examined how to use the tool to achieve course goals but rather had put the cart before the horse, so to speak. The purpose of the listserv and the expectation for students to post messages was not explicitly provided to the students and, as a result, the students did not perceive a clear-cut reason to dialogue with each other. The few instructors who viewed the lists as an avenue of collaborative learning were satisfied with the discussions that were taking place online. In fact, one professor actually was overwhelmed by the amount of dialogue taking place and, about mid-semester, gave up trying to read all of the postings. For professors who were satisfied with student participation, therefore, the listserv was merely an extension of the activity that took place in the traditional classroom.

The second theme that emerged was that instructors would be unable to tap into the full potential of online discussions until the issues of "real and imagined access" to computers were resolved. If faculty members believe they have to spend valuable time teaching their students how to use the technology or do not believe the support from information services is keeping up with their needs, they will jettison this teaching tool. In fact, Edwards and Shaffer (1999) found faculty are reluctant to try listservs if they perceive a lack of institutional and technological support for the investment of faculty time and if they do not have confidence that the investment will result in improved student learning. Likewise, students feeling overwhelmed by techno-stress and receiving conflicting instructions that do not seem to resolve the technological problems they are encountering may eventually give up, in some cases seriously jeopardizing their grade.

To summarize, faculty recognize the potential power of the listserv to improve student learning when included in their teaching. They understand that it can be used for topical discussions, to gauge student learning, and as means of communication that expands the classroom environment. However, most of those interviewed for this study stated that they were unable to tap into the listserv's potential. Two themes emerged from this study. The majority of the faculty did not have predetermined teaching goals regarding their course listserv. As a result, students did not engage in the expected discussions, and some students used the listserv inappropriately. The second theme was that instructors have a concern regarding the time involved in having the listserv and whether the listserv requirement was inadvertently punishing students who do not have ready access to the required technology and the skills to use it efficiently. Despite the concerns, 19 out of the 20 professors interviewed indicated they would continue to use listservs because of their potential to positively impact student learning.

References

Batson, T. & Bass, R. (1996). Primacy of process: Teaching and learning in the computer age. *Change,* (March/April), 42-47.

Breen, R., Lindsay, R., Jenkins, A., & Smith, P. (2001). The role of information and communication technologies in a university learning environment. *Studies in Higher Education, 26,* 95-114.

Bump, J. (1990). Radical changes in class discussion using networked computers. *Computers and the Humanities, 24,* 49-65.

Davis, M. & Ralph, S. (2001). Stalling the learning process: Group dynamics in cyberspace. *Studies in the Education of Adults, 33,* 217-230.

Dewey, J. (1900). *The School and society and the child and the curriculum.* Chicago, IL: The University of Chicago Press.

Edwards, S. & Shaffer, C. (1999). An analysis of a course-oriented electronic mailing list. *Computer Science Education, 9,* 8-22.

Gizzi, M. (1995). *Cyperspace and the political science classroom: Reflections on using the Internet and on-line conferencing.* Paper presented at the 1995 Annual Meeting of the American Political Science Association, Chicago, IL. (ERIC Document Reproduction Service No. ED 392 695).

Grassie, W. (1995). *Computer-mediated communications as an enhancement of the core-curriculum at Temple University.* Intellectual Heritage Program. Philadelphia, PA: Temple University.

Hardy, V., Hodgson, V., & McConnell, D. (1994). Computer conferencing: A new medium for investigating issues in gender and learning. *Higher Education, 28,* 403-418.

Harrington, H. (1993). The essence of technology and the education of teachers. *Journal of Teacher Education, 44,* 5-15.

Karayan, S. & Crowe, J. (1997). Student perceptions of electronic discussion groups. *Technological Horizons in Education Journal, 24*(9), 69-71. Retrieved from http://www.thejournal.com.

McFann, J. (2000). Correlates of listserv usage for traditional and nontraditional university students. (Doctoral dissertation, Temple University). *Dissertation Abstracts International, 61,* 1293.

McMahen, C. & Dawson, A. (1995). The design and implementation of environmental computer-mediated communication (CMC) projects. *Journal of Research on Computing in Education, 27,* 318-335.

Miller, M. (1991). Electronic conferencing in the networked classroom. *College Teaching, 39*(4), 136-139.

Morrison, J. (1993). Empowerment by technology: Using electronic dialogue to promote critical thinking. *Business Education Forum, 47*(3), 13-15.

networked computer. This reduced the labor intensiveness previously associated with PSI while training students to learn through distance education. The combination of PSI and the Internet produced an effective instructional strategy, reviving Keller's (1968) original PSI model while setting the stage both for more advanced PSI research and Internet-based instruction.

Background

In this chapter, we examine the merger of a long-established instructional method, Fred Keller's Personalized System of Instruction (PSI), with a modern technological medium, the Internet, to create a more flexible learning environment for university students. Keller and colleagues conducted the first PSI class in 1964 at the University of Brasilia. Five features distinguished it from a traditional lecture-based course: (a) students were permitted to move through the course at their own pace, (b) students were required to master each unit before proceeding to the next one, (c) lectures were used as vehicles for motivation rather than as sources of necessary information, (d) stress was placed on the written word in teacher-student communication, and (e) proctors were used to provide testing, feedback, tutoring, and personalized interaction with students (Keller, 1968).

By the late 1970s, PSI's effectiveness in a variety of classroom and training settings was evident. Results from empirical studies, the establishment of the Center for Personalized Instruction at Georgetown University in 1973, the *PSI Newsletter*, and the *Journal of Personalized Instruction* led Keller and others to believe that PSI would thrive, thus reducing use of the traditional lecture-based method. However, this was not the case. Multiple problems inherent within the PSI system discouraged instructors from employing it within their courses. Specifically, both instructors and students found the course to be too labor intensive (Sherman, 1974). Unlike traditional lecture-based courses with comprehensive examinations, PSI students were required to maintain a steady rate of studying in order to achieve mastery on the frequent quizzes. Consequently, there were a high number of student withdrawals in PSI courses. In addition, because students were permitted to self-pace, many procrastinated and were not able to complete the course (Robin, 1976). Instructors and proctors struggled with the amount of work necessary to personalize instruction for each student. For example, the frequent creation, distribution, and grading of quizzes, the provision of feedback, the constant need for record keeping, and the training of proctors were rigorous and time consuming. This often resulted in the neglect of many students in need of assistance (Born & Moore, 1978). Inevitably, the problems associated with PSI led to ineffective course modifications by various instructors.

Can teaching a PSI course through the Internet mitigate the amount of student and instructor labor while enhancing the learning environment? In traditional lecture-based courses, students are required to attend lectures, meet with their instructors, and take examinations—all at a specified place and time. Similarly, in previous PSI courses, students were required to meet with their proctors for quizzing and provision of feedback during scheduled office hours. The initial use of computers in PSI courses required space and time obligations from students who had to take quizzes at computer laboratories during specified hours of the day (Hantula, Boyd, & Crowell, 1989). An aspect of the course discussed in this chapter that was novel to typical university students and instructors was the elimination of both spatial and temporal limitations.

By using a server-based template program such as Blackboard (created by Blackboard, Inc., Washington DC) and the Internet, it is possible to provide frequent automatic and asynchronous testing and grading, and extensive and immediate feedback. Another advantage of the Internet is that it allows students to interact with the instructor in a virtual environment in which there are no longer space and time limitations. It was therefore predicted that teaching a PSI course through the Internet would significantly reduce instructor/proctor responsibilities and increase instructor-student interaction. To test these hypotheses, two iterations of a PSI Internet-based undergraduate Social Psychology course were taught by one of the authors of this chapter, Erica Davis, at Temple University (Fall 2001 and Spring 2002).

Kock, McQueen, and Scott's (1997) multiple-cycle Action Research (AR) model was used to evaluate each course. As shown in Figure 1, the model is made up of Susman and Evered's (1978) five stages of action research. First, in the diagnosing stage, the researcher and client must identify and define the problem or process in need of improvement. Second, in the action planning stage, the researcher and client consider alternative solutions/interventions to address the problem. Third, in the action-taking stage, the researcher and client decide on the most effective course of action from the previous stage and begin implementation. Fourth, in the evaluation stage, the researcher and client examine the consequences of their action. Last, in the specifying learning stage, the researcher identifies the more significant findings while adding to the knowledge base derived after each research cycle. Two AR cycles were employed for this study; one cycle for each course.

First Iteration

Participants

Twenty-one students originally registered for the course. Two students never entered the course and eventually dropped out, another student left after the second week because of her frustration with the Blackboard system, the fourth withdrawal was due to personal problems and an inability to enter the Blackboard system, and the fifth student dropped out midway through the course without providing a reason. The 16 remaining students gave their consent for the instructor to collect and record data on their achievement and attitudes for research purposes, but only 14 course evaluation forms were returned at the end of the semester. Of the 14 students, 11 were females and three were males. Their ages ranged from 21 to 50 years, and the majority of students were juniors and seniors. Most students were psychology majors and education majors. Students identified themselves as White (11), African-American (2), or West Indian (1). All of the students owned a computer and reported that they used it regularly for both online and offline functions.

Figure 1: The AR cycle (After Kock et al., 1997)

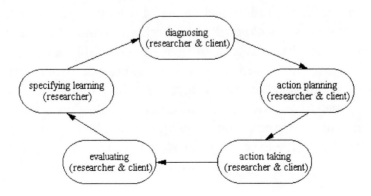

Setting

The course was created in Blackboard, a server-based template program for online courses. Upon entering the course, students were presented with an introductory message outlining the course content and PSI structure, with directions to click on the "Course Information" button. Six documents were posted under this button: an introductory message, information about obtaining help with Blackboard, an explanation of PSI, the required text and articles for the course, and a course structure document with the quiz mastery and examination due dates.

Course Structure

Lectures were posted by 10:00 a.m. every Friday throughout the semester. Students were instructed to read and study the lectures, the assigned modules in the text, and the assigned academic articles. From Tuesday until Thursday students were required to take a timed, unit quiz in Blackboard. Those who reached the set criterion during the specified days received bonus points towards an examination (Lloyd, 1971). Students who passed a unit quiz by Tuesday or Wednesday received two bonus points, while students who achieved mastery on a unit quiz by Thursday at midnight received 1 bonus point. Overall, the accumulation of 10 bonus points towards the midterm and 12 bonus points towards the final was possible. With these bonus points, a student's examination score could be elevated an entire grade or more. Those students who did not achieve mastery on a quiz after their initial attempt were instructed to retake the unit quiz sometime between Friday and Tuesday, without the possibility of earning bonus points.

Students were also required to participate in weekly asynchronous class discussions posted on Blackboard. Although not required, students were encouraged to e-mail the instructor with questions regarding all aspects of the course. Similar to lecture-based courses, time was designated during the week by the instructor to check e-mail and respond to student questions. She generally refrained from answering e-mails after 11:00 PM during the week and not at all from Friday evening to Sunday evening. Overall, student achievement was evaluated by the mean score of the weekly quizzes (20%), a midterm examination (30%), a final examination (35%), and participation in class discussions (15%).

Readings

Students were assigned weekly readings from both the course textbook, *Exploring Social Psychology* (Myers, 2000), and six articles that could be found in most academic libraries (Byrne, 1961; Darley & Latane, 1968; Hovland & Sears, 1940; Isen & Levin, 1972; Lapiere, 1934; Milgram, 1963). All lectures were posted under the "Course Documents" button and were made available according to the dates on the syllabus. The lectures were 7 to 10 single-spaced pages. Each lecture included thought-provoking questions, diagrams, and examples to assist with the demonstration of complex concepts. All graphics were simple, with minimal color and style, so that even the most archaic computer and/or Internet browser would be able to download them.

Nielson's (1999) criteria for web design were used as a guide for creating all course web pages: ease of use, minimal download time, frequent updating, and high quality content. For effective lecture design, Hantula's (1998) presentation strategies for online lectures were applied: (a) major points were broken down into small, easily read paragraph units, (b) paragraphs were no longer than the computer screen, (c) direct questions about the material were presented after each major concept, (d) white space was used to separate and highlight material, (e) different text positions as well as colors and font sizes were included for emphasis and variety, and (f) direct requests for responding, such as links to other websites, were incorporated into the lectures.

Teaching effectiveness is enhanced if students actively engage with the course material (Keller, 1968; Skinner, 1968). Links embedded within the lectures required students to respond to the technology, thus increasing the probability of maintaining their interest and attention while improving learning and retention (Tudor, 1995). In one lecture, for example, students were able to click on a link for Zimbardo's website (http://www.prisonexp.org), which contained a detailed explanation and a slideshow of his prison experiment (Zimbardo, 1999). By viewing Zimbardo's extensive website, students were able to study social psychological concepts through a more dynamic and interactive medium. Some links were added to spark student interest in a topic or to provide external information not presented in the lecture or textbook, such as the biography of Stanley Milgram (http://www.stanleymilgram.com).

Unit Quizzes

Weekly unit quizzes were usually made up of 10 multiple-choice questions with occasional true/false or open-ended questions. The questions required students to recognize and identify concepts. Half of the questions were based on the lecture and half of the questions were based on the textbook. When articles were assigned, one or two questions were included that were based on the articles. Students were permitted to have their notes and texts open during each quiz, but were advised to study prior to each quiz. Quizzes were timed, allowing students 20 minutes to fill in and submit their answers. A descending clock was located at the bottom of each quiz.

Blackboard automatically recorded the total amount of time spent taking each quiz. The number of correct responses was automatically recorded in the automated gradebook and provided students with their score immediately after they submitted their answers. To prevent cheating, students were only permitted to enter each quiz one time so that it was impossible to enter the quiz, print it out and return later to fill in the answers. Students were required to obtain at least 7 out of 10 questions correct on each quiz to show their mastery of the subject matter. If students failed to reach the designated criterion on their initial attempt, they were instructed to contact the instructor via e-mail so that their initial attempt could be cleared and they could retake the quiz without a mastery criterion. These students were not given the opportunity to earn bonus points.

Examinations

The midterm examination consisted of 30 multiple-choice questions, four of which were taken from the quizzes worth two points each, and six essay questions (with students required to answer five) worth eight points each. Students were given a three-day examination period, but once they started the multiple-choice part of the examination they were required to complete and submit it within two hours. The final examination consisted of 35 multiple-choice questions worth two points each (none of which were on the quizzes), and short essay questions worth six points each where students were again instructed to answer 5 out of the 6 questions. Rather than including the essay questions within Blackboard, they were e-mailed to the students five days before the due date allowing students as much time as necessary to provide well thought out and grammatically correct answers. Students were given more than an hour to complete the multiple-choice section of the examination.

The multiple-choice questions in both the midterm and final examinations required students to apply their knowledge of the material, rather than to simply define terminology as they did for the unit quizzes. For example, students would be provided with a brief scenario and were asked to identify the social psychological concept represented in the scenario. Similar to the unit quizzes, students were permitted to have their notes and books open during both examinations. It was suggested, however, that they study beforehand so that they did not waste valuable time sifting through their materials during the examination.

Discussions

During the class discussions scheduled throughout the semester, forum questions based on the assigned article or the weekly topic were posted under the "Discussion Board." These mandatory, asynchronous, discussion forums gave students the opportunity to comment on the topics and articles while interacting with other members of the class. The instructor and a teaching assistant added their own comments to facilitate postings and to clarify concepts. After every forum, the teaching assistant would give each student a grade based on the amount and quality of their participation.

Second Iteration

Participants

Twenty-five students originally registered for the course. One student never entered the course and eventually dropped out, another student withdrew after the third week because she was leaving school, and the third student left after the midterm because of health reasons. Of the 22 remaining students, 21 gave their consent for the instructor to collect and record data on their achievement and attitudes towards the course for research purposes. All 21 background surveys and evaluation forms were returned to the teaching assistant at the end of the semester. Of the 21 students, 19 were females and two were males. Their ages ranged from 18 to 48 years, and most were seniors. Almost half of the students were psychology majors. Other majors included speech pathology, film, computer science, therapeutic recreation, education, and business. Students identified themselves as White (10), African-American (6), Asian Indian (2), or Hispanic (1). Two students did not reveal their ethnicity. Of the 21 students, 18 owned a computer and reported that they used it regularly for both online and offline functions.

Setting

The course was once again created in Blackboard on the Temple University server. Although Temple still implemented the same version of Blackboard, a number of improvements on the system were promised (e.g., better downloading of images and less time needed to take Blackboard offline for troubleshooting).

Course Structure

After examining the results of student performance and student reactions to the course from the first iteration, significant modifications were made to the second iteration. The most noteworthy change was the self-pacing feature. Students were now permitted to self-pace throughout the entire course (after they completed the first practice unit) so that they would have more freedom to schedule their quizzes. There were only two necessary deadlines: one for the first six units, which included the midterm exam that needed to be completed by a certain date and time or the student would earn an F; and one for the last six units, which included the final exam that needed to be taken by a certain date and time or the student would receive an F. The recommended schedule included suggested due dates for readings, quizzes, and discussion forums, and was posted to assist students with self-pacing. Consistent with the previous iteration, each unit began on a Friday and ended on the subsequent Friday. According to the recommended schedule, lectures were to be read between Friday and Tuesday, and the quiz was to be mastered between Tuesday and the following Friday.

A second change was the increase in the amount of class e-mails sent by the instructor over the course of the semester. Because some students chose to follow the recommended schedule while others self-paced according to their own schedules, it was necessary for the instructor to keep meticulous records of each student's progress. E-mails, including information about the number of unit quizzes mastered by each student, were sent to the entire class every couple of weeks, with a total of six e-mails sent throughout the semester. This not only increased the amount of instructor-student interaction, but also demonstrated that the instructor was knowledgeable regarding each student's progress. Students were encouraged to e-mail the instructor regarding questions on any aspect of the course, but as in the previous iteration, she generally refrained from answering e-mails after 11:00 p.m. during the week and not at all from Friday evening to Sunday evening.

Another significant change from the first to the second iteration was the elevation in mastery criterion. The first iteration required 7 out of 10 correct answers on a quiz as an indication of mastery; the second iteration initially required 9 out of 10 correct answers (for the first quiz) and then 8 out of 10 correct answers as an indication of mastery, thus guaranteeing all students a high quiz average of eight or above. Asynchronous class discussions were again posted, but in the second iteration, there was more of an emphasis on participation in class discussions and less emphasis on quiz performance. Consistent with the first iteration, students obtained bonus points towards their midterm or final examinations for timely mastery of unit quizzes. Students were required to complete each quiz by the suggested Friday date (posted on a recommended schedule) in order to earn bonus points. Unlike the previous iteration, however, students were given an extra day to obtain bonus points for each unit. If a student mastered a quiz before the recommended date on the first attempt, the student obtained two bonus points regardless of the day of the week. Ten bonus points for both the midterm and final examinations were possible, which gave students the chance to raise their examination scores an entire grade.

Overall, student achievement was evaluated by the average score of the weekly quizzes (15%), a midterm examination (30%), a final examination (35%), and participation in class discussions (20%).

Readings

Both the content units, which consisted of the assigned modules in the textbook, and the lectures, which the instructor had designed for the previous iteration, were used for the second iteration.

Unit Quizzes

The unit quizzes were again posted in Blackboard under the "Assignments" button and consisted of 10 multiple-choice questions with occasional true/false or open-ended questions that asked students to identify and define concepts. Many of the questions were the same or similar to the questions that comprised the quizzes in the previous iteration. Consistent with the previous iteration, students were given 20 minutes to complete the quiz and were permitted to have their notes and texts open. If a student failed a quiz, he/she was required to inform the instructor via e-mail so that his or her initial attempt could be cleared in the electronic gradebook and he/she could retake the quiz. Self-pacing was not officially employed until after the first unit quiz (the practice quiz) so that the first quiz score did not count toward the overall quiz average. In addition, students were not required to take a quiz on the last content unit because the due date would have been too close to the final examination.

Examinations

In general, the examination questions were similar to or the same as those in the examinations from the previous iteration. The midterm examination consisted of 30 multiple-choice questions (worth two points each) and six essay questions (with students required to answer five) worth eight points each. The final examination consisted of 35 multiple-choice questions worth two points each, and six essay questions (with students required to answer five) worth six points each. Students had to log in using the security password and could enter the multiple-choice part of the examinations only once, which required them to complete it upon entry. As soon as the essays and password were e-mailed to them, students had three days to finish both parts of the examination.

Discussions

Discussions were listed on the recommended schedule for various content units throughout the semester. Students were required to post responses to questions that had been posted by the instructor to the discussion forum and to other student's comments after reading through the corresponding content unit. To increase participation in the discussions, students were reminded — both with an announcement on the course website and with e-mails — that new forums were posted and that participation was mandatory. For every forum, the teaching assistant monitored the discussion, answered student questions, recorded the names of students who participated, and graded their comments on clarity, insight and frequency.

Results and Discussion

During both AR iterations of the course, a formative evaluation was conducted to diagnose problems and to make immediate improvements. At the end of each course, a summative evaluation was conducted to assess overall effectiveness (Scriven, 1967). Kirkpatrick (1976) outlined four criteria for training evaluations: reaction criteria, learning criteria, behavioral criteria, and results criteria. In this study, behavioral criteria were examined in terms of attendance and completion, learning criteria in terms of performance on quizzes and examinations, reaction criteria in terms of students' attitudes toward the course and material and usability of computer-based programs (e.g., how well the components of the program work together) (Rubin, 1994). Overall, the results of this study indicate that PSI taught through the Internet was an effective instructional strategy for yielding high student performance and satisfaction in these two undergraduate social psychology courses.

To summarize, there were three structural differences between the first and second iteration of the course. First, students in the first iteration were permitted to self-pace only within the weekly four-day testing periods, while students in the second iteration were permitted to self-pace through all of the content units with only two examination deadlines. Second, to increase instructor-student interaction, frequent e-mails were sent to the entire class that included updates of each student's achievement. Third, to improve student quiz performance, the mastery criterion for the quizzes was raised from 7 out of 10 correct answers for the first iteration, to 8 out of 10 correct answers for the second iteration.

As expected, the labor-intensive problems previously associated with PSI were mitigated. For the first iteration, the instructor found the course to be labor intensive during pre-course preparation, but the amount of time and energy needed to maintain the course was not overwhelming throughout the rest of the semester. Similar to an instructor preparing a lecture-based course for the second time, the pre-course preparation for the second iteration was minimal. Students in the first iteration also did not report a heavy workload. These students were able to master all of the content units in a timely fashion. More students in the second iteration, however, had difficulty managing their schedules and passing units in a timely fashion. This was due to a higher mastery criterion and fewer quiz deadlines. Second iteration students, however, were still able to complete all of the content units by the end of the semester.

Overall, students in both iterations obtained high course grades and performed well on the midterm and final examinations. Satisfaction with the course, from both the students' and instructor's perspectives, was high for most of the course components with only minimal variation. There were, however, some notable performance differences between the first and second iterations in re-quiz frequencies, timeliness in mastering units, bonus points earned, attitudes towards the instructor, and the instructor's assessment. To determine whether the modifications made in the second iteration were effective in enhancing the course, a comparison of student performance and satisfaction is presented.

Student Performance

Course Grades
Similar to the course participants in the study discussed by Keller (1968), the majority of the students in both iterations earned grades in the A-B range as shown in Figures 2a and 2b. Consistent with Kulik, Jaksa, and Kulik's (1978) review (which compared the effectiveness of PSI courses taught with and without instructor deadlines), the grade distribution between the two iterations did not differ significantly. With the implementation of a higher mastery criterion and self-pacing with only minimal deadlines in the second iteration, 28.6 % of the class obtained scores in the C and D range. Although none of the second iteration students failed the course, a higher percentage of students obtained a B- or above in the first iteration, when there were more stringent deadlines.

Minimal quiz deadlines in the second iteration gave students more freedom to procrastinate, which resulted in poor scheduling by some of the students. Further, because some students in the second iteration did not take their quizzes in a timely manner, they were required to cram before the examination. Cramming prevented them from having enough time to post comments in the discussion board and from earning bonus points. Without the bonus points and

Figure 2a: Course Grades and Withdrawals (W) for Students in the First Iteration of the AR Cycle

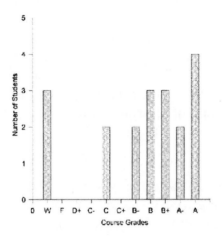

without especially high discussion-board grades, high course grades were not earned. Implementation of weekly deadlines in the first iteration was successful in reducing procrastination, but it limited students' ability to schedule quizzes around external pressures. Perhaps the most efficient way to reduce procrastination, while simultaneously improving course grades, would be to implement a moderate pacing schedule with quarterly due dates (after every three weeks of the course) (Wesp & Ford, 1982).

Figure 2b: Course Grades and Withdrawals (W) for Students in the Second Iteration of the AR Cycle

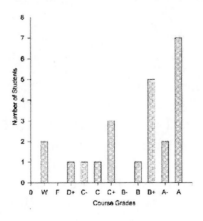

The majority of students in both iterations received high course grades, regardless of the number of attempts they made on each quiz or how long it took them to master each unit, as long as they did not procrastinate. Because mastery was required for progression through the material, students had to continually perform well to stay in the course. As a result, the inflated grade distribution more realistically represents student achievement and does not adversely affect student satisfaction. If the primary purpose of a course is to enable student mastery of the subject matter, rather than to challenge their overall intellectual ability, then PSI is the appropriate instructional method.

Withdrawal Rate

The withdrawal rates for both classes were moderately low at less than 20%. Although these percentages fall in the bottom of the withdrawal rate range of 14% to 25% reported in Robin's (1976) review of PSI studies, the students in both of these courses were not forced to withdraw from the class because of their inability to master units by a set date (e.g., Malott & Svinicki, 1969). Rather, students withdrew because of technical problems, for personal reasons, for health reasons, or they left without providing a reason.

There is no evidence that students withdrew from the courses because of the uniqueness of the PSI structure or because the course was taught via the Internet. Discounting the two students who experienced technical difficulties and the one student who left without providing a reason, the two remaining students not only withdrew from this course, but most likely withdrew from school altogether. Further, it should be noted that if Blackboard were working properly at all times, the two students who withdrew from the first iteration because of technical frustration may have stayed in the course, thereby lowering the withdraw rate to 6.3%. Unlike previous PSI studies without the use of the Internet, this implementation of PSI did not yield high withdrawal rates.

Quiz Performance

The quiz means in the second iteration of the course, when the criterion was set at 8 out of 10, were not statistically significantly higher than the quiz means in the first iteration, when the criterion was set at 7 out of 10. Consistent with previous PSI studies (e.g., Davis, 1975; Johnston & O'Neil, 1973; Semb, 1974), the students modified their quiz performance according to the established mastery 7 out of 10 or 8 out of 10 criteria. A problem with a higher mastery criterion, however, was an increase in the number of times students attempted mastery per quiz. The criterion of 7 out of 10 for the first iteration was more lenient than the 8 out of 10 criterion employed during the second iteration and was easily achieved by most students with one quiz attempt. The instructor intended to make the course challenging by setting the criterion at 9 out of 10 in the second iteration, but this made the quizzes too difficult for most of the students. Because so many students had to retake the quizzes more than once when the criterion was set at 9 out of 10, the instructor was inundated with e-mails to clear quiz attempts. As a result, an 8 out of 10 criterion was then employed. In sum, it is the responsibility of the instructor to find a mastery criterion that is somewhat challenging yet attainable by all of the students so that they do not become discouraged and withdraw from the class (Kulik et al., 1978).

Re-Quiz Frequency

During the first iteration, when the criterion was 7 out of 10, only one or two students had to retake quizzes more than once for half of the units. When the criterion was raised to 8 out of 10 in the second iteration, however, there were between one and seven students who were required to retake all of the quizzes a second time, between one and two students who were required to retake three of the quizzes a third time, and one student who was required to retake one quiz a fourth time. Therefore, although there were minimal differences between quiz means for each quiz, some students in the second iteration required more time to master quizzes with the higher mastery criterion than students in the first iteration. This made it difficult for some students to keep up with the recommended schedule.

It is important to note that the increase in re-quiz frequencies by second iteration students did not negatively affect the skewed distribution of course grades towards the A and B range. Consistent with various previous PSI courses (e.g., McMichael & Corey, 1969), students were permitted to retake quizzes as many times as needed to achieve mastery. As a result, students who required multiple quiz retakes for almost every quiz earned similar quiz means to the students who did not require any retakes. Only the allocation of bonus points revealed whether a student achieved mastery on an initial attempt, but it was impossible to discern the number of times students required re-quizzing by looking at their overall quiz means.

Because of this grading issue, a student's mean score for the unit quizzes accounted for only 20% of the final course grade in the first iteration and only 15% of the final course grade in the second iteration with the majority of the course grade dependent upon a student's examination performance. Despite the higher re-quiz frequency for students in the second iteration, the examination scores between the two iterations of the course did not differ. Therefore, to gain a better understanding of each student's intellectual abilities, it may be worthwhile for future researchers to incorporate re-quiz frequency into final course grades.

Timeliness in Mastering Units

Students in both iterations of the course were able to complete the content units by the designated due dates, even though students in the first iteration were given weekly deadlines and students in the second iteration were given two examination deadlines. Consistent with previous research (e.g., Morris, Surber, & Bijou 1978), the frequent quiz deadlines in the first iteration helped students to complete their quizzes in a timely fashion but did not have an effect on course grades or examination performance. As a result of the deadlines, all of the students in the first iteration had plenty of time to study for each content unit, to retake quizzes if necessary, to prepare for the examinations, and to do work for other courses. The bonus points motivated students to master the units in a timely matter because many of them attempted mastery at the beginning of each week in order to obtain the maximum amount of extra credit.

For the second iteration of the course, there were two examination deadlines where students were required to complete five unit quizzes before each examination date. Even without the weekly deadlines, many students opted to plan quizzes, according to or close to the recommended schedule posted by the instructor. It is highly probable that without the recommended schedule more students would have procrastinated. The degree of self-pacing employed in the second iteration was novel for many of them, and without any instructor guidance they might not have been as successful in budgeting their time. To further urge students to maintain their pacing schedules, the instructor sent out frequent e-mails to publicly inform the class of the progress of all of the students. Despite these e-mails, the same six students usually delayed mastery.

Perhaps these second iteration students who continually delayed mastery had low self-control. They may have engaged in behavior that results in a smaller, more immediate reward rather than behavior that results in a delayed but a greater reward (Ainslie, 2001). For example, the procrastinators in the second iteration may have chosen to postpone studying so that they could engage in more immediate rewards, such as getting together with friends, attending a party, or engaging in an extracurricular activity. In general, self-control increases as children become adults (Mischel & Metzner, 1962), but consistent with what was observed in the present study, adults vary in their abilities to understand the value of delayed rewards. Therefore, it is possible that the students in this study who needed more study time to master each unit may have had low self-control and were not able to self-pace effectively. In general, the students who were capable of putting in more study time and were willing to do so earned high course grades. Consistent with previous research (Ainsworth, 1979), procrastination was the most noteworthy reason for poor performance. Therefore, a possible enhancement of future PSI courses may be instructor monitoring of those students with low self-control, providing additional prompts and incentives for timely completion of quizzes. Further, because self-control and intellectual ability are related (Mischel, Shoda, & Rodriguez, 1989), students with comparatively low intellectual ability may not do as well on the quizzes and examinations, perhaps becoming more likely to procrastinate to avoid a stressful and punishing class and ultimately failing. This is the irony of PSI classes; although multiple attempts at mastery may sound appealing for students of lower intellectual ability, the combination of the extra work and the additional demands of greater self-pacing may entrap these students into failing.

Bonus Points

All of the students in the first iteration of the course obtained bonus points toward both the midterm and final examinations and were able to successfully pace themselves throughout each content unit. This was not the case for the second iteration of the course: two students did not obtain any bonus points and five students obtained bonus points only toward the midterm examination. These students also did not master quizzes according to the recommended schedule, which may be attributed either to their inability to reach the mastery criterion after one or more trials or to their propensity to procrastinate. Consistent with results from previous studies (Bijou, Morris, & Parsons, 1976; Bitgood & Segrave, 1975; Lloyd, 1971; Semb, Conyers, Spencer, & Sanchez Sosa, 1975), the allocation of bonus points for timely unit completion according to the recommended schedule was effective for 14 out of 21 of the second iteration students. Specifically, bonus points provided an immediate reward for some of those students who had difficulty pacing. Those students who did not accumulate bonus points over the semester earned lower examination and course grades.

Examination Performance

The means for all four of the examinations, prior to the addition of bonus points, ranged from 76.81% to 80.29%. There were no statistically significant differences between the midterm examination means from the first to the second iteration, and there were no statistically significant differences between the final examination means from the first to the second iteration. It was expected that students in the second iteration would perform significantly better on the midterm and final examinations for two reasons. First, the mastery criterion for the quizzes was 1 point higher in the second iteration. However, the increase of 1 mastery point for the quizzes was not significant enough to enhance performance by raising examination scores. Second, the students in the first iteration experienced fewer technical challenges during the examination periods. Perhaps because these students were accustomed to technical challenges associated with Blackboard from taking the weekly quizzes, they were less likely to be challenged by technical problems during the midterm and final examinations.

Also inconsistent with expectations were the minimal differences between the means for the midterm and final examinations in both iterations. In traditional lecture-based classes, instructors can expect students to perform better on the final than on the midterm examination because, after the first examination, students gain an understanding of the instructor's examination style. Even though the questions for all of the examinations were taken from the same pool for both iterations, the mean examination score did not improve from the midterm to the final. Perhaps the required mastery of unit quizzes, which both familiarized the students with the instructor's examination style and with important social psychological terminology, contributed to the lack of variance between the scores.

Student Attitudes

Student attitudes towards the course were measured by the survey shown in the Appendix, which was sent to the students via e-mail before final course grades were distributed. Using a 5-point Likert scale, students rated their agreement with statements relating to all of the course's components.

Overall Course Satisfaction
The students enjoyed most aspects of the course. Students in both iterations reported high agreement that the course was interesting, that they would recommend this course, and that they had a desire to learn more about social psychology. Open-ended responses revealed student satisfaction with the course format, the convenience of the course, and the freedom and indepen-

dence given to students. Mostly, statements focused on students' overall satisfaction with the class and the lack of areas in need of improvement.

Instructor Effectiveness

Even though students in both iterations reported moderate to high satisfaction with instructor effectiveness, first-iteration students found the instructor to be more effective than second-iteration students. This finding is attributed to a higher degree of personalization experienced by students who, in the first iteration of the course maintained a constant one-to-one e-mail relationship with the instructor to troubleshoot technical problems related to Blackboard. Further, because quizzes were due every week in the first iteration, the instructor was often required to answer questions about content on a weekly basis instead of sporadically throughout the semester. In general, first-iteration students developed the perception that the instructor was always available to help them on an individual basis, thus enhancing their perception of instructor effectiveness.

During the second iteration, the instructor sent out group e-mails to the class to provide them with performance information. Unlike the first iteration, there was not as much need for technical assistance, which made personalized instructor-student contact less frequent. There were more students who needed to retake quizzes more often in the second iteration, but they kept their e-mail contact with the instructor to a minimum. At some points throughout the semester, it appeared that there were students who did not check their class e-mail accounts for weeks at a time, further decreasing interaction with the instructor. To enhance direct instructor-student interaction, instructors should send occasional personalized e-mails to each student, even though it may increase the amount of instructor labor.

Blackboard Usability and Internet as an Instructional Medium

Despite the technical challenges, such as being knocked offline, not being able to download graphics, and difficulties entering the course website (mostly experienced in the first iteration), students in both courses reported high satisfaction with Blackboard usability and moderate to high satisfaction with the Internet as an instructional medium. Interestingly, students in both iterations were not entirely convinced that this course helped to improve their computer and online interaction skills. Students may have already been well versed in computer-based communication prior to this course, leaving little room for improvement.

Lecture, Textbook, and Discussion Board Satisfaction

Teaching this course on the Internet, where the lectures, course materials, quizzes and examinations, and instructor-student interaction were all text-based, was consistent with Keller's (1968) original idea for "the related stress upon the written word in teacher-student communication" (p. 83). Therefore, student satisfaction with these aspects of the course was highly important for the course's success. Students in both iterations reported notably high satisfaction with the lectures, finding them interesting, full of examples, and appropriate in format and length.

Students in both iterations also reported high satisfaction with the textbook and moderate satisfaction with the effectiveness of the discussion board. Some students found that participating in the discussion board was helpful for clarifying material while others, especially in the second iteration, found it tedious to post two to three comments for every content unit. It may be that some of these second iteration students were rushing to complete their quizzes before the examination date, leaving them little time to read the textbook and to participate in the discussion board forums, thus reducing their satisfaction with this feature of the course.

Quiz and Examination Satisfaction

In general, students reported moderate to high satisfaction with the quiz format. Students in the second iteration were disappointed that they were not given the correct responses to wrong answers on quizzes. Similar to those who were dissatisfied with the textbook and the discussion forums, it is probable that these students who complained were those who required multiple quiz retakes and wanted a shortcut to the correct answers.

Students were only moderately satisfied with the examination format. Some students may not have been prepared to answer questions that required direct application of the concepts, rather than simply defining them, as they had in the quizzes. Further, there were students, especially in the first iteration, who had extreme difficulties with Blackboard during the midterm examination period. Also, because the evaluation survey was distributed prior to the final examination, students in the second iteration were asked to evaluate only the midterm. Perhaps these students would have perceived the examination format as more satisfactory if they had been asked to evaluate both the midterm and final examinations.

Bonus Point and Mastery Effectiveness

There was a difference in the perception of the mastery component between the students in the first iteration and the students in the second iteration. Factor analysis of the survey data showed that students in the first iteration included mastery as part of the quiz category, and students in the second iteration included mastery as part of the bonus point effectiveness category. This difference in grouping can be attributed to the variation of pacing contingencies. Students in the first iteration related mastery to quiz satisfaction, most likely because the mastery criterion determined whether they would pass each quiz within the designated week. Students in the second iteration may have also related mastery to quiz satisfaction, but because there was no pressure to master units according to weekly deadlines, students perceived the recommended due dates as an opportunity to master quizzes in a timely fashion. These students perceived a strong relationship between the mastery criterion and earning bonus points. Despite these differences, students in both iterations reported moderate to high bonus-point effectiveness in addition to finding the mastery criteria fair and attainable.

Self-Pacing Satisfaction

Consistent with previous studies (Nelson & Scott, 1974), students in both iterations reported high satisfaction with the ability to self–pace. Students in the first iteration were not entirely satisfied with the designated days for self-pacing, and their desire for more freedom to schedule quizzes promoted the changes to the self-pacing component in the second iteration. Students in the second iteration also reported satisfaction with self-pacing, with some students admitting that it was difficult to schedule their own quizzes. Interestingly, the timeliness data revealed that there were many more students in the second iteration who procrastinated quiz mastery until close to the examination due dates.

Because of Institutional Review Board (IRB) restrictions on data collection in this project, the instructor was not able to determine whether the students who reported high satisfaction with the pacing component were the same students who procrastinated. If this were the case, it would be necessary to decide whether it is worthwhile to enhance student satisfaction by increasing self-pacing if it is simultaneously detrimental to some students. Although students may prefer to self-pace through their courses, it is the responsibility of future instructors to determine the degree of self-pacing that can be instituted without being detrimental to student achievement.

Instructor Assessment

Overall, the instructor enjoyed both teaching on the Internet and implementing PSI. As predicted, characteristics of the Internet eliminated many of the administrative responsibilities, such as quizzing, grading, and providing feedback, which made PSI so onerous to instructors. Instead, the instructor was now able to monitor student progress and course quality, interact with students both in the public discussion group and privately via e-mail without devoting an inappropriate amount of time to administrative matters. Finally, teaching via the Internet was convenient, allotting the instructor more freedom to schedule course work around external pressures.

Conclusions

The Internet and the Blackboard system were successful in supporting all of the components of PSI. Unlike previous computer-based PSI courses, the asynchronous nature of the Internet and the automated features built into Blackboard made it possible for students to attend lectures, to take quizzes and examinations, and to communicate with the instructor and other class members at any time, from any networked computer. This reduced the labor intensiveness previously associated with PSI and distance education.   It was the combination of PSI, the Internet, and Blackboard that produced an effective instructional strategy. The success of this study revived Keller's (1968) original PSI model, while setting the stage both for more advanced PSI research and Internet-based instruction.

References

Ainslie, G. (2001). *Breakdown of will*. New York: Cambridge University Press.

Ainsworth, L. L. (1979). Self-paced instruction: An innovation that failed. *Teaching of Psychology*, 6, 42-46.

Bijou, S. W., Morris, E. K., & Parsons, J. A. (1976). A PSI course in child development with a procedure for reducing student procrastination. *Journal of Personalized Instruction, 1*, 36-40.

Bitgood, S. C. & Segrave, K. (1975). A comparison of graduated and fixed point systems of contingency managed instruction. In J. Johnston (Ed.), *Behavior Research and Technology in Higher Education,* (pp. 202-213). Springfield, IL: Charles C. Thomas Co.

Born, D. G. & Moore, M. C. (1978). Some belated thoughts on pacing. *Journal of Personalized Instruction, 3*, 33-36.

Byrne, D. (1961). Interpersonal attraction and attitude similarity. *Journal of Abnormal and Social Psychology, 62*, 713-715.

Darley, J. M. & Latane, B. (1968). Bystander intervention in emergencies: Diffusion of responsibility. *Journal of Personality and Social Psychology, 8*, 377-383.

Davis, M. L. (1975). Mastery test proficiency requirement affects mastery test performance. In J. Johnston (Ed.), *Behavior Research and Technology in Higher Education,* (pp. 185-201). Springfield, IL: Charles C. Thomas Co.

Hantula, D. A. (1998). The virtual industrial/organizational psychology class: Learning and teaching in cyberspace in three iterations. *Behavior Research Methods, Instruments, & Computers, 30*, 205-216.

Hantula, D. A., Boyd, J. H., & Crowell, C. R. (1989). Ten years of behavioral instruction with computers: Trials, tribulations and reflections. In *Proceedings of the Academic Microcomputer Conference,* (pp. 81-92). Indianapolis, IN: Indiana University.

Hovland, C. I. & Sears, R. R. (1940). Minor studies of aggression: VI. Correlation of lynchings with economic indices. *The Journal of Psychology, 9*, 301-310.

Isen, A. M. & Levin, P. F. (1972). Effect of feeling good on helping: Cookies and kindness. *Journal of Personality and Social Psychology, 21*, 384-388.

Johnston, J. M. & O'Neill, G. (1973). The analysis of performance criteria defining course grades as a determinant of college student academic performance. *Journal of Applied Behavior Analysis, 6*, 261-268.

Keller, F. S. (1968). "Good-bye teacher…" *Journal of Applied Behavior Analysis,* 1, 79-89.

Kirkpatrick, D. L. (1976). Evaluation of training. In R. L. Craig (Ed.), *Training and Development Handbook (2nd ed.),* (pp. 18-1 to 18-27). New York: McGraw-Hill.

Kock, N. F., McQueen, R. J., & Scott, J. L. (1997). Can action research be made more rigorous in a positivist sense? The contribution of an iterative approach. *Journal of Systems and Information Technology,* 1, 1-24.

Kulik, J. A., Jaksa, P., & Kulik, C. C. (1978). Research on component features of Keller's personalized system of instruction. *Journal of Personalized Instruction,* 3, 2-14.

Lapiere, R. T. (1934). Attitude vs. action. *Social Forces,* 13, 230-237.

Lloyd, K. E. (1971). Contingency management in university courses. *Educational Technology,* 11, 18-23.

Malott, R. W. & Svinicki, J. G. (1969). Contingency management in an introductory psychology course for one thousand students. *The Psychological Record,* 19, 545-556.

McMichael, J. S. & Corey, J. R. (1969). Contingency management in an introductory psychology course produces better learning. *Journal of Applied Behavior Analysis,* 2, 79-83.

Milgram, S. (1963). Behavioral study of obedience. *Journal of Abnormal and Social Psychology,* 67, 371-378.

Mischel, W. & Metzner (1962). Preference for delayed reward as a function of age, intelligence, and length of delay interval. *Journal of Abnormal and Social Psychology,* 64, 425- 431.

Mischel, W., Shoda, Y., & Rodriguez, M. L. (1989). Delay of gratification in children. *Science,* 244, 933-938.

Morris, E. K., Surber, C. F., & Bijou, S. W. (1978). Self- versus instructor-pacing: Achievement, evaluations, and retention. *Journal of Educational Psychology,* 70, 224-230.

Myers, D. G. (2000). *Exploring social psychology, (2nd ed.)* Boston, MA: McGraw-Hill.

Nelson, T. F. & Scott, D. W. (1974). Personalized instructional in educational psychology. In J. G. Sherman (Ed.), *Personalized System of Instruc-*

tion: 41 Germinal Papers, (pp. 36-44). Menlo Park, CA: W. A. Benjamin, Inc.

Nielson, J. (1999). *Designing web usability.* Indianapolis, IN: New Riders Publishing.

Robin, A. L. (1976). Behavior instruction in the college classroom. *Review of Educational Research*, 46, 313-354.

Rubin, J. (1994). *Handbook of usability testing.* New York: John Wiley & Sons, Inc. Scriven, M. (1967). The methodology of evaluation. In R. W. Tyler, R. M. Gagne, & M.

Scriven (Ed.), *Perspectives of Curriculum Evaluation,* (pp. 39-83). Chicago, IL: Rand McNally.

Semb, G. (1974). The effects of mastery criteria and assignment length on college student test performance. *Journal of Applied Behavior Analysis*, 7, 61-69.

Semb, G., Conyers, D., Spencer, R., & Sanchez Sosa, J. J. (1975). An experimental comparison of four pacing contingencies. In J. Johnston (Ed.), *Behavior Research and Technology in Higher Education,* (pp. 348-368). Springfield, IL: Charles C. Thomas Co.

Sherman J. G. (1974). PSI: Some notable failures. In J. G. Sherman (Ed.), *Personalized System of Instruction: 41 Germinal Papers,* (pp. 120-124). Menlo Park, CA: W. A. Benjamin, Inc.

Skinner, B. F. (1968). *The technology of teaching.* Englewood Cliffs, NJ: Prentice-Hall.

Susman, G.I. & Evered, R.D. (1978). As assessment of the scientific merits of action research. *Administrative Science Quarterly,* 23, 582-603.

Tudor, R. M. (1995). Isolating the effects of active responding in computer-based instruction. *Journal of Applied Behavior Analysis*, 28, 343-344.

Wesp, R. & Ford, J. E. (1982). Flexible instructor pacing assists student progress in a personalized system of instruction. *Teaching of Psychology*, 9, 160-162.

Zimbardo, P. G. (1999). Stanford prison experiment. Retrieved from http://www.prisonexp.org.

Appendix

Course Evaluation: Spring 2001

Directions: Answer all of the following questions about this course using the answer choices below (type your answer, 1-5, in the space provided).

Strongly Disagree	Somewhat Disagree	Neither Agree nor Disagree	Somewhat Agree	Strongly Agree
1	2	3	4	5

Example: I enjoyed this course. __5__

1.   The instructor was available to answer my questions. ____
2.   The instructor provided rapid feedback to my comments and questions. ____
3.   The instructor's feedback was helpful. ____
4.   I felt that the instructor knew me personally. ____
5.   I felt that I knew the instructor personally. ____
6.   Taking this course was convenient. ____
7.   The Internet is an effective way of to teach social psychology. ____
8.   The web links embedded within the lectures helped to clarify concepts. ____
9.   Overall I found this course to be interesting. ____
10. I would recommend this course to friends who are interested in social psychology. ____
11. The study material downloaded quickly. ____
12. I felt better about the knowledge of the subject as the class went along. ____
13. The computer system responded quickly to my quiz answers. ____
14. The graphics included in the lectures were appropriate. ____
15. There was sufficient text in the lectures to explain the concepts. ____
16. There were sufficient examples to illustrate the concepts in the lectures. ____
17. In general, the length of the lectures was appropriate. ____

18. The lectures held my interest. ____
19. The format of the lectures was clear. ____
20. The lectures were easy to read. ____
21. I enjoyed reading the textbook. ____
22. The amount of reading assigned weekly was appropriate. ____
23. I found the textbook to be informative. ____
24. The quizzes accurately tested my knowledge of the subject matter. ____
25. The number of test questions for each lesson was appropriate. ____
26. I liked the format of the unit quiz questions. ____
27. The feedback to the quiz questions was presented in a useful format. ____
28. The midterm accurately tested my knowledge of the subject matter. ____
29. I liked the format of the midterm examination questions. ____
30. I never felt lost or confused while navigating through Blackboard. ____
31. Blackboard was easy to use. ____
32. I became impatient while using Blackboard. ____
33. It was easy to find course information and assignments in Blackboard.
____
34. The course guidelines were clear. ____
35. I enjoyed the self-pacing feature of the course. ____
36. It was easy for me to schedule my quizzes on my own time. ____
37. As a result of this course I am interested in learning more about social psych. ____
38. As a result of this course my computer skills improved. ____
39. As a result of this course I am more comfortable interacting with people online. ____
40. As a result of this course I will take more online courses. ____
41. The recommended schedule helped me pace myself through this course.
____
42. The quizzes helped me to prepare for the midterm and final examinations.
____
43. The bonus points motivated me to read and study the material in a timely fashion. ____
44. The bonus points motivated me to do well on the quizzes. ____
45. The passing quiz score of 8/10 was fair. ____
46. The passing quiz score of 8/10 was difficult to achieve. ____
47. Doing well in this course took self-discipline. ____
48. Because the passing grade was 8/10, I often aimed to achieve this score rather than aiming for 10/10. ____
49. The discussion board facilitated interaction among class members. ____

50. The discussion board helped me to clarify terms and theories. ____
51. The TA's involvement in the discussion board generated discussion. ____
52. What did you think of the self-pacing feature of this course?

_____

53. Do you have any suggestions that would help to improve this course?
     Please be specific!

_____

54. Was there anything specific that you *did not* like about the course (e.g.,
     lectures, quizzing, Blackboard, discussion board or the instructor)?

_____

55. Was there anything specific that you did like about the course (e.g.,
     lectures, pacing, Blackboard, discussion board or the instructor)?

_____

Thank you for completing the survey!!! These comments will help me to
make improvements on the course.

Endnote

*   The writer is a Senior Research Analyst with TIAA-CREF. The views
       expressed in this chapter are those of the Author, and do not necessarily
       represent the views of anyone else at TIAA-CREF

Conclusion

Dominique Monolescu

Temple University, USA

This book has reviewed some of the issues that Temple University faced when it launched its distance education program. The Temple University OnLine Learning (TU-OLL) Program was created in order to explore ways of enhancing the institution's overall educational goals through emerging new technologies. Its initiatives were expanded as students and faculty assimilated new possibilities to replace their traditional classroom experiences with technological means of sharing content, interacting with each other, and ultimately creating knowledge.

The editors hope that this book is representative of the distance education issues that we were faced with in our institution, and demonstrates the important current issues in the field such as planning to start a distance education program, finding different ways of teaching an online course, choosing appropriate interaction communication technologies, establishing program evaluation measures, and resolving issues of accessibility and intellectual property.

Although online students may never have a reason to come to campus, they are as affected by university policies and operations as traditional on-campus students. Determining the students' satisfaction with their online learning experience, curriculum, and interaction with faculty helps reshape the University's distance education policies and educational goals. By having a strong commitment and support from the University's administration, a distance education program is able to provide (a) faculty incentives for online course development,

(b) different technological tools for faculty, (c) means for new online teaching solutions to be discovered, and, most importantly, (d) policies and procedures that extend the University's on-campus services to distance students and faculty.

Although none of the initiatives described above comes without a cost to the institution, many of the solutions found for the online learning environment have proven to help implementation at the traditional university level as well. For instance, in the past decade, course management tools (such as Blackboard Inc. and WebStudy Inc.) have been very beneficial to distance education course organization, content presentation, content evaluation, and to online student and faculty interactions. Even though the online teaching and learning experience originally benefited most from the adoption of such course management tools, they have also enhanced the traditional on-campus experience as well. Tools initially considered necessary for online courses can also impact the on-campus courses, allowing the university to reallocate and share resources in a synergistic manner.

In addition to providing a good distance education experience to students, the chapter on virtual teams describes how the online student body's needs are changing, and it highlights the importance of institutional efforts to find ways to provide online students with the same social opportunities that it provides to its on-campus students. In this vein, the authors of this chapter suggest various ways of promoting virtual communities among higher education online students. Distance education programs can take charge of generating such a virtual social experience by creating virtual "spaces" for students to "gather" via chat rooms or virtual cafes.

All of the preceding chapters attempt to highlight issues such as *access*, *cost*, *quality*, *flexibility*, and *innovation*, which are extremely important when discussing any institutional distance education initiatives. As universities plan to extend their knowledge product to remote students, they need to ensure accessibility. The cost of a distance education program must also be considered because without an established distance education budget, it is difficult for higher education institutions to meet the educational goals of their remote students. In addition, quality distance education programs must consider the differences in both the experiences and needs of their students. With the lifelong learning trends that we have experienced in the past decades, higher education institutions need to be innovative and have within their educational goals flexible and convenient ways for students to pursue their academic endeavors while also advancing their careers and personal life goals.

The following quote from the UNESCO's 2002 Teacher Educational Guidelines emphasizes the relevance of distance education:

> *Distance education still remains, at heart, a reflection of individual national infrastructures and a wide complex of educational, social, cultural and economic issues, including the willingness and capacities of teachers themselves to become engaged in these modes in their various learning institutions and communities (John Daniel, p. 4).*

In conclusion, distance education has evolved throughout the years and most likely will continue to evolve. The history of distance education has demonstrated that, regardless of the form, many societies in every corner of the globe have benefited from the effort to expand education beyond the walls of the classroom. Whether the purpose is to provide access to education for young adults who live in rural areas via television broadcasts, to promote the opportunity for professionals to pursue a new degree through the Internet, or to allow older students to complete an unfinished bachelor's program via online or videoconferencing courses, distance education is a significant component of current higher education institutional curriculum reform and will continue to be so in the future.

Reference

International Research Foundation for Open Learning. (2001). *Teacher education guidelines: Using open and distance learning* (UNESCO Report). Retrieved from http://unesdoc.unesco.org/images/0012/001253/125396e.pdf.

About the Authors

Dominique Monolescu, Ph.D., is the Interim Director of Temple University's OnLine Learning Program and an Adjunct Faculty Member at Arcadia University's Corporate Communications Program. Her research, primarily in distance education, student and faculty interaction, online focus groups, desktop videoconferencing, and virtual conferences, has appeared in such journals as *Internet and Higher Education* and the *American Journal of Distance Education*. She holds M.A. and Ph.D. degrees from Temple University, and a B.A. in Business and a B.A. in Special Education from Mackenzie University, Brazil. Dr. Monolescu's email address is dominiq@temple.edu.

Catherine Schifter, Ph.D., is an Associate Professor in Curriculum, Instruction and Technology in Education at Temple University, USA, was a Carnegie Scholar (2000-2001), and Director of the Temple Online Learning Program from 1996 through 2000. In 2002 and 2003, Dr. Schifter was the first Faculty Fellow for the Temple University Teaching and Learning Center that was established to support faculty in all endeavors of teaching and learning in traditional and online environments. Her most recent scholarship has been in reviewing national trends for DE faculty support models in higher education, and evaluation of faculty development programs for infusing technology into classrooms in K-12 education. Dr. Schifter's email address is catherine.schifter@temple.edu.

Linda Greenwood is a doctoral student in the Mass Media and Communication Program in the School of Communications and Theater at Temple University, USA. As an Adjunct Lecturer and Teaching Assistant, she has taught courses in public speaking, political communication, and media studies and received the International Communication Association (ICA) award for excellence in Graduate Assistance Teaching. Linda graduated summa cum laude from Rutgers University with a B.A. in English and earned an M.A. in rhetoric and communication from Temple University. She is currently writing her dissertation on the effects of virtual desktop environments and computer-mediated communication on political attitudes and behavior. Her email address is linda.greenwood@temple.edu.

*   *   *

Erica Davis Blann, Ph.D., is a Research Analyst in the Corporate Research Division at Teachers Insurance and Annuity Association College Retirement Equities Fund (TIAA-CREF), a large financial service provider that serves the faculty and staff of America's education and research communities. Her primary responsibilities are designing, directing, and reporting marketing research projects for Retirement Services, Enterprises and Corporate Research staff areas. Erica earned her M.A. and Ph.D. in social and organizational psychology from Temple University, where she researched Internet-based training and methods for evaluating training effectiveness. She holds a B.A. in Psychology from Brandeis University. Her email address is erdavis@tiaa-cref.org.

Rosangela K. Boyd, Ph.D., is an Associate Professor at the Department of Therapeutic Recreation, College of Allied Health Professions, at Temple University, USA. She is also an Associate Director at the Institute on Disabilities, Temple University's Center for Excellence in Developmental Disabilities. Dr. Boyd received one of Temple's first grants to develop an online class. She has been teaching both online courses and courses augmented by online components since 1999. She was a presenter at the International Conference on Distance Education held in Sao Paulo, Brazil, in 2000. She has written and presented extensively on topics related to disabilities and aging. Her email address is rosangela.boyd@temple.edu.

Gisela Gil-Egui is a doctoral student in the Mass Media and Communication Program, Temple University, USA. She holds a B.A. in Journalism from

Central University of Venezuela (1992), and an M.A. in Communication from Temple University (1999). Her research has been focused on telecommunications policy and economics, distance education, media law, and international regimes of ICT governance, with an emphasis on issues related to universal access, public interest, discourse ethics, and the boundaries between private and public domains. Currently, she is a staff member of the Online Learning Program at Temple University. Her email address is ggil@temple.edu.

Donald A. Hantula, Ph.D., is Associate Professor and Director of the Graduate Program in Social & Organizational Psychology at Temple University and Executive Editor of the *Journal of Social Psychology*. His research in consumer and financial decision making and in computer applications has appeared in such journals as *Behavior Research, Methods, Instruments & Computers, Computers in Human Behavior, Journal of Applied Psychology, Journal of Organizational Behavior Management, Organizational Behavior & Human Decision Processes*, and *Managerial & Decision Economics*. He has been using computer technology in education since 1985 and has been teaching on the Internet and its precursors since 1992. Professor Hantula holds a B.A. from Emory University, and an M.A. and Ph.D. from the University of Notre Dame. His email address is hantula@temple.edu.

Sandy Kyrish, Ph.D., is Assistant Dean of Technology and Planning in the School of Communications and Theater at Temple University in Philadelphia, USA. She was the Founding Director of Temple's On Line Learning Program, and she has also directed four grant programs for the Commonwealth of Pennsylvania that awarded more than $20 million in educational technology funds to colleges and universities across the state. Her research has appeared in journals including *Convergence* and *Media Information Australia*. Dr. Kyrish holds a Ph.D. from Temple University and an M.A. and B.S. from the University of Texas at Austin. Her email address is skyrish@temple.edu.

Elizabeth J. Leebron, Ph.D., is Chair of the Department of Broadcasting, Telecommunications and Mass Media at Temple University, USA, where she teaches media entrepreneurship, video production, and production management. Her research and production interests are in creating and evaluating programming for young audiences. Her production credits include programming for Juvenile Diabetes Research Foundation, Philadelphia Department of

Human Services, The Franklin Institute Science Museum, The Environmental Protection Agency, Domestic Abuse Project of Delaware County, Head Start, Planned Parenthood, and organizations that serve today's youth. Her email address is betsy@temple.edu.

Julie-Ann M. McFann, Ph.D., is Faculty Development Coordinator in the Office of Instructional Development at the University of California, Los Angeles, USA. Prior to her current appointment, she was an Assistant Professor of Educational Psychology at Purdue University, North Central and the Coordinator of the Teaching Enhancement Center in the College of Education at Temple University. Her research interests involve how faculty development can ensure academic success for all students. Her email address is jmcfann@oid.ucla.edu.

Bonnie M. Moulton, M.Ed., OTR, is a staff member at the Institute on Disabilities, Pennsylvania's University Center for Excellence in Developmental Disabilities at Temple University. She has been involved in co-teaching online courses at the Institute on Disabilities. Her interests in accessible information technologies and inclusive educational practices arise from her experiences on a professional level and on a personal level as a person with a life-long disability. Her email address is bonnie.moulton@temple.edu.

Darleen M. Pawlowicz is a doctoral student at Temple University, USA, whose primary research interests include virtual teamwork, computer-mediated learning, and research methodology. Darleen received a distinguished graduate teaching award from Temple University and a Temple University New Directions Grant to study virtual teams. Her research has been presented at many academic meetings including the American Psychological Society, the Society for Industrial Organizational Psychology, and the Southern Academy of Management. She received her B.A. from the College of the Holy Cross and her M.A. from Temple University. Her email address is zach5@worldnet.att.net.

Stella F. Shields, Ph.D., is a Faculty Member of the Department of Telecommunications, Indiana University, USA. Previously, she taught at Rutgers University, the State University of New Jersey, and Fordham University. She has designed and taught online courses at Temple University and serves as Senior Associate to TLT Group. Prior to her Ph.D., she lived in Venezuela. After leaving Venezuela, she held positions in industry in Montreal, Quebec, Canada, and Nigeria. Her research centers on global telecommunications and distance learning as they relate to minorities in the U.S. and developing countries. The intersection of economic, technical, and policy issues is her focus. Her email address is sfshield@indiana.edu.

John A. Sorrentino is an Associate Professor in the Economics Department at Temple University, USA. His research is primarily in the economics of energy and the environment, but he has presented work on environmental information systems and the costs and benefits of distance education at the M.B.A. level. Some of his research has appeared in journals such as the *American Economic Review, Ecological Modelling,* and the *Journal of Environmental Economics and Management.* His short article on computer-assisted face-to-face teaching appeared in *The Teaching & Learning Forum.* One of his articles on online teaching was included in *Technology Tools for Today's Campuses,* a CD-ROM produced by Microsoft. He was honored with a Lindback Foundation Award for Distinguished Teaching in 1999, and was the first professor in the School of Business and Management at Temple University to offer an online course for M.B.A. students. He has taught Economic Analysis since 1997, and has added an online version of the upper-level Economic Decision Making in the Firm in the Spring of 2002. His email address is jsorrent@temple.edu.

Concetta M. Stewart, Ph.D., is Dean of the School of Communications and Theater at Temple University, USA. Prior to joining the faculty there, Dr. Stewart worked at AT&T for 12 years at its corporate headquarters. She is also a Senior Associate for the American Association of Higher Education's Teaching, Learning and Technology Group and has presented and published on a variety of topics related to the introduction, evaluation, and impact of communication and information technology. In addition, she has served on the editorial boards of several journals including *Academy of Management Executive, Journal of Applied Communication Research,* and *Studies in Technological Innovation and Human Resources.* Her email address is cstewart@temple.edu.

Karen M. Turner, J.D., is an Associate Professor and the Chairperson of the Department of Journalism, Public Relations and Advertising at Temple University, USA. Professor Turner teaches courses in broadcast journalism, performance, race studies and media law and ethics. Before joining the Temple faculty in 1992, she was the Press Secretary to then Philadelphia Mayor Edward Rendell. She has extensive experience as a radio journalist and talk radio interviewer, having worked in such markets as Philadelphia, Cincinnati, and New Brunswick, NJ. Professor Turner has earned an A.B. degree with honors in Psychology and Urban Studies from Dartmouth College, a M.S. from Columbia University Graduate School of Journalism, and a J.D. from Northwestern University School of Law. Her email address is kturner@temple.edu.

Maurice W. Wright was born in Front Royal, VA, in 1949. He attended Duke University (B.A., 1972), and Columbia (M.A., 1974, D.M.A., 1989) where he received the Charles Ives Scholarship and the Guggenheim Fellowship. Since 1980 he has taught at Temple University, USA. In 1988, he received the Recording Award from the American Academy of Arts and Letters and was named Laura H. Carnell Professor of Music Composition. Performed by the Boston Symphony, the Emerson Quartet, and the American Brass Quintet, he scored the PBS series, "Strokes Of Genius" and "The Human Language." His music is recorded on CRI and New World Records. His email address is wright@temple.edu.

Index

online discussion group 259
online focus groups 176
online learning 2
online students 127
online survey 173
online teaching 241
overload pay 31

P

participant observation 264
Paulos, John Allen 196
personal needs 26
personalized system of instruction (PSI) 287
physical disability 69
private correspondence 246
profitability 10
program development 164
program evaluation 164

Q

qualified individuals with disabilities 75
QuickTime 194

R

race 215
Race and Racism in the News 216
reasonable accommodations 75
Rehabilitation Act 72

S

Section 508 88
server-based template program 288
short circuits stereotypes 270
social psychology 286
speech and motor disabilities 82
structured trust 131
student populations 243
student satisfaction 164
student writing 260
studies-in-race course 216
supplier 45
sustainability 10
swift trust 129
synchronous 42

synchronous online sessions 245

T

teaching assistants (TA) 33
teaching online 217
team-based learning 152
technical infrastructure 11
technoliteracy 151
technology beachhead 4
technology objectives 5
Telecommunications Act 72
Temple University 164
Temple University OnLine Learning Program 164
Test of Economic Knowledge (TEK) 47
Test of Economic Literacy (TEL) 47
Test of Understanding Economic Knowledge (TUCE) 47
trade journal article review 223
trust 127

U

universal design 69
university teaching 258
unmet needs 5

V

value net 44
videoconference (VDC) course 172
virtual classroom 241
virtual environment 116
virtual lecture hall 198
virtual teams 152
virtual teamwork 116, 123

W

weekly journal 223
World Wide Web Consortium (W3C) 85

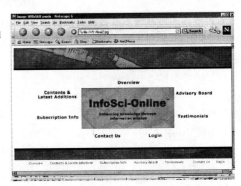